Connected Mathematics 2™

Growing, Growing, Growing

Exponential Relationships

2.7×10^{12}

Glenda Lappan
James T. Fey
William M. Fitzgerald
Susan N. Friel
Elizabeth Difanis Phillips

PEARSON

Boston, Massachusetts · Glenview, Illinois · Shoreview, Minnesota · Upper Saddle River, New Jersey

Connected Mathematics™ was developed at Michigan State University with financial support from the Michigan State University Office of the Provost, Computing and Technology, and the College of Natural Science.

This material is based upon work supported by the National Science Foundation under Grant No. MDR 9150217 and Grant No. ESI 9986372. Opinions expressed are those of the authors and not necessarily those of the Foundation.

The Michigan State University authors and administration have agreed that all MSU royalties arising from this publication will be devoted to purposes supported by the Department of Mathematics and the MSU Mathematics Enrichment Fund.

Acknowledgments appear on page 129, which constitutes an extension of this copyright page.
Acknowledgments for the student pages appear on student page 86, which constitutes an extension of this copyright page.

13-digit ISBN 978-0-13-366203-0
10-digit ISBN 0-13-366203-9
1 2 3 4 5 6 7 8 9 10   11 10 09 08

Authors of Connected Mathematics

(from left to right) Glenda Lappan, Betty Phillips, Susan Friel, Bill Fitzgerald, Jim Fey

Glenda Lappan is a University Distinguished Professor in the Department of Mathematics at Michigan State University. Her research and development interests are in the connected areas of students' learning of mathematics and mathematics teachers' professional growth and change related to the development and enactment of K–12 curriculum materials.

James T. Fey is a Professor of Curriculum and Instruction and Mathematics at the University of Maryland. His consistent professional interest has been development and research focused on curriculum materials that engage middle and high school students in problem-based collaborative investigations of mathematical ideas and their applications.

William M. Fitzgerald (*Deceased*) was a Professor in the Department of Mathematics at Michigan State University. His early research was on the use of concrete materials in supporting student learning and led to the development of teaching materials for laboratory environments. Later he helped develop a teaching model to support student experimentation with mathematics.

Susan N. Friel is a Professor of Mathematics Education in the School of Education at the University of North Carolina at Chapel Hill. Her research interests focus on statistics education for middle-grade students and, more broadly, on teachers' professional development and growth in teaching mathematics K–8.

Elizabeth Difanis Phillips is a Senior Academic Specialist in the Mathematics Department of Michigan State University. She is interested in teaching and learning mathematics for both teachers and students. These interests have led to curriculum and professional development projects at the middle school and high school levels, as well as projects related to the teaching and learning of algebra across the grades.

CMP2 Development Staff

Teacher Collaborator in Residence
Yvonne Grant
Michigan State University

Administrative Assistant
Judith Martus Miller
Michigan State University

Production and Field Site Manager
Lisa Keller
Michigan State University

Technical and Editorial Support
Brin Keller, Peter Lappan, Jim Laser, Michael Masterson, Stacey Miceli

Assessment Team
June Bailey and **Debra Sobko** (Apollo Middle School, Rochester, New York), **George Bright** (University of North Carolina, Greensboro), **Gwen Ranzau Campbell** (Sunrise Park Middle School, White Bear Lake, Minnesota), **Holly DeRosia, Kathy Dole,** and **Teri Keusch** (Portland Middle School, Portland, Michigan), **Mary Beth Schmitt** (Traverse City East Junior High School, Traverse City, Michigan), **Genni Steele** (Central Middle School, White Bear Lake, Minnesota), **Jacqueline Stewart** (Okemos, Michigan), **Elizabeth Tye** (Magnolia Junior High School, Magnolia, Arkansas)

Development Assistants
At Lansing Community College *Undergraduate Assistant:* **James Brinegar**

At Michigan State University *Graduate Assistants:* **Dawn Berk, Emily Bouck, Bulent Buyukbozkirli, Kuo-Liang Chang, Christopher Danielson, Srinivasa Dharmavaram, Deb Johanning, Wesley Kretzschmar, Kelly Rivette, Sarah Sword, Tat Ming Sze, Marie Turini, Jeffrey Wanko;** *Undergraduate Assistants:* **Daniel Briggs, Jeffrey Chapin, Jade Corsé, Elisha Hardy, Alisha Harold, Elizabeth Keusch, Julia Letoutchaia, Karen Loeffler, Brian Oliver, Carl Oliver, Evonne Pedawi, Lauren Rebrovich**

At the University of Maryland *Graduate Assistants:* **Kim Harris Bethea, Kara Karch**

At the University of North Carolina (Chapel Hill) *Graduate Assistants:* **Mark Ellis, Trista Stearns;** *Undergraduate Assistant:* **Daniel Smith**

Advisory Board for CMP2

Thomas Banchoff
Professor of Mathematics
Brown University
Providence, Rhode Island

Anne Bartel
Mathematics Coordinator
Minneapolis Public Schools
Minneapolis, Minnesota

Hyman Bass
Professor of Mathematics
University of Michigan
Ann Arbor, Michigan

Joan Ferrini-Mundy
Associate Dean of the College of
Natural Science; Professor
Michigan State University
East Lansing, Michigan

James Hiebert
Professor
University of Delaware
Newark, Delaware

Susan Hudson Hull
Charles A. Dana Center
University of Texas
Austin, Texas

Michele Luke
Mathematics Curriculum
Coordinator
West Junior High
Minnetonka, Minnesota

Kay McClain
Assistant Professor of
Mathematics Education
Vanderbilt University
Nashville, Tennessee

Edward Silver
Professor; Chair of Educational
Studies
University of Michigan
Ann Arbor, Michigan

Judith Sowder
Professor Emerita
San Diego State University
San Diego, California

Lisa Usher
Mathematics Resource Teacher
California Academy of
Mathematics and Science
San Pedro, California

Field Test Sites for CMP2

During the development of the revised edition of *Connected Mathematics* (CMP2), more than 100 classroom teachers have field-tested materials at 49 school sites in 12 states and the District of Columbia. This classroom testing occurred over three academic years (2001 through 2004), allowing careful study of the effectiveness of each of the 24 units that comprise the program. A special thanks to the students and teachers at these pilot schools.

Arkansas

Magnolia Public Schools
Kittena Bell*, Judith Trowell*; *Central Elementary School:* Maxine Broom, Betty Eddy, Tiffany Fallin, Bonnie Flurry, Carolyn Monk, Elizabeth Tye; *Magnolia Junior High School:* Monique Bryan, Ginger Cook, David Graham, Shelby Lamkin

Colorado

Boulder Public Schools
Nevin Platt Middle School: Judith Koenig

St. Vrain Valley School District, Longmont
Westview Middle School: Colleen Beyer, Kitty Canupp, Ellie Decker*, Peggy McCarthy, Tanya deNobrega, Cindy Payne, Ericka Pilon, Andrew Roberts

District of Columbia

Capitol Hill Day School: Ann Lawrence

Georgia

University of Georgia, Athens
Brad Findell

Madison Public Schools
Morgan County Middle School: Renee Burgdorf, Lynn Harris, Nancy Kurtz, Carolyn Stewart

Maine

Falmouth Public Schools
Falmouth Middle School: Donna Erikson, Joyce Hebert, Paula Hodgkins, Rick Hogan, David Legere, Cynthia Martin, Barbara Stiles, Shawn Towle*

Michigan

Portland Public Schools
Portland Middle School: Mark Braun, Holly DeRosia, Kathy Dole*, Angie Foote, Teri Keusch, Tammi Wardwell

Traverse City Area Public Schools
Bertha Vos Elementary: Kristin Sak; *Central Grade School:* Michelle Clark; Jody Meyers; *Eastern Elementary:* Karrie Tufts; *Interlochen Elementary:* Mary McGee-Cullen; *Long Lake Elementary:* Julie Faulkner*, Charlie Maxbauer, Katherine Sleder; *Norris Elementary:* Hope Slanaker; *Oak Park Elementary:* Jessica Steed; *Traverse Heights Elementary:* Jennifer Wolfert; *Westwoods Elementary:* Nancy Conn; *Old Mission Peninsula School:* Deb Larimer; *Traverse City East Junior High:* Ivanka Berkshire, Ruthanne Kladder, Jan Palkowski, Jane Peterson, Mary Beth Schmitt; *Traverse City West Junior High:* Dan Fouch*, Ray Fouch

Sturgis Public Schools
Sturgis Middle School: Ellen Eisele

Minnesota

Burnsville School District 191
Hidden Valley Elementary: Stephanie Cin, Jane McDevitt

Hopkins School District 270
Alice Smith Elementary: Sandra Cowing, Kathleen Gustafson, Martha Mason, Scott Stillman; *Eisenhower Elementary:* Chad Bellig, Patrick Berger, Nancy Glades, Kye Johnson, Shane Wasserman, Victoria Wilson; *Gatewood Elementary:* Sarah Ham, Julie Kloos, Janine Pung, Larry Wade; *Glen Lake Elementary:* Jacqueline Cramer, Kathy Hering, Cecelia Morris,

Robb Trenda; *Katherine Curren Elementary:* Diane Bancroft, Sue DeWit, John Wilson; *L. H. Tanglen Elementary:* Kevin Athmann, Lisa Becker, Mary LaBelle, Kathy Rezac, Roberta Severson; *Meadowbrook Elementary:* Jan Gauger, Hildy Shank, Jessica Zimmerman; *North Junior High:* Laurel Hahn, Kristin Lee, Jodi Markuson, Bruce Mestemacher, Laurel Miller, Bonnie Rinker, Jeannine Salzer, Sarah Shafer, Cam Stottler; *West Junior High:* Alicia Beebe, Kristie Earl, Nobu Fujii, Pam Georgetti, Susan Gilbert, Regina Nelson Johnson, Debra Lindstrom, Michele Luke*, Jon Sorensen

Minneapolis School District 1
Ann Sullivan K–8 School: Bronwyn Collins; Anne Bartel* (Curriculum and Instruction Office)

Wayzata School District 284
Central Middle School: Sarajane Myers, Dan Nielsen, Tanya Ravnholdt

White Bear Lake School District 624
Central Middle School: Amy Jorgenson, Michelle Reich, Brenda Sammon

New York

New York City Public Schools
IS 89: Yelena Aynbinder, Chi-Man Ng, Nina Rapaport, Joel Spengler, Phyllis Tam*, Brent Wyso; *Wagner Middle School:* Jason Appel, Intissar Fernandez, Yee Gee Get, Richard Goldstein, Irving Marcus, Sue Norton, Bernadita Owens, Jennifer Rehn*, Kevin Yuhas

---

* indicates a Field Test Site Coordinator

Ohio
Talawanda School District, Oxford
Talawanda Middle School: Teresa Abrams, Larry Brock, Heather Brosey, Julie Churchman, Monna Even, Karen Fitch, Bob George, Amanda Klee, Pat Meade, Sandy Montgomery, Barbara Sherman, Lauren Steidl

Miami University
Jeffrey Wanko*

Springfield Public Schools
Rockway School: Jim Mamer

Pennsylvania
Pittsburgh Public Schools
Kenneth Labuskes, Marianne O'Connor, Mary Lynn Raith*; *Arthur J. Rooney Middle School:* David Hairston, Stamatina Mousetis, Alfredo Zangaro; *Frick International Studies Academy:* Suzanne Berry, Janet Falkowski, Constance Finseth, Romika Hodge, Frank Machi; *Reizenstein Middle School:* Jeff Baldwin, James Brautigam, Lorena Burnett, Glen Cobbett, Michael Jordan, Margaret Lazur, Tamar McPherson, Melissa Munnell, Holly Neely, Ingrid Reed, Dennis Reft

Texas
Austin Independent School District
Bedichek Middle School: Lisa Brown, Jennifer Glasscock, Vicki Massey

El Paso Independent School District
Cordova Middle School: Armando Aguirre, Anneliesa Durkes, Sylvia Guzman, Pat Holguin*, William Holguin, Nancy Nava, Laura Orozco, Michelle Peña, Roberta Rosen, Patsy Smith, Jeremy Wolf

Plano Independent School District
Patt Henry, James Wohlgehagen*; *Frankford Middle School:* Mandy Baker, Cheryl Butsch, Amy Dudley, Betsy Eshelman, Janet Greene, Cort Haynes, Kathy Letchworth, Kay Marshall, Kelly McCants, Amy Reck, Judy Scott, Syndy Snyder, Lisa Wang; *Wilson Middle School:* Darcie Bane, Amanda Bedenko, Whitney Evans, Tonelli Hatley, Sarah (Becky) Higgs, Kelly Johnston, Rebecca McElligott, Kay Neuse, Cheri Slocum, Kelli Straight

Washington
Evergreen School District
Shahala Middle School: Nicole Abrahamsen, Terry Coon*, Carey Doyle, Sheryl Drechsler, George Gemma, Gina Helland, Amy Hilario, Darla Lidyard, Sean McCarthy, Tilly Meyer, Willow Nuewelt, Todd Parsons, Brian Pederson, Stan Posey, Shawn Scott, Craig Sjoberg, Lynette Sundstrom, Charles Switzer, Luke Youngblood

Wisconsin
Beaver Dam Unified School District
Beaver Dam Middle School: Jim Braemer, Jeanne Frick, Jessica Greatens, Barbara Link, Dennis McCormick, Karen Michels, Nancy Nichols*, Nancy Palm, Shelly Stelsel, Susan Wiggins

---

* indicates a Field Test Site Coordinator

Reviews of CMP to Guide Development of CMP2

Before writing for CMP2 began or field tests were conducted, the first edition of *Connected Mathematics* was submitted to the mathematics faculties of school districts from many parts of the country and to 80 individual reviewers for extensive comments.

School District Survey Reviews of CMP

Arizona
Madison School District #38 (Phoenix)

Arkansas
Cabot School District, Little Rock School District, Magnolia School District

California
Los Angeles Unified School District

Colorado
St. Vrain Valley School District (Longmont)

Florida
Leon County Schools (Tallahassee)

Illinois
School District #21 (Wheeling)

Indiana
Joseph L. Block Junior High (East Chicago)

Kentucky
Fayette County Public Schools (Lexington)

Maine
Selection of Schools

Massachusetts
Selection of Schools

Michigan
Sparta Area Schools

Minnesota
Hopkins School District

Texas
Austin Independent School District, The El Paso Collaborative for Academic Excellence, Plano Independent School District

Wisconsin
Platteville Middle School

Individual Reviewers of CMP

Arkansas
Deborah Cramer; Robby Frizzell *(Taylor)*; Lowell Lynde *(University of Arkansas, Monticello)*; Leigh Manzer *(Norfork)*; Lynne Roberts *(Emerson High School, Emerson)*; Tony Timms *(Cabot Public Schools)*; Judith Trowell *(Arkansas Department of Higher Education)*

California
José Alcantar *(Gilroy)*; Eugenie Belcher *(Gilroy)*; Marian Pasternack *(Lowman M. S. T. Center, North Hollywood)*; Susana Pezoa *(San Jose)*; Todd Rabusin *(Hollister)*; Margaret Siegfried *(Ocala Middle School, San Jose)*; Polly Underwood *(Ocala Middle School, San Jose)*

Colorado
Janeane Golliher *(St. Vrain Valley School District, Longmont)*; Judith Koenig *(Nevin Platt Middle School, Boulder)*

Florida
Paige Loggins *(Swift Creek Middle School, Tallahassee)*

Illinois
Jan Robinson *(School District #21, Wheeling)*

Indiana
Frances Jackson *(Joseph L. Block Junior High, East Chicago)*

Kentucky
Natalee Feese *(Fayette County Public Schools, Lexington)*

Maine
Betsy Berry *(Maine Math & Science Alliance, Augusta)*

Maryland
Joseph Gagnon *(University of Maryland, College Park)*; Paula Maccini *(University of Maryland, College Park)*

Massachusetts
George Cobb *(Mt. Holyoke College, South Hadley)*; Cliff Kanold *(University of Massachusetts, Amherst)*

Michigan
Mary Bouck *(Farwell Area Schools)*; Carol Dorer *(Slauson Middle School, Ann Arbor)*; Carrie Heaney *(Forsythe Middle School, Ann Arbor)*; Ellen Hopkins *(Clague Middle School, Ann Arbor)*; Teri Keusch *(Portland Middle School, Portland)*; Valerie Mills *(Oakland Schools, Waterford)*; Mary Beth Schmitt *(Traverse City East Junior High, Traverse City)*; Jack Smith *(Michigan State University, East Lansing)*; Rebecca Spencer *(Sparta Middle School, Sparta)*; Ann Marie Nicoll Turner *(Tappan Middle School, Ann Arbor)*; Scott Turner *(Scarlett Middle School, Ann Arbor)*

Minnesota
Margarita Alvarez *(Olson Middle School, Minneapolis)*; Jane Amundson *(Nicollet Junior High, Burnsville)*; Anne Bartel *(Minneapolis Public Schools)*; Gwen Ranzau Campbell *(Sunrise Park Middle School, White Bear Lake)*; Stephanie Cin *(Hidden Valley Elementary, Burnsville)*; Joan Garfield *(University of Minnesota, Minneapolis)*; Gretchen Hall *(Richfield Middle School, Richfield)*; Jennifer Larson *(Olson Middle School, Minneapolis)*; Michele Luke *(West Junior High, Minnetonka)*; Jeni Meyer *(Richfield Junior High, Richfield)*; Judy Pfingsten *(Inver Grove Heights Middle School, Inver Grove Heights)*; Sarah Shafer *(North Junior High, Minnetonka)*; Genni Steele *(Central Middle School, White Bear Lake)*; Victoria Wilson *(Eisenhower Elementary, Hopkins)*; Paul Zorn *(St. Olaf College, Northfield)*

New York
Debra Altenau-Bartolino *(Greenwich Village Middle School, New York)*; Doug Clements *(University of Buffalo)*; Francis Curcio *(New York University, New York)*; Christine Dorosh *(Clinton School for Writers, Brooklyn)*; Jennifer Rehn *(East Side Middle School, New York)*; Phyllis Tam *(IS 89 Lab School, New York)*; Marie Turini *(Louis Armstrong Middle School, New York)*; Lucy West *(Community School District 2, New York)*; Monica Witt *(Simon Baruch Intermediate School 104, New York)*

Pennsylvania
Robert Aglietti *(Pittsburgh)*; Sharon Mihalich *(Freeport)*; Jennifer Plumb *(South Hills Middle School, Pittsburgh)*; Mary Lynn Raith *(Pittsburgh Public Schools)*

Texas
Michelle Bittick *(Austin Independent School District)*; Margaret Cregg *(Plano Independent School District)*; Sheila Cunningham *(Klein Independent School District)*; Judy Hill *(Austin Independent School District)*; Patricia Holguin *(El Paso Independent School District)*; Bonnie McNemar *(Arlington)*; Kay Neuse *(Plano Independent School District)*; Joyce Polanco *(Austin Independent School District)*; Marge Ramirez *(University of Texas at El Paso)*; Pat Rossman *(Baker Campus, Austin)*; Cindy Schimek *(Houston)*; Cynthia Schneider *(Charles A. Dana Center, University of Texas at Austin)*; Uri Treisman *(Charles A. Dana Center, University of Texas at Austin)*; Jacqueline Weilmuenster *(Grapevine-Colleyville Independent School District)*; LuAnn Weynand *(San Antonio)*; Carmen Whitman *(Austin Independent School District)*; James Wohlgehagen *(Plano Independent School District)*

Washington
Ramesh Gangolli *(University of Washington, Seattle)*

Wisconsin
Susan Lamon *(Marquette University, Hales Corner)*; Steve Reinhart *(retired, Chippewa Falls Middle School, Eau Claire)*

Growing, Growing, Growing
Exponential Relationships

> The Student Edition pages for the Unit Opener follow page 18.

Growing, Growing, Growing
Exponential Relationships

Goals of the Unit

- Recognize situations in which one variable is an exponential function of another variable

- Recognize the connections between exponential equations and growth patterns in tables and graphs of those equations

- Construct equations to express exponential patterns that appear in data tables, graphs, and problem conditions

- Understand and apply the rules for operating on numerical expressions with exponents

- Solve problems about exponential growth and decay from a variety of different subject areas, including science and business

- Compare exponential and linear relationships

Developing Students' Mathematical Habits

The overall goal of *Connected Mathematics* is to help students develop sound mathematical habits. Through their work in this and other algebra units, students learn important questions to ask themselves about any situation that can be represented and modeled mathematically, such as:

- *What are the variables?*

- *Is the relationship between variables an example of exponential growth or decay?*

- *How can the relationship be detected in a table, graph, or equation? What is the growth or decay factor?*

- *What equation models the data in the table?*

- *What equation models the pattern in the graph?*

- *What can I learn about this situation by studying a table, graph, or equation of the exponential relationship?*

- *How does the relationship compare to other types of relationships that I have studied?*

Overview

One of the central goals of algebra is describing and reasoning about relationships among quantitative variables. That goal has been addressed in many *Connected Mathematics* units. In grade 6, students looked for connections among sides and angles in regular polygons in *Shapes and Designs* and connections among dimensions, perimeters, and areas of various figures in *Covering and Surrounding*. In grade 7, students explored general techniques for representing quantitative relationships with words, pictures, tables, graphs, and symbols in *Variables and Patterns,* and then, in *Moving Straight Ahead,* focused on an important family of quantitative relationships: those with linear graphs illustrating constant, additive rates of change. In the grade 8 unit *Thinking With Mathematical Models*, students continued to explore linear patterns of change and contrasted these patterns with inverse patterns of change.

This algebra unit, *Growing, Growing, Growing,* focuses students' attention on a family of useful nonlinear relationships: those that model exponential growth and exponential decay. Studies of biological populations, from bacteria and amoebas to mammals (including humans), often reveal exponential patterns of growth. The populations increase over time and at increasing rates of growth. Graphs of the (*time, population*) data curve upward. This same pattern of growth at increasing rates is seen when money is invested in accounts paying compound interest or when inflation is tracked.

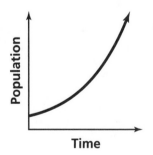 

In other situations, quantities decline as time passes, but the actual amount of decline diminishes over time (unlike the constant rate of decline for decreasing linear relationships). For example, radioactive substances and many medicines decay in nonlinear patterns in the body. These patterns of change are multiplicative. As the independent variable changes by a constant amount, the dependent variable changes by a constant factor.

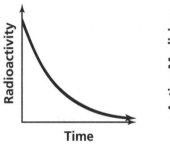 

Summary of Investigations

Investigation 1

Exponential Growth

In Investigation 1, students explore situations that involve repeated doubling, tripling, and quadrupling. Students are introduced to one of the essential features of many exponential patterns: rapid growth.

Students make and study tables and graphs for exponential situations, describe the patterns they see, and write equations for them, looking for a general form of an exponential equation. Students also compare and contrast linear and exponential patterns of growth.

Investigation 2
Examining Growth Patterns

Investigation 2 focuses on exponential relationships with y-intercepts greater than 1. The standard form of an exponential equation is $y = a(b)^x$. When $x = 0$, the equation becomes $y = a$ since $b^0 = 1$. Thus a, the coefficient of the exponential term, generally indicates the initial value of the exponentially growing quantity. This initial value is the y-value corresponding to $x = 0$, or the y-intercept. Each problem in the investigation presents information about an exponential pattern in a different form—in a verbal description, in an equation, and as a graph—helping students develop flexibility in moving among representations.

Investigation 3
Growth Factors and Growth Rates

In Investigation 3, students study non-whole-number growth factors other than 1 and relate these growth factors to *growth rates*. As an example, consider money invested at 6% annual interest. To find the amount of money for a given year, multiply the amount from the previous year by 1.06. The growth factor in this case is 1.06, while the growth rate is 6% (or 0.06). Students also explore how the growth rate and the initial value affect the growth pattern.

Investigation 4
Exponential Decay

Investigation 4 introduces students to *exponential decay*—patterns of change that exhibit successive, non-constant decreases rather than increases. These decreasing relationships are generated by repeated multiplication by factors between 0 and 1, called *decay factors*. Strategies for finding decay factors and initial population and for representing decay patterns are similar to those used for exponential growth patterns.

Investigation 5
Patterns With Exponents

Investigation 5 develops rules for operating with exponents. Students examine patterns among the ones digits of powers and use these patterns to predict ones digits for powers that would be tedious to find directly. Then, they look for relationships among numbers written in exponential form. This leads to the rules for operating on numerical expressions with exponents. Finally, students use graphing calculators to study the effects of the values of a and b on the graph of $y = a(b^x)$.

Mathematics Background

The basic goal in *Growing, Growing, Growing* is for students to learn to recognize situations, data patterns, and graphs that are modeled by exponential equations and to use tables, graphs, and equations to answer questions about exponential patterns. This unit is designed to introduce the topic and to give students a sound, intuitive foundation on which to build later.

Exponential Growth

An exponential pattern of change can often be recognized in a verbal description of a situation or in the pattern of change in a table of (x, y) values.

Suppose you offer one of your classes a reward for days on which everyone works diligently for the entire class period. At the start of the year, you put 1 cent in a party fund. You promise that on the first good-work day, you will contribute 2 cents; on the second good-work day, you will contribute 4 cents; and on each succeeding good-work day, you will double the reward of the previous good-work day.

Class Party Fund

Good-Work Day	Reward (cents)
0 (start)	1
1	2
2	4
3	8
4	16
5	32
6	64
7	128
8	256

Growth Factor

For each good-work day, the monetary reward doubles. You multiply the previous reward by 2 to get the new reward. This constant factor can also be obtained by dividing each successive y-value by the previous y-value: $\frac{2}{1} = 2, \frac{4}{2} = 2$, and so on. This ratio is called the *growth factor* of the pattern.

The exponential growth in rewards for good-work days in the example can be represented in a graph. The increasing rate of growth is reflected in the upward curve of the plotted points.

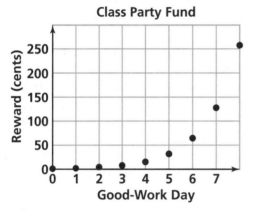

Exponential Equations

Examining the growth pattern in the class reward leads to an equation.

Day	Calculation	Reward (cents)
0	1	1
1	$1 \times 2 = 2^1$	2
2	$1 \times 2 \times 2 = 2^2$	4
3	$1 \times 2 \times 2 \times 2 = 2^3$	8
⋮	⋮	⋮
6	$1 \times 2 \times 2 \times 2 \times 2 \times 2 \times 2 = 2^6$	64
⋮	⋮	⋮
n	$1 \times 2 \times 2 \times \ldots \times 2 = 2^n$	2^n

This growth pattern can be summarized in symbolic form using exponents. For example, the reward on the tenth good-work day can be expressed as $1 \times 2 \times 2 \times 2 \times 2 \times 2 \times 2 \times 2 \times 2 \times 2 \times 2 = 2^{10}$.

On the nth good-work day, the reward r will be $r = 2^n$. Because the independent variable in this pattern appears as an exponent, the growth

pattern is called *exponential*. The growth factor is the *base*, 2. The *exponent n* tells the number of times the 2 is a factor.

It is important to distinguish between a constant growth *factor* (multiplicative), as just illustrated in an exponential pattern, and the constant *additive* pattern in linear relationships. In the graphs of $y = 2^x$ and $y = 2x + 1$ below, the horizontal change is the same. On the graph of $y = 2x + 1$, the vertical change is a constant. On the graph of $y = 2^x$, the vertical change increases by a multiple of the growth factor as the graph rises.

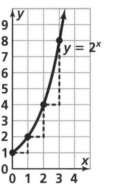 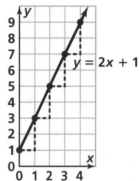

In a linear situation with equation $y = mx + b$, as x increases by 1, the value m is added to get the new y-value. The difference between any two consecutive terms in a linear relationship is that constant additive change m. In contrast, an exponential growth pattern, $y = a(b)^x$, may increase slowly at first but grows at an increasing rate because its growth is multiplicative. The growth factor is b.

y-Intercept or Initial Value

In the preceding example, the y-intercept was $(0, 1)$. The following example illustrates a y-intercept that is not equal to 1.

The class party fund began with only 1 cent. That might strike students as a tiny seed for the fund, so suppose you made a more generous initial offer of 5 cents. The table and graph for this new reward scheme follow; an equation (with the usual variable names, x and y) to represent it would be $y = 5(2^x)$.

Note that the growth factor is still 2. The reward on any given good-work day is twice that of the previous day. The reward is five times the reward for the same day in the original scheme, and the new starting amount is reflected in the equation by multiplying the original reward by 5. The equation is $y = 5(2^x)$. In the standard form for exponential equations, $y = a(b^x)$, a is the y-intercept, and b is the growth factor.

Class Party Fund

Good-Work Day	Reward (cents)
0 (start)	5
1	10
2	20
3	40
4	80
5	160
6	320

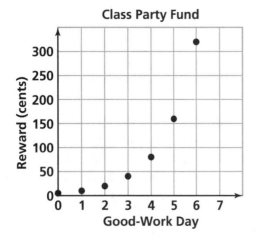

Class Party Fund

Note that students sometimes refer to the y-intercept (or initial value) as the "starting point." For exponential situations, they use the starting point and the growth factor to generate a table by multiplying the previous term by a constant factor. For a linear situation, they use the starting point (y-intercept) and the constant rate of change to generate a table by adding a constant amount to the previous term.

Growth Rates

A growth rate is different from, but related to, a growth factor. The following example will illustrate the connection between the two concepts.

Suppose you put 5 cents in the Class Party Fund and then increase the reward by 8% for each succeeding good-work day. Figure 1 shows the calculations required to find the reward for each day.

The 8% increase is the growth rate. By examining the pattern in the reward column, you can see that the growth factor is 1.08. (Divide each reward value by the previous reward value.) The equation for the relationship between the work day n and reward r is: $r = 5(1.08)^n$

Another way to find the growth factor is to apply the distributive property at each stage of the calculations:

Day 1: $5 + 0.08 \times 5 = 5(1 + 0.08) = 5 \times 1.08$

Day 2: $(5 \times 1.08) + 0.08 \times (5 \times 1.08)$
$= (5 \times 1.08)(1 + 0.08)$
$= (5 \times 1.08)(1.08)$
$= 5 \times (1.08)^2$

Continuing this process gives
Day n: $5 \times (1.08)^n$

In general, a growth rate of r is associated with a growth factor of $(1 + r)$. Similarly, if the growth factor is f, then the growth rate is $(f - 1)$. Growth rates are often expressed as percents.

Figure 1

Good-Work Day	Calculation	Reward (cents)
0 (start)	5	5
1	5 + 0.08 × 5	5.4
2	5.4 + 0.08 × 5.4	5.832
3	5.832 + 0.08 × 5.832	6.29856
4	6.29856 + 0.08 × 6.29856	6.8024448
5	6.8024448 + 0.08 × 6.8024448	7.346640384
6	7.346640384 + 0.08 × 7.346640384	7.934371615
⋮	⋮	⋮
n		$5(1.08)^n$

Exponential Decay

Exponential models also describe patterns in which the value of a dependent variable decreases as time passes. In this case, the constant multiplicative factor is referred to as the decay factor. Decay factors work just like growth factors, only they result in decreasing relationships because they are between 0 and 1.

Suppose another teacher offers a different incentive for good-work days. At the start of the school year, the teacher puts $50 in a class party fund. For each day the class does not work diligently, she cuts the party fund in half.

As the days pass, the class party fund will decrease in the pattern shown in the following table. The exponential decay pattern is also represented in the graph. The plotted points begin at (0, 50) and drop from left to right. Notice that, although half the amount is removed at each stage, the amount removed each time decreases.

Class Party Fund

Bad-Work Day	Reward
0 (start)	$50.00
1	$25.00
2	$12.50
3	$6.25
4	$3.13
5	$1.56
6	$0.78
7	$0.39
8	$0.20

The decay factor for this exponential decay pattern is $\frac{1}{2}$. The amount in the party fund f after n bad-work days is given by the equation $f = 50(\frac{1}{2})^n$.

This exponential model is similar to that for exponential growth except that the repeating factor, the base, is a positive number less than 1.

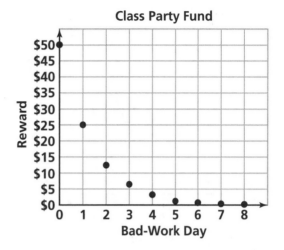

Class Party Fund

Graphs of Exponential Relationships

The basic patterns of exponential growth and exponential decay involve change from one point in time to the next by some constant factor. For growth, the change factor is a number greater than 1 and the graph curves upward from left to right. For decay, the change factor is between 0 and 1 and the graph curves downward from left to right, approaching the x-axis but never reaching it.

Exponential relationships can also be defined for negative and non-integer values of the exponent. The related graphs are *continuous curves* (rather than graphs of plotted points) with shapes similar to those shown.

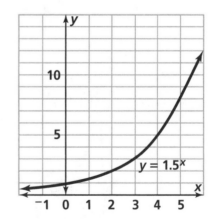

$y = 1.5^x$

Students will recall from the unit *Variables and Patterns* the difference between graphs where the dots are connected and those where the dots are not connected. In this unit, that distinction is not an important one. In fact, it is often useful to connect the dots to highlight a pattern. In such a case, though, it is important to remember that the points

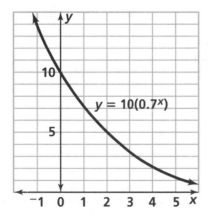

corresponding to non-integer values of x may not arise from the data of the problem at hand.

The focus of this unit is primarily on positive integer exponents, so the graphs will generally occur in the first quadrant. Depending on the situation, the graph will show discrete points (with or without a curve through the points) or a continuous curve.

It is illuminating to occasionally ask students what information the continuous graphs produced by graphing calculators communicate at non-integer points. For example, in many contexts where time is the independent variable, the corresponding y-values have quite natural interpretations.

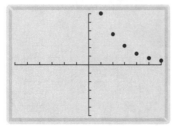

Graph of plotted points

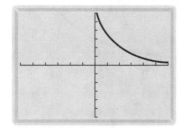

Graph of related equation

The formal definition of exponential expressions for non-integer exponents is delayed until a later course.

Tables of Exponential Relationships: Recursive or Iterative Processes

Students usually generate each value in their tables based on the previous value. Either they add a constant to the previous value (in the case of linear relationships) or they multiply the previous value by a constant (in the case of exponential relationships). This process of generating a value from a previous value is called *recursion* or *iteration*.

Equivalence of Two Forms of Exponential Equations

In the first investigation of this unit, students may end up writing two different, but equivalent, exponential equations for this situation:

A king places 1 ruba on the first square of a chessboard, 2 rubas on the second square, 4 on the third square, 8 on the fourth square, and so on, until he has covered all 64 squares. Each square has twice as many rubas as the previous square.

By examining the patterns in a table, students write an equation for the number of rubas r on square n.

Square Number	Number of Rubas
1	1
2	2
3	4
4	8
5	16

Some students will note that the number of rubas on a given square n is a product of $n - 1$ twos and write $r = (2^{n-1})$.

Other students will reverse the pattern and find the number of rubas on "square 0" by dividing by the number of rubas on square 1 by 2. This gives them the y-intercept, $\frac{1}{2}$. (Square 0 has no meaning in this context, but many students find it useful to use the y-intercept as a starting point when they write an equation.) They then note that the number of rubas on square n is half the product of n twos, and write $r = \frac{1}{2}(2^n)$.

It is important for students to recognize that the two forms, $r = (2^{n-1})$ and $r = \frac{1}{2}(2^n)$, are equivalent. They can verify the equivalence by generating tables or graphs.

The following is a general argument for why b^{x-1} is equivalent to $\frac{1}{b}(b^x)$ for any value of b. (In the example above, $b = 2$.)

The equation $y = (b^{x-1})$ is equivalent to $y = (b^x) \times b^{-1}$. Because $b^{-1} = \frac{1}{b}$, this is equivalent to $y = \frac{1}{b}(b^x)$.

This argument is provided for your information. Students do not need to understand it at this point in their development.

Logarithms

Understanding logarithms is *not* a goal of this unit. Logarithms are not mentioned to students. Nonetheless, there are several questions in the unit that push students to think about the ideas behind logarithms. For example, in Problem 1.1, students examine a situation in which a sheet of paper is cut in half, the resulting two pieces are stacked and the stack is cut in half, the resulting four pieces are stacked and the stack is cut in half, and so on. Students write the equation $y = 2^x$ to describe the relationship between the number of cuts x and the number of pieces of paper y. In one question, they are asked how many cuts it would take to create at least 500 pieces of paper. The answer is the solution to $500 = 2^x$.

Students will and should estimate the solution by using a guess-and-check method or by generating a calculator table or graph. In high school, they will learn to use logarithms to solve such an equation exactly.

Logarithmic functions are the inverses of exponential functions, just as division is the inverse of multiplication. We can rewrite the preceding equation as:

$x = \log_2 500$

Some calculators can compute logarithms using any base (here the base is 2). Most scientific calculators are limited to the bases 10 and e. In this case, the solution is more complicated:

$500 = 2^x$

$\log_{10}(500) = \log_{10}(2^x)$

$\log_{10}(500) = x\log_{10}(2)$ (by laws of exponents)

So, $x = \dfrac{\log_{10} 500}{\log_{10} 2}$.

Remember that all of this is far beyond what we ask students to do in this unit.

Not all problems can be solved by applying standard algorithms. For example, there is no algebraic technique for finding the point of intersection of an exponential relationship and a linear relationship, such as $y = (2^x)$ and $y = 5x + 15$. The best we can do is estimate the intersection point of the graphs of the equations. Sophisticated estimation techniques exist, but it is impossible to solve such a problem directly.

Rules of Exponents

Students begin to develop understanding of the rules of exponents by examining patterns in the powers charts for the first 10 whole numbers. (See Figure 2.)

Students observe that several numbers occur more than once in the table. For example, 64 occurs as 2^6, 8^2, and 4^3. By examining the multiplicative structure of the bases, they find that $8^2 = (2 \times 2 \times 2)^2 = (2^3)^2 = 2^6$. After several examples, students conjecture that $(b^m)^n = b^{mn}$.

Students multiply pairs of numbers in the same column, say 9 and 27 in column 3: $9 \times 27 = 243$ or $3^2 \times 3^3 = 3^5$. After looking at several examples, students conjecture that $(b^m)(b^n) = b^{m+n}$.

Students also multiply pairs of numbers in the same row, say 4 and 25 in row 2:
$4 \times 25 = 2^2 \times 5^2 = (2 \times 5)^2 = 10^2 = 100$.
The general pattern is $(a^m b^m) = (ab)^m$. Similar explorations lead to the rule $\frac{a^m}{a^n} = a^{m-n}$.

Students also note that the ones digits for the powers repeat in cycles of 1, 2, or 4 and apply this observation to predict ones digits of powers and to estimate the value of exponential expressions.

Figure 2

Powers Table

x	1^x	2^x	3^x	4^x	5^x	6^x	7^x	8^x	9^x	10^x
1	1	2	3	4	5	6	7	8	9	10
2	1	4	9	16	25	36	49	64	81	100
3	1	8	27	64	125	216	343	512	729	1,000
4	1	16	81	256	625	1,296	2,401	4,096	6,561	10,000
5	1	32	243	1,024	3,125	7,776	16,807	32,768	59,049	100,000
6	1	64	729	4,096	15,625	46,656	117,649	262,144	531,441	1,000,000
7	1	128	2,187	16,384	78,125	279,936	823,543	2,097,152	4,782,969	10,000,000
8	1	256	6,561	65,536	390,625	1,679,616	5,764,801	16,777,216	43,046,721	100,000,000
Ones Digits of Powers	1	2, 4, 8, 6	3, 9, 7, 1	4, 6	5	6	7, 9, 3, 1	8, 4, 2, 6	9, 1	0

Big Idea	Prior Work	Future Work
Building and analyzing an exponential model	Looking for graphical or symbolic models to describe a pattern in data *(Variables and Patterns; Moving Straight Ahead; Thinking With Mathematical Models)*	Extending the analysis to include all positive real numbers for the domain *(high school)*
Reasoning with and about exponential relationships	Reasoning relationships such as connections among attributes of geometric figures *(Covering and Surrounding)* Representing relationships with words, tables, graphs, and equations *(Variables and Patterns; Moving Straight Ahead; Thinking With Mathematical Models)*	Using tabular, graphical, and symbolic methods to solve problems that involve exponential functions, such as finding half-life or solving equations of the type $a^x = b$ *(high school)*
Exploring the significance of shapes of graphs and patterns in tables of exponential relationships	Exploring the significance of shapes of graphs and patterns in tables *(Variables and Patterns; Moving Straight Ahead; Thinking With Mathematical Models)*	Exploring the significance of shapes of graphs and patterns in tables *(Frogs, Fleas, and Painted Cubes)* Extending the experiences to include recognition of logarithmic and trigonometric relationships *(high school)*
Making sense of the symbols in the equation $y = a(b^x)$	Attaching meaning to the symbols in a linear equation of the form $y = mx + b$ *(Variables and Patterns; Moving Straight Ahead; Thinking With Mathematical Models)*	Making sense of the symbols in quadratic relationships, expressed in expanded or factored form *(Frogs, Fleas, and Painted Cubes)* Reviewing and extending the analysis of exponential and quadratic functions *(high school)* Analyzing symbolic expressions of trigonometric and logarithmic functions *(high school)*
Exploring rates of growth	Recognizing the significance of constant additive growth *(Moving Straight Ahead)*; reasoning about percent change *(Comparing and Scaling)*	Recognizing the significance of the pattern of change in quadratic relationships *(Frogs, Fleas, and Painted Cubes)* Analyzing patterns of change in exponential, logarithmic, and trigonometric functions *(high school)*
Recognizing and describing situations that can be modeled by an exponential function	Recognizing and describing situations that can be modeled by linear relationships *(Variables and Patterns; Moving Straight Ahead; Thinking With Mathematical Models)*	Recognizing and describing situations that can be modeled by quadratic functions *(Frogs, Fleas, and Painted Cubes)* Extending recognition to logarithmic and trigonometric functions *(high school)*
Using exponents	Using exponents to express large and small quantities *(Data Around Us ©2004)*	Applying rules for exponents to interpret more complex algebraic expressions and exponential equations *(high school)*

Planning for the Unit

Pacing Suggestions and Materials

Investigations and Assessments	Pacing 45–50 min. classes	Materials for Students	Materials for Teachers
1 Exponential Growth	4 days	Graph paper, blank paper, Labsheet 1.2 (optional), counters	Blank paper, Transparencies 1.1, 1.2A, 1.2B, 1.3A and 1.3B, 1.4 (optional)
Mathematical Reflections	$\frac{1}{2}$ day		
2 Examining Growth Patterns	3 days	Graph paper	Transparencies 2.1 and 2.3 (optional)
Mathematical Reflections	$\frac{1}{2}$ day		
Assessment: Check Up	$\frac{1}{2}$ day		
3 Growth Factors and Growth Rates	3 days	Graph paper	Transparency 3.1 (optional)
Mathematical Reflections	$\frac{1}{2}$ day		
4 Exponential Decay	3 days	Grid paper, scissors, hot water, cups for holding hot liquid, thermometers, watches or clocks with second hands, CBLs (optional)	Inch grid paper, Transparencies 4.1 and 4.2 (optional), CBL (optional), thermometer for measuring the room temperature
Mathematical Reflections	$\frac{1}{2}$ day		
Assessment: Partner Quiz	1 day		
5 Patterns With Exponents	4 days	Labsheet 5.1	Transparencies 5.1A, 5.1B, 5.2A, 5.2B; overhead graphing calculator (optional)
Mathematical Reflections	$\frac{1}{2}$ day		
Looking Back and Looking Ahead	$\frac{1}{2}$ day		
Assessment: Unit Project	Optional		
Assessment: Self Assessment	Take Home		
Assessment: Unit Test	1 day		

Total Time $22\frac{1}{2}$ days

For detailed pacing for Problems within each Investigation, see the Suggested Pacing at the beginning of each investigation.

For pacing with block scheduling, see next page.

Materials for Use in All Investigations	
Graphing calculators, student notebooks	Blank transparencies and transparency markers (optional)

Pacing for Block Scheduling (90-minute class periods)

Investigation	Suggested Pacing	Investigation	Suggested Pacing	Investigation	Suggested Pacing
Investigation 1	$2\frac{1}{2}$ days	**Investigation 3**	2 days	**Investigation 5**	3 days
Problem 1.1	$\frac{1}{2}$ day	Problem 3.1	$\frac{1}{2}$ day	Problem 5.1	1 day
Problem 1.2	$\frac{1}{2}$ day	Problem 3.2	$\frac{1}{2}$ day	Problem 5.2	1 day
Problem 1.3	$\frac{1}{2}$ day	Problem 3.3	$\frac{1}{2}$ day	Problem 5.3	$\frac{1}{2}$ day
Problem 1.4	$\frac{1}{2}$ day	Math Reflections	$\frac{1}{2}$ day	Math Reflections	$\frac{1}{2}$ day
Math Reflections	$\frac{1}{2}$ day	**Investigation 4**	2 days		
Investigation 2	2 days	Problem 4.1	$\frac{1}{2}$ day		
Problem 2.1	$\frac{1}{2}$ day	Problem 4.2	$\frac{1}{2}$ day		
Problem 2.2	$\frac{1}{2}$ day	Problem 4.3	$\frac{1}{2}$ day		
Problem 2.3	$\frac{1}{2}$ day	Math Reflections	$\frac{1}{2}$ day		
Math Reflections	$\frac{1}{2}$ day				

Vocabulary

Essential Terms Developed in This Unit	Useful Terms Referenced in This Unit	Terms Developed in Previous Units
base	doubling time	factor
compound growth	evaluate	linear relationship
decay factor	investment rate	rate
decay rate	linear growth	ratio
exponent	rate of decay	relationship
exponential decay	standard form	power
exponential form		scientific notation
exponential growth		
exponential relationship		
growth factor		
growth rate		

Components

Use the chart below to quickly see which components are available for each Investigation.

Investigation	Labsheets	Additional Practice	Transparencies		Formal Assessment		Assessment Options	
			Problem	Summary	Check Up	Partner Quiz	Multiple-Choice	Question Bank
1	1.2	✔	1.1, 1.2A, 1.2B, 1.3A, 1.3B, 1.4				✔	✔
2		✔	2.1, 2.3		✔			✔
3		✔						✔
4		✔	4.1, 4.2			✔	✔	✔
5	5.1	✔	5.1A, 5.1B, 5.2A, 5.2B				✔	✔
For the Unit		*ExamView* CD-ROM, Web site	LBLA		Unit Test, Notebook Check, Self Assessment		Multiple-Choice, Question Bank, *ExamView* CD-ROM	

Also Available For Use With This Unit

- Parent Guide: take-home letter for the unit
- Implementing CMP

- Spanish Assessment Resources
- Additional online and technology resources

Technology

The Use of Calculators

Connected Mathematics was developed with the belief that calculators should be available and that students should learn when their use is appropriate. For this reason, we do not designate specific problems as "calculator problems."

Students will need access to graphing calculators for most of their work in this unit. Ideally, the calculators should be able to display a function table. It is also helpful if you have an overhead display model of the calculator. Extensive exploration of exponential patterns with the assistance of graphing calculators, and frequent class discussions to share observations and formulate explanations, will add a great deal to the impact of this unit.

The instructions here are written for the TI-83 graphing calculator. If your students use a different calculator, consult the manual for instructions on these various procedures.

Performing Recursive Multiplication

Because the essence of an exponential relationship is recursive multiplication, there are efficient calculator algorithms to shorten the process. Here is the output from a calculator that, beginning with 5, is repeating the process of multiplying an answer by 2.

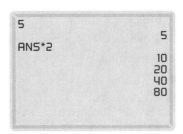

To accomplish this, press 5 and ENTER. To enter the formula ANS × 2, press 2nd (−) × 2. Now, by repeatedly pressing ENTER, you will generate a list of values, each of which is double the previous value.

Entering Exponents

When entering equations in which the exponent consists of more than one character, such as $r = 2^{n-1}$, the entire exponent must be enclosed in parentheses. For instance, the right side of this equation would be entered as 2^(X−1). This is because the calculator follows the correct order of operations. So, when evaluating 2^X−1, the calculator first finds 2^X and then subtracts 1.

Converting Decimals to Fractions

There are occasions in this unit when it is convenient to work with fractions rather than with decimals to see a pattern in the data. To convert a displayed decimal to a fraction, press MATH. Select choice 1 to convert the decimal to a simple fraction and then press ENTER.

Displaying a Function Table

Once an equation has been entered, you can display (x, y) pairs that satisfy the equation in a table. The values in a table can be displayed in decimal increments by changing the settings in the TABLE SETUP menu. Press 2nd WINDOW to access the menu and enter a new value for △TBL.

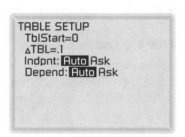

Then press 2nd GRAPH to display the table. Below is a table for the equation $y = 1.4^x$.

Entering Data

Data given as (x, y) pairs can be entered into the calculator and plotted. To enter a list of (x, y) data pairs, press STAT and then press ENTER to select the Edit mode. Then enter the pairs into the L1 and L2 columns: Enter the first number and press ENTER, use the arrow keys to change columns, enter the second number and press ENTER, then use the arrow keys to return to the L1 column.

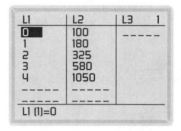

Plotting the Points

To plot the data you have entered, use the commands in the STAT PLOT menu. Display the STAT PLOT menu, which looks like the following screen, by pressing 2nd Y=.

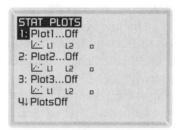

Press ENTER to select PLOT1. Use the arrow keys and ENTER to move around the screen and highlight the elements shown (ON, icon of discrete points, L1, L2, and open circle for mark).

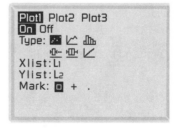

Next, press WINDOW, which will display a screen similar to the one below. To accommodate the data you have for input, adjust the window settings by entering values and pressing ENTER.

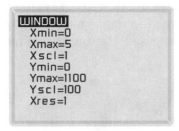

Press GRAPH.

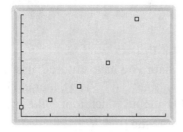

Exploring Sums of Sequences

The sum of a geometric sequence is a bit beyond what we hope to accomplish in this unit, but students can use their calculators to derive sums of sequences fairly easily.

The following screen shows how to find the sum of terms in the sequence 2^n for $n = 0$ to $n = 10$. The calculation involves two operations. The SUM operation gives the sum of all elements in a list. This operation is found in the LIST MATH menu, which is accessed by pressing 2nd STAT, selecting MATH, and choosing option 5, sum(. The SEQ operation defines a sequence. This operation is found in the LIST OPS menu. It is accessed by pressing 2nd STAT, selecting OPS, and choosing option 5, seq(.

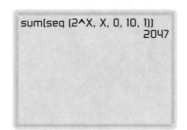

Student CD-ROM

Includes interactive activities to enhance the learning in the Problems within Investigations.

PHSchool.com

For Students Multiple-choice practice with instant feedback, updated data sources, and data sets for Tinkerplots data software.

For Teachers Professional development, curriculum support, downloadable forms, and more.

See also www.math.msu.edu/cmp for more resources for both teachers and students.

ExamView® CD-ROM

Create multiple versions of practice sheets and tests for course objectives and standardized tests. Includes dynamic questions, online testing, student reports, and all test and practice items in Spanish. Also includes all items in the *Assessment Resources* and *Additional Practice*.

Teacher Express™ CD-ROM

Includes a lesson planning tool, the Teacher's Guide pages, and all the teaching resources.

LessonLab Online Courses

LessonLab offers comprehensive, facilitated professional development designed to help teachers implement CMP2 and improve student achievement. To learn more, please visit PHSchool.com/cmp2.

Assessment Summary

Ongoing Informal Assessment

Embedded in the Student Unit
Problems Use students' work from the Problems to check student understanding.

ACE exercises Use ACE exercises for homework assignments to assess student understanding.

Mathematical Reflections Have students summarize their learning at the end of each Investigation.

Looking Back and Looking Ahead At the end of the unit, use the first two sections to allow students to show what they know about the unit.

Additional Resources
Teacher's Edition Use the Check for Understanding feature of some Summaries and the probing questions that appear in the *Launch, Explore,* or *Summarize* sections of all Investigations to check student understanding.

Summary Transparencies Use these transparencies to focus class attention on a summary check for understanding.

Self Assessment
Notebook Check Students use this tool to organize and check their notebooks before giving them to their teacher. Located in *Assessment Resources*.

Self Assessment At the end of the unit, students reflect on and provide examples of what they learned. Located in *Assessment Resources*.

Formal Assessment

Choose the assessment materials that are appropriate for your students.

Assessment	For Use After	Focus	Student Work
Check Up	Invest. 2	Skills	Individual
Partner Quiz	Invest. 3	Rich problems	Pair
Unit Test	The Unit	Skills, rich problems	Individual
Unit Project	The Unit	Rich problems	Pair or Group

Additional Resources
Multiple-Choice Items Use these items for homework, review, a quiz, or add them to the Unit Test.

Question Bank Choose from these questions for homework, review, or replacements for Quiz, Check Up, or Unit Test questions.

Additional Practice Choose practice exercises for each Investigation for homework, review, or formal assessments.

***ExamView* CD-ROM** Create practice sheets, review quizzes, and tests with this dynamic software. Give online tests and receive student progress reports. (All test items are available in Spanish.)

Spanish Assessment Resources
Includes Partner Quizzes, Check Ups, Unit Test, Multiple-Choice Items, Question Bank, Notebook Check, and Self Assessment. Plus, the *ExamView* CD-ROM has all test items in Spanish.

Correlation to Standardized Tests

Investigation	NAEP	Terra Nova		ITBS	SAT10	Local Test
		CAT6	CTBS			
1 Exponential Growth	A1a, A1b, A1e, A2g					
2 Examining Growth Patterns	A1a, A1b, A1e, A2g					
3 Growth Factors and Growth Rates	A1a, A1b, A1e, A2g					
4 Exponential Decay	A1a, A1b, A1e, A2g					
5 Patterns With Exponents	N5e					

NAEP National Assessment of Educational Progress   **CAT6/Terra Nova** California Achievement Test, 6th Ed.   **CTBS/Terra Nova** Comprehensive Test of Basic Skills   **ITBS** Iowa Test of Basic Skills, Form M   **SAT10** Stanford Achievement Test, 10th Ed.

Introducing Your Students to *Growing, Growing, Growing*

One way to introduce *Growing, Growing, Growing* is to find an interesting graph of exponential growth—the return on a bond mutual fund, or the growth of the world's population, for example. Ask students to identify the variables and to describe the relationship between them. Discuss whether the relationship is linear and how students can tell that it is not. Tell students that in this unit they will study relationships like these, which are called exponential relationships.

Using the Unit Opener

Refer students to the three questions posed on the opening page of the student edition. The questions are designed to start students thinking about nonlinear relations between variables. Invite students to share personal experiences they have had with any of these situations. Then explain that all of these examples involve a similar type of pattern called exponential change.

Each question is posed again in the investigations, after the students have learned the mathematical concepts required to answer it. Ask your students to keep these questions in mind as they work through the investigations and to think about how they might use the ideas they are learning to help them determine the answers.

Using the Mathematical Highlights

The Mathematical Highlights page in the student edition provides information to students, parents, and other family members. It gives students a preview of the mathematics and some of the overarching questions that they should ask themselves while studying *Growing, Growing, Growing*.

As they work through the unit, students can refer back to the Mathematical Highlights page to review what they have learned and to preview what is still to come. This page also tells students' families what mathematical ideas and activities will be covered as the class works through *Growing, Growing, Growing*.

Using the Unit Project

As a final assessment in *Growing, Growing, Growing*, you may administer the Unit Test or assign the Unit Project, Half-Life. In this optional project, students investigate the phenomenon of radioactive decay. They simulate the decay of a substance, collect and analyze data, and look for patterns.

We recommend that students work on the project with a partner. Each pair will need 100 cubes (wooden, plastic, or sugar) to conduct the simulation. If it is not possible to have students mark on the cubes, supply them with stickers that can be removed later. Students could also use dice and choose one number to represent the marked side. The cubes can be shared.

The material in Investigation 4 is necessary for this project. Some teachers launch the project at the start of Investigation 4 and use the last several minutes of class each day for a few groups to experiment and collect data. By the end of Investigation 4, all groups have their data. A class period is then used for groups to finish the project.

Sample results and answers to the questions are given in the Assessment Resources section.

Connected  Mathematics 2™

Growing, Growing, Growing

Exponential Relationships

$$2.7 \times 10^{12}$$

Glenda Lappan

James T. Fey

William M. Fitzgerald

Susan N. Friel

Elizabeth Difanis Phillips

PEARSON

Boston, Massachusetts · Glenview, Illinois · Shoreview, Minnesota · Upper Saddle River, New Jersey

Notes _____

_____

_____

_____

Growing, Growing, Growing

Exponential Relationships

When the water hyacinth was introduced to Lake Victoria, it spread quickly over the lake's surface. At one point, the plant covered 769 square miles, and its area was doubling every 15 days. What equation models this growth?

When Sam was in seventh grade, his aunt gave him a stamp collection worth $2,500. The value of the collection increased by 6% each year for several years in a row. What was the value of Sam's collection after four years?

What pattern of change would you expect to find in the temperature of a hot drink as time passes? What would a graph of the (time, drink temperature) data look like?

2   Growing, Growing, Growing

Notes _____

_____

_____

_____

One of the most important uses of algebra is to model patterns of change. You are already familiar with linear patterns of change. Linear patterns have constant differences and straight-line graphs. In a linear relationship, the y-value increases by a constant amount each time the x-value increases by 1.

In this unit, you will study exponential patterns of change.

Exponential growth patterns are fascinating because, although the values may change gradually at first, they eventually increase very rapidly. Patterns that decrease, or decay, exponentially may decrease quickly at first, but eventually they decrease very slowly.

As you work through the investigations in this unit, you will encounter problems like those the on the facing page.

Notes _____

_____

_____

_____

Mathematical Highlights

Exponential Relationships

In *Growing, Growing, Growing,* you will explore exponential relationships, one of the most important types of nonlinear relationships.

You will learn how to

- Identify situations in which a quantity grows or decays exponentially
- Recognize the connections between exponential equations and the growth patterns in tables and graphs of those equations
- Construct equations to express exponential patterns in data tables, graphs, and problem situations
- Solve problems about exponential growth and decay from a variety of different areas, including science and business
- Compare exponential and linear relationships
- Understand the rules for working with exponents

As you work on the problems in this unit, ask yourself questions about situations that involve nonlinear relationships:

What are the variables?

Is the relationship between variables an example of exponential growth or decay?

How can the relationship be detected in a table, graph, or equation?

What is the growth or decay factor?

What equation models the data in the table?

What equation models the pattern in the graph?

What can I learn about this situation by studying a table, graph, or equation of the exponential relationship?

How does the relationship compare to other types of relationships that I have studied?

Notes _____

_____

_____

_____

Investigation 1 · Exponential Growth

Mathematical and Problem-Solving Goals

- Gain an intuitive understanding of basic exponential growth patterns

- Begin to recognize exponential patterns in tables, graphs, and equations

- Solve problems involving exponential growth

- Understand the role of the growth factor in exponential relationships

- Express a product of identical factors in both exponential form and standard form

- Write equations for exponential relationships represented by tables and graphs

- Make a table from the graph of an exponential relationship

- Compare different exponential growth patterns and compare exponential and linear growth

Summary of Problems

Problem 1.1 Making Ballots

This hands-on introduction to the unit offers a review of exponents. Students investigate the growth in the number of ballots created by repeatedly cutting a piece of paper in half.

Problem 1.2 Requesting a Reward

Students investigate an exponential situation set in the fictitious ancient kingdom of Montarek. One coin is placed on the first square of a chessboard, two on the second square, four on the third square, and so on. Students explore patterns of change in this exponential relationship.

Problem 1.3 Making a New Offer

Students consider two variations on the previous problem. In the first, the number of coins is tripled on each square. In the second, the number is quadrupled. Students make tables and graphs for the variations, describe patterns, and write equations for them, looking for a general form for exponential equations. The term *growth factor* is introduced.

Problem 1.4 Getting Costs in Line

Students compare a linear relationship to the exponential relationships in the preceding problems.

	Suggested Pacing	Materials for Students	Materials for Teachers	ACE Assignments
All	$4\frac{1}{2}$ days	Graphing calculators, student notebooks	Blank transparencies and transparency markers (optional)	
1.1	1 day	Blank paper	Transparency 1.1 (optional), blank paper	1–4, 31
1.2	1 day	Labsheet 1.2 or chessboards (optional), counters (about 65 per group)	Transparencies 1.2A and 1.2B (optional)	5–21, 32, 33, 39–46
1.3	1 day	Labsheet 1.2 or chessboards (optional), counters (about 65 per group)	Transparencies 1.3A and 1.3B (optional)	22, 23, 34, 47–49
1.4	1 day		Transparency 1.4 (optional)	24–30, 35–38, 50
MR	$\frac{1}{2}$ day			

1.1 Making Ballots

Goals

- Gain an intuitive understanding of basic exponential growth patterns
- Begin to recognize exponential patterns in tables

In earlier units, students explored relationships between variables and found patterns that helped them express those relationships symbolically. They used graphs, tables, and equations to represent situations. With this paper-cutting activity, students begin an exploration of exponential growth by representing the data in a table.

Launch 1.1

Describe Chen's ballot-making task. You might ask students to jot down predictions for the number of ballots that would result from three, four, or even ten cuts. Later, they can compare their predictions to the results they obtain in the activity.

Have students work on the problem in groups of two to four.

Explore 1.1

Have students cut and stack paper for the first two or three cuts. This provides a visual aid to help them understand the relationship between the number of cuts and the number of ballots created.

Suggested Questions Encourage students to look for the multiplicative pattern in the table by asking questions like these:

- *How did you find each of the entries in your table?*

- *What is the relationship between this number of ballots and the previous number of ballots?* (It is twice the previous number.)

- *Explain that relationship in terms of the number of cuts.* (When the number of cuts increases by 1, the number of ballots doubles.)

As students work on Questions C and D, look for interesting strategies to share in the summary.

Students might be using exponential notation rather than listing all the factors of 2 that are needed for each cut. Some will begin to reason using the general relationship between cuts and number of ballots.

You may want to distribute blank transparencies for some groups to record their answers for sharing during the summary.

Summarize 1.1

Suggested Questions As groups share their answers to the problem, you may want to ask questions like these:

- *How do your results compare to the predictions you made earlier?*

- *How is the number of ballots after each cut related to the number of ballots before the cut?* (The number of ballots doubles with each successive cut.)

- *Question C asked how many ballots are made after 20 cuts and after 30 cuts. Describe how you found your answers.*

- *Question D asked you to work in reverse to predict the number of cuts needed to make enough ballots for 500 students. Describe your method.* (Students generally find it more difficult to work in reverse, especially because no exact power of 2 is equal to 500. Because 8 cuts gives 256 ballots and 9 cuts gives 512 ballots, 9 cuts are needed to guarantee at least 500 ballots.)

By asking about patterns in the table relating the number of cuts to the number of ballots, lead the class to a discussion of exponents.

Suggested Questions Display the table from Problem 1.1 on the overhead and ask:

- *How did you get the number of ballots for 5 cuts?* (Most students will say they started with 1 cut and 2 ballots and then multiplied the number of ballots by 2 for each cut until they reached 5 cuts.)

Add a third column to the table and illustrate each calculation, showing each factor of 2. Stop after showing the calculation for 5 cuts. (Figure 1)

Suggested Questions

• *How many times is 2 used as a factor to find the number of ballots after 1 cut? After 2 cuts? After 3 cuts? After 4 cuts? After 5 cuts?*

• *Can you predict how many factors of 2 will be used to find the number of ballots after 6 cuts? After 10 cuts? After 30 cuts?*

Explain to students that they can use shorthand notation, rather than writing the factor of 2 over and over again. Write the following on the board:

$2 \times 2 \times 2 \times 2 \times 2 \times 2 \times 2 \times 2 \times 2 \times 2 = 2^{10}$

Make sure students see that there are 10 factors of 2 on the left side of the equation and a raised number 10 on the right side.

Point to the expression 2^{10}. Explain that the number 2 is the *base*, the number 10 is the *exponent*, and the expression 2^{10} is in *exponential form*. Explain that 1,024 is the *standard form* of 2^{10}.

Suggested Questions

• *How many ballots are there after 0 cuts?* (1 ballot)

• *How could we show this in our table?* (Add a row at the top that has 0 in the Number of Cuts column and 1 in the Number of Ballots column.)

Figure 1

Number of Cuts	Number of Ballots	Calculation
1	2	2
2	4	2 × 2
3	8	2 × 2 × 2
4	16	2 × 2 × 2 × 2
5	32	2 × 2 × 2 × 2 × 2
6	64	
7	128	
8	256	
9	512	
10	1,024	

1.1 Making Ballots

Mathematical Goals

- Gain an intuitive understanding of basic exponential growth patterns
- Begin to recognize exponential patterns in tables

Launch

Describe Chen's ballot-making task.

You might ask students to jot down predictions for the numbers of ballots that would result from three, four, or even ten cuts. Later, they can compare their predictions to the results they obtain in the activity.

Have students work on the problem in groups of two to four.

Materials
- Transparency 1.1 (optional)
- Paper for demonstration

Explore

Have students cut and stack paper for the first two or three cuts. This provides a visual aid to help them understand the relationship between the number of cuts and the number of ballots created.

Encourage students to look for the multiplicative pattern in the table.

- *How did you find each of the entries in your table?*
- *What is the relationship between this number of ballots and the previous number of ballots?*
- *Explain that relationship in terms of the number of cuts.*

As students work on Questions C and D, look for interesting strategies to share in the summary.

You may want to distribute blank transparencies for some groups to record their answers to the problem for sharing during the summary.

Materials
- Blank paper (1 sheet per pair or group)

Summarize

As groups share their answers to the problem, ask questions such as:

- *How do your results compare to the predictions you made earlier?*
- *How is the number of ballots obtained with each cut related to the number of ballots before the cut?*
- *Question C asked how many ballots are made after 20 cuts and after 30 cuts. Describe how you found your answers.*
- *Question D asked you to work in reverse to predict the number of cuts needed to make enough ballots for 500 students. Describe your method.*

By asking about patterns in the table relating the number of cuts to the number of ballots, lead the class to a discussion of exponents.

Display the table from Problem 1.1 on the overhead and ask:

- *How did you get the number of ballots for 5 cuts?*

Materials
- Student notebooks

Vocabulary
- base
- exponent
- standard form
- exponential form

continued on next page

Add a third column to the table and illustrate each calculation, showing each factor of 2.

Use the example below to introduce the terms *base, exponent, exponential form,* and *standard form.*

$$2 \times 2 \times 2 \times 2 \times 2 \times 2 \times 2 \times 2 \times 2 \times 2 = 2^{10}$$

Explain that 1,024 is the standard form of 2^{10}.

- *How many ballots are there after 0 cuts?*
- *How could we show this in our table?*

ACE Assignment Guide for Problem 1.1

Core 1–4
Other *Applications* 5–7; *Connections* 31
Adapted For suggestions about adapting ACE exercises, see the *CMP Special Needs Handbook.*

Answers to Problem 1.1

A.

Number of Cuts	Number of Ballots
1	2
2	4
3	8
4	16
5	32
6	64
7	128
8	256
9	512
10	1,024

B. For each cut, the number of ballots doubles. See the table for the number of ballots for up to 10 cuts.

C. If Chen could make 20 cuts, he would have 1,048,576 ballots. If he could make 30 cuts, he would have 1,073,741,824 ballots.

D. It would take 9 cuts to make at least 500 ballots.

1.2 Requesting a Reward

Goals

- Express a product of identical factors in both exponential form and standard form
- Gain an intuitive understanding of basic exponential growth patterns
- Begin to recognize exponential patterns in tables, graphs, and equations
- Write an equation for an exponential relationship

This problem gives students another opportunity for hands-on involvement. In this classic problem, one item is placed on the first square of a chessboard; the number placed on each successive square is twice the number on the previous square. The equation for the ballot-cutting situation was $b = 2^n$, where n is the number of cuts and b is the number of ballots. In this problem, the equation is $r = 2^{n-1}$ or $r = \frac{1}{2}(2^n)$, where n is the number of the square and r is the number of items (rubas) on that square. Students discuss the patterns in the table and graph for the chessboard situation and compare the patterns to those for the ballot-cutting situation.

Launch 1.2

The terms *exponential form, exponent, base,* and *standard form* are formally introduced in the opening paragraph. Review these terms with students (or introduce them if you did not do so in the Problem 1.1 summary).

Suggested Questions Use the Getting Ready to give students practice with these new ideas.

- *Write each expression in exponential form.*
  a. $2 \times 2 \times 2$ (2^3)
  b. $5 \times 5 \times 5 \times 5$ (5^4)
  c. $1.5 \cdot 1.5 \cdot 1.5 \cdot 1.5 \cdot 1.5 \cdot 1.5 \cdot 1.5$ (1.5^7)

- *Write each expression in standard form.*
  a. 2^7 (128)
  b. 3^3 (27)
  c. $(4.2)^3$ (74.088)

- *Most calculators have a $\boxed{\wedge}$ or $\boxed{y^x}$ key for evaluating exponents. Use your calculator to find the standard form for each expression.*
  a. 2^{15} (Press the number 2, the $\boxed{\wedge}$ or $\boxed{y^x}$ key, then 15, then the equals sign or $\boxed{\text{ENTER}}$. The standard form is 32,768.)
  b. 3^{10} (59,049)
  c. $(1.5)^{20}$ ($\approx$3,325.26)

- *Explain how the meanings of $5^2, 2^5,$ and 5×2 differ.* (5^2 has two factors of 5; 2^5 has five factors of 2 and 5×2 has one factor of 5 and one factor of 2. Also, $5^2 = 25, 2^5 = 32,$ and $5 \times 2 = 10$.)

Tell the story of the peasant and the king of Montarek. You may want to demonstrate, or have a student demonstrate, the square-filling process using a transparency of Labsheet 1.2 and small counters.

Suggested Questions To check that students understand the situation, you could ask the following:

- *How many rubas will there be on square 1? On square 2? On square 3? On square 4?* (1; 2; 4; 8)

- *Which square will have 64 rubas?* (Square 7)

Pose the following questions, and record all student responses. Later, students can compare their predictions to their findings.

- *How many rubas do you think will be placed on the last square of the chessboard?*

- *If a Montarek ruba is worth 1 cent, do you think the peasant's plan is a good deal for her?*

Have students work in groups of two to four on the problem.

Explore 1.2

Encourage students to actually place counters on a chessboard or a paper model of a chessboard (as on Labsheet 1.2), for at least the first five or six squares.

The doubling pattern should be fairly easy for students.

Suggested Questions If some students struggle, ask them:

- *How did the number of rubas increase from square 1 to square 2? From square 2 to square 3? From square 3 to square 4?*

Some students might suggest adding 1, then 2, then 4, and so on, rather than a multiplicative pattern. If so, encourage them to think of another way to explain the growth.

You may want to have one or two groups put their graphs on transparencies to share with the class.

Students may need some help with writing the equation for exponential growth. They may recognize that it is similar to the last problem and write $r = 2^n$. If this happens, ask them to check a few values. Students generally come up with either $r = 2^{n-1}$ or $r = \frac{1}{2}(2^n)$. These equations, which are equivalent, are discussed in the summary.

Suggested Questions These questions can be used to guide students to find the equation $r = 2^{n-1}$:

- *How many rubas are on square 4?* (8)

  How can you write this as a power of 2? (2^3 **Note:** Students will be formally introduced to the term "power" in Investigation 5. If they have difficulty with this term now, you may want to add, "in other words, 8 equals 2 to what exponent?")

- *How many rubas are on square 5?* (16)
  How can you write this as a power of 2? (2^4)

- *How many rubas are on square 6?* (32)
  How can you write this as a power of 2? (2^5)

- *In all these cases, how is the exponent related to the number of the square?* (It is 1 less.)

- *How can you write the number of rubas on the nth square as a power of 2?* (2^{n-1})
  So what is the equation? ($r = 2^{n-1}$)

Encourage students to check their equations for another value in the table, such as $n = 9$ or $n = 10$, to make sure the equation works.

If students are making sense of the problem, ask:

- *How many rubas will be on square 64?*

The number of rubas on the chessboard escalates quickly. Because it is often easier to express large numbers using scientific notation, you may want to review scientific notation with students when they try to write the number of rubas on square 64 in standard form. Scientific notation is defined in ACE Exercise 39 (and in the ©2004 unit *Data Around Us*).

Summarize 1.2

Have some students share their graphs. Ask students to describe the graph. Choose points in the table and ask students where they are on the graph. Choose points on the graph and ask where they are in the table. Ask how the growth pattern shows up in the graph. You may want to draw horizontal and vertical segments showing the "rise" and the "run" between consecutive points on the graph.

Here are two ways students have come up with equations for the relationship between the number of the square n and the number of rubas r on the square:

Method 1: Students recognize that the number of times 2 is used as a factor is 1 less than the number of the square. This is because on square 1 we start with 1 ruba; on square 2, we place 1×2 rubas; on square 3, we place $1 \times 2 \times 2$ rubas, and so on. So, the number of rubas on the nth square is the product of $(n - 1)$ 2s, which is 2^{n-1}. The equation is then $r = 2^{n-1}$. Students will get this same equation if they write the exponential forms and notice that there are 2^1 rubas on square 2, 2^2 rubas on square 3, 2^3 rubas on square 4, and so on. From this form, it is apparent that the exponent is always 1 less than the number of the square.

Method 2: Students go back one step in the table to find the y-intercept—that is, the number of rubas on "square 0." Moving up the rubas column, each value is half the value below it. Because there is 1 ruba on square 1, there would be $\frac{1}{2}$ ruba on square 0. Students use this as a starting point and double the rubas for each successive square. This gives the equation $r = \frac{1}{2}(2^n)$.

The use of the y-intercept as a starting point begins in the grade 7 unit *Moving Straight Ahead*, and the y-intercept becomes a strong reference point for many students. The y-intercept for exponential relationships is discussed in the next investigation.

Square Number	Number of Rubas
0	$\frac{1}{2}$
1	$\frac{1}{2} \times 2 = 1$
2	$\frac{1}{2} \times 2 \times 2 = 2$
3	$\frac{1}{2} \times 2 \times 2 \times 2 = 4$
4	$\frac{1}{2} \times 2 \times 2 \times 2 \times 2 = 8$
5	$\frac{1}{2} \times 2 \times 2 \times 2 \times 2 \times 2 = 16$
⋮	⋮
n	$\frac{1}{2} \times 2 \times 2 \ldots \times 2 = \frac{1}{2}(2^n)$

Another way students might come up with the equation $r = \frac{1}{2}(2^n)$ is by comparing the ruba table to the ballot table from Problem 1.1. The number of rubas on square n is half the number of ballots after n cuts. Because there are 2^n ballots after n cuts, there are $\frac{1}{2}(2^n)$ rubas on square n.

Suggested Questions This is an appropriate time to discuss the fact that $2^0 = 1$.

- *What do we get when we substitute 1 for* n *in the equation* r = 2^{n-1}? ($r = 2^{1-1} = 2^0$)

- *You know that this value, 2^0, is the number of rubas on square 1. How many rubas are on that square?* (1) *So what is 2^0 equal to?* (1)

You might tell students that $a^0 = 1$ for any nonzero number a. Students will explore why this is true in Problem 5.2.

Discuss the answers to Question F. Ask students how they found the first square that had at least one million rubas. Students may have repeatedly multiplied by 2, keeping track of the number of 2s, until the product exceeded one million, then counted the number of 2s and subtracted 1. Or, they may have evaluated 2^n for increasingly large values of n until the result was over one million, and then subtracted 1 from the last value of n.

Suggested Questions Discuss the questions you posed in the Launch and compare the answers to students' predictions. The numbers are much easier to work with if students write them in scientific notation.

- *How many rubas will be on the last square?* (about 9.2×10^{18})

- *How did you find that number?* (by finding 2^{63} or by multiplying 63 factors of 2)

- *If each ruba is worth 1 cent, what is the value of the rubas on the last square in dollars?* (about 9.2×10^{16} dollars)

- *How did you find this answer?* (To change 9.2×10^{18} cents to dollars, you need to divide by 100, or 10^2. This gives 9.2×10^{16}.)

- *Is this plan a good deal for the peasant?* (Yes!)

To emphasize how much money 9.2×10^{16} dollars is, you might write the value in standard form:

$92,000,000,000,000,000

Tell students this number is read, "ninety-two quadrillion."

Suggested Questions End by asking students to compare the ballot-cutting and chessboard situations.

- *In what ways are the chessboard and ballot-cutting situations similar?*

- *In what ways are the two situations different?*

Requesting a Reward

Mathematical Goals

- Express a product of identical factors in both exponential form and standard form
- Gain an intuitive understanding of basic exponential growth patterns
- Begin to recognize exponential patterns in tables, graphs, and equations
- Write an equation for an exponential relationship
- Solve problems involving exponential growth

Launch

Use the Getting Ready to give students practice with exponents.

Tell the story of the peasant and the king of Montarek.

- *How many rubas will there be on square 1? On square 2? On square 3? On square 4?*
- *Which square will have 64 rubas?*

Pose the following questions, and record all student responses. Later, students can compare their predictions to their findings.

- *How many rubas do you think will be placed on the last square of the chessboard?*
- *If a Montarek ruba is worth 1 cent, do you think the peasant's plan is a good deal for her?*

Have students work in groups of two to four on the problem.

Materials
- Transparencies 1.2A and 1.2B (optional)

Vocabulary
- base
- exponent
- standard form
- exponential form

Explore

Encourage students to actually place counters on a Labsheet 1.2 or a chessboard for at least the first five or six squares. The doubling pattern should be fairly easy for students. If some students struggle, ask them:

- *How did the number of rubas increase from square 1 to square 2? From square 2 to square 3? From square 3 to square 4?*

Have one or two groups put their graphs on transparencies to share with the class. Students may need some help with writing the equation for exponential growth. Ask such students,

- *How many rubas are on square 4? How can you write this as a power of 2?*
- *How many rubas are on square 5? How can you write this as a power of 2?*
- *How many rubas are on square 6? How can you write this as a power of 2?*
- *How can you write the number of rubas on the nth square as a power of 2? So what is the equation?*

If students are making sense of the problem, ask:

- *How many rubas will be on square 64?*

Materials
- Labsheet 1.2 (optional; 1 per pair or group)
- Counters (optional; about 65 per pair or group)

Summarize

Discuss the graph and how it represents the growth pattern. Have students share the methods they used for finding the equation.

Discuss the questions you posed in the Launch and compare the answers to students' predictions.

- *How many rubas will be on the last square? How did you find that number?*
- *If each ruba is worth 1 cent, what is the value of the rubas on the last square in dollars? How did you find this answer?*
- *Is this plan a good deal for the peasant?*

Ask students to compare the ballot-cutting and chessboard situations.

- *In what ways are the chessboard and ballot-cutting situations similar? In what ways are they different?*

Materials
- Student notebooks

ACE Assignment Guide for Problem 1.2

Core 5–7, 10–11, 15–21, 39–42
Other *Applications* 8, 9, 12–14, *Connections* 32, 33, 43–46; unassigned choices from previous problems

Adapted For suggestions about adapting ACE exercises, see the *CMP Special Needs Handbook.*

Answers to Problem 1.2

A. 1.

Square Number	Number of Rubas
1	1
2	2
3	4
4	8
5	16
6	32
7	64
8	128
9	256
10	512

2. The number of rubas doubles from one square to the next.

B.

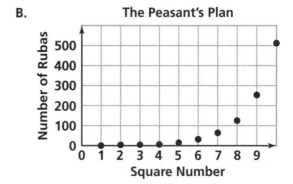

The Peasant's Plan

C. $r = 2^{n-1}$ or $r = \frac{1}{2}(2^n)$

D. In the graph, you can see the doubling pattern if you look at the y-values for the plotted points. The y-value doubles each time the number of the square increases by 1. In the equation, the base of 2 means that you are multiplying by another 2 each time the number of the square n increases by 1.

E. Square 31. The number of factors of 2 for a square is 1 less than the number of the square. For example, on square 4 there are $2 \cdot 2 \cdot 2 = 8$ rubas, which has three factors of 2. Or, if you write 2^{30} in the form 2^{n-1}, you get 2^{31-1}, so $n = 31$.

F. Square 21; 1,048,576 rubas. On square 20, there are $2^{20-1} = 2^{19} = 524,288$ rubas. On square 21, there are $2^{21-1} = 2^{20} = 1,048,576$. So square 21 is the first square with over 1 million rubas.

Making a New Offer

Goals

- Continue to recognize exponential patterns in tables, graphs, and equations

- Compare different exponential growth patterns

- Understand the role of the growth factor in exponential relationships

- Make a table from the graph and equation of an exponential relationship

- Write equations for exponential relationships represented by tables and graphs

- Solve problems involving exponential growth

In this problem, students are presented with two more reward plans. One plan is presented as a graph and the other is given as an equation. As with the original plan, these new plans show exponential growth. One has a tripling pattern and the other has a quadrupling pattern. This problem formally introduces *growth factor*.

Launch 1.3

The introduction to this problem discusses the terms *exponential growth, exponential relationship,* and *growth factor.* Use the situations in Problems 1.1 and 1.2 to illustrate these terms.

Suggested Questions

- *What are the growth factors for the situations in Problems 1.1 and 1.2?* (In both the ballot situation and the ruba-reward situation, the growth factor is 2.)

Tell the class about the next chapter in the peasant's saga. Both the king and the queen have offered new plans. Have students examine the graph and the equation.

Suggested Questions Check for understanding by asking questions.

- *How many squares are on the board for each new plan?*

- *For each plan, how many rubas are placed on the first square?*

- *What is the rule for placing rubas on each successive square?*

Ask students to indicate, by a show of hands, which plan they think is best for the king and which they think is best for the peasant.

Have students work in pairs on the problem.

Explore 1.3

When finding the equation for Plan 2, some students will write $r = 3^{n-1}$. Others will be more comfortable finding the y-intercept and use it as a starting point, giving them the equation $r = \frac{1}{3}(3^n)$. (See the discussion of Method 2 in the Summarize section below.)

For Question D, students can graph the data by hand or enter the data pairs in their graphing calculators and make a plot. (See page 15 for a description of how to enter data pairs and make a plot.) Students may need help choosing suitable scales for the axes. Some students may use the equation to graph Plan 3.

You may want to have one or two pairs put their graphs on transparencies. Have at least one group put all three graphs on the same set of axes.

Going Further

Ask students to find and compare the total reward for the three plans. Suggest that they use their calculators to find the totals. (See page 16 for a description of how to use a calculator to find the sum of a sequence.)

Students will find that the total reward for Plan 2 is less than the number on individual squares in the later stages of Plan 1. In fact, the total reward for Plan 2 is 21,523,360 rubas, less than the number of rubas on square 26 of Plan 1. The total reward for Plan 3 is 5,592,405 rubas. The totals show that Plan 1 is best for the peasant and Plan 3 is best for the king.

- *For Plan 1, look at how the total number of rubas on the board changes with each square. What pattern do you see?*

- *Do you find similar patterns for Plans 2 and 3?*

If students keep a running total, they may see that for Plan 1, the sum for the first n squares is $2^n - 1$. Each sum is 1 less than a power of 2.

Students may think of $r = 2^n - 1$ as an exponential pattern, but they will not be able to determine the growth factor.

Square Number	Rubas	Total Rubas
1	1	1
2	2	3
3	4	7
4	8	15
5	16	31
6	32	63
7	64	127
8	128	255
9	256	511
10	512	1,023
n	2^{n-1} or $\frac{1}{2}(2^n)$	$2^n - 1$

For the teacher: Similar patterns hold for sums of powers of 3 and 4. The sum of the first n powers of 3, $3^0 + 3^1 + 3^2 + \dots + 3^{n-1}$, is $\frac{1}{2}(3^n - 1)$, and the sum of the first n powers of 4, $4^0 + 4^1 + 4^2 + \dots + 4^{n-1}$, is $\frac{1}{3}(4^n - 1)$.

Summarize 1.3

Begin the summary by asking for another show of hands about which plan is best for the peasant and which is best for the king. Then discuss the answers to the problem.

Discuss Question B. Students should understand that the growth pattern for each plan is exponential because the number of rubas for any square is a fixed number times the number on the previous square. For Plan 2, the fixed number, or growth factor, is 3, and for Plan 3, it is 4.

Students will eventually be comparing four plans. A large visual record of essential information about each plan will facilitate making comparisons. Work with students to start a class chart and graph for the plans. In the chart, include the number of squares on the board, the equation, and the number of rubas on the last square. Students can enter information on the class chart as they find it.

This is how the chart might look at the end of Problem 1.3:

Reward Plans

Plan	Squares	Equation	Rubas on Last Square
Plan 1	64	$r = 2^{n-1}$	9.2×10^{18}
Plan 2	16	$r = 3^{n-1}$	14,348,907
Plan 3	12	$r = 4^{n-1}$	4,194,304

Ask students to compare the graphs. Discuss how the growth patterns show up in the tables and graphs. Be sure students identify the growth factor for each plan and can describe how this number affects the table, graph, and equation.

Question E is intended to help you discuss the standard form of an exponential equation, $y = a(b)^x$. The equation $r = \frac{1}{4}(4)^n$ is in standard form, while the equation $r = 4^{n-1}$ is not. If you have not yet discussed equations in standard form, do so now. Students need not master this form here, but they should begin thinking about it and about how they can check that the two forms of the equation are equivalent.

Suggested Questions

- *What are the growth factors for the relationships in Plans 1, 2, and 3?* (2, 3, and 4)

- *How does the growth factor show up in the table for each relationship?* (It is the constant factor that is used to generate the next entry.)

- *How does the growth factor show up in the equation for each relationship?* [It is the base of the exponential expression, or the value of b in the equation, $y = a(b)^x$.]

- *How does the growth factor affect the shape of the graph?* (It causes the graph to increase slowly at first and then zoom upward.)

- *In the last problem, you saw that $2^0 = 1$. Do 3^0 and 4^0 also equal 1? Explain.* (Yes; the equation $r = 3^{n-1}$ is the number of rubas on square n for Plan 3. When $n = 1$, $r = 3^{1-1} = 3^0$. We know this is equal to 1 because there is 1 ruba on square 1. Using the same argument for Plan 4 gives $4^0 = 1$.)

You could pose the Going Further questions from the Explore for homework or discuss them as a class.

Making a New Offer

Mathematical Goals

- Continue to recognize exponential patterns in tables, graphs, and equations
- Compare different exponential growth patterns
- Understand the role of the growth factor in exponential relationships
- Make a table from the graph and equation of an exponential relationship
- Write equations for exponential relationships represented by tables and graphs
- Solve problems involving exponential growth

Launch

Have students read about the new plans and study the graph and equation.

- *How many squares are on the board for each new plan?*
- *For each plan, how many rubas are placed on the first square?*
- *What is the rule for placing rubas on each successive square?*

Ask students which plan they think is best for the king and which they think is best for the peasant.

Materials
- Transparencies 1.3A and 1.3B (optional)

Vocabulary
- exponential growth
- exponential relationships
- growth factor

Explore

Students may come up with different, but equivalent, equations for Plan 2.

For Question D, students can graph the data by hand or make a plot on their calculators. Students may need help choosing scales for the axes.

You might want to have one or two pairs put their graphs on transparencies.

Going Further

Ask students to find the total reward for each plan.

Materials
- Labsheet 1.2 (optional)
- Counters (optional, 65 per group)
- Blank transparencies

Summarize

Ask again which plan is best for the peasant and which is best for the king. Then, discuss the answers to the problem.

For Question B, make sure students understand why the two new plans are exponential relationships and can explain how to find the growth factor in each case.

Work with students to start a class chart and graph showing the essential information about each plan. Include the number of squares on the board, the equation, growth factors, and the number of rubas on the last square.

Use Question E to facilitate a discussion of the standard form of an exponential equation.

Materials
- Student notebooks

Core 22, 23, 47
Other *Connections* 34; *Extensions* 48, 49;
unassigned choices from previous problems

Adapted For suggestions about adapting
Exercise 22 and other ACE exercises, see the
CMP Special Needs Handbook.
Connecting to Prior Units 34: *Moving Straight
Ahead*

Answers to Problem 1.3

A.

Reward Plans

Square Number	Number of Rubas		
	Plan 1	Plan 2	Plan 3
1	1	1	1
2	2	3	4
3	4	9	16
4	8	27	64
5	16	81	256
6	32	243	1,024
7	64	729	4,096
8	128	2,187	16,384
9	256	6,561	65,536
10	512	19,683	262,144

B. **1.** All three plans start with 1 ruba on square
1, and all grow very rapidly. In each plan,
the number of rubas for a square is found
by multiplying the number on the previous
square by a fixed number. The plans are
different in that the number of rubas doubles
with each square in Plan 1, triples in Plan 2,
and quadruples in Plan 3. The number of

squares on the board is also different for
each plan. There are 64 squares in Plan 1,
16 in Plan 2, and 12 in Plan 3.

2. Yes, both plans are exponential. The growth
factor for Plan 2 is 3, and the growth factor
for Plan 3 is 4.

C. $r = 3^{n-1}$ or $r = \frac{1}{3}(3^n)$

D. Because the numbers get fairly large, students
may estimate the points on their graphs or
use a graphing calculator to produce a sketch.

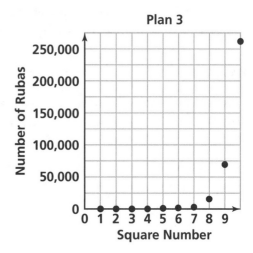

The graphs of Plans 1, 2, and 3 all have a
starting point of $(1, 1)$ and all increase in a
similar, curved pattern. However, the graph
of Plan 3 grows at a faster rate than the
graphs of Plan 1 and Plan 2. You can begin
to look at vertical changes as the horizontal
increases by one each time.

E. No; this is the same plan. Students may check
this by generating a table or a graph and
seeing that the value for each square is the
same for each equation.

F. Plan 1: 9.22×10^{18} rubas
Plan 2: 14,348,907 rubas
Plan 3: 4,194,304 rubas

Getting Costs in Line

Goals

- Continue to investigate the role of the growth factor in exponential relationships

- Compare and contrast exponential and linear growth

In this problem, data are presented in a table rather than in an equation. Students must infer the pattern and equation from the table.

Students investigate a fourth reward plan, which involves linear growth. This provides a connection to students' previous work with linear models (as in the grade 7 unit *Moving Straight Ahead*), as well as a contrast to the exponential models explored earlier in this investigation.

Launch 1.4

Review the terms *exponential growth, exponential relationship,* and *growth factor.* Use Reward Plans 1–3 to illustrate the terms. These plans are summarized on Transparency 1.4.

Describe the last episode in the saga of the king and the peasant.

Suggested Questions To make sure students understand Plan 4, you might ask these questions:

- *How many rubas are on square 1?* (20) *On square 2?* (25)

- *How many squares does the board contain?* (64)

- *What kind of relationship do you see between the number of the square and the number of rubas?* (a linear relationship)

- *How do you know the relationship is linear?* (There is a constant change of 5 in the number of rubas for every change of 1 in the number of the square.)

Ask students who think the peasant should accept the new plan to raise their hands.

Have students work in groups of three or four on the problem.

Explore 1.4

You may want to distribute blank transparencies and have each group record their work for a part of the problem. They can share their work during the summary.

Summarize 1.4

In a class discussion, talk about the groups' findings for the problem. The important idea to explore in this discussion is the distinction between the exponential model (Plan 1) and the linear model (Plan 4).

Suggested Questions Ask questions to check students' understanding.

- *Which plan would you advise the peasant to accept?*

- *Do the plans increase in the same way?* (No, Plan 4 increases along a straight line, which means the rate of increase is constant. Plan 1 increases along a curve that gets steeper and steeper, indicating that the number of rubas increases at a faster and faster rate.)

- *What would the graphs look like if we extended them?* (The graph for Plan 4 would continue along the same straight line. The graph for Plan 1 would increase along a steeper and steeper curve.)

- *What causes this difference in their patterns of change?* (In Plan 4, a constant number of rubas is added with each square, so the rate of change is constant. In Plan 1, the number of rubas is multiplied by a constant factor for each square, so the amount of increase gets greater and greater with each square.)

Discuss the fact that Plan 4 favors the peasant for the first six squares, but that Plan 1 is more favorable thereafter.

Suggested Questions Ask students about the equations for Plans 1 and 4.

- *What do the numbers and variables mean in the equations for Plans 1 and 4?*

This question offers an opportunity to review equations for exponential and linear relationships.

As part of learning to reason using symbols, students need to be able to read information from equations and interpret what each part of an equation reveals about the situation. This is challenging, and students need time and many occasions to consider these ideas. Whenever the opportunity arises, ask students to explain what each part of an equation means in terms of the situation.

Have a student add the information for Plan 4 to the class chart. Figure 2 shows how the chart might look at the end of Problem 1.4.

Check for Understanding

Have each student create a table showing a linear relationship and a table showing an exponential relationship. If there is time, display some of these pairs of tables, and have the class decide which table in each pair shows a linear relationship and which shows an exponential relationship.

Figure 2

Reward Plans

Plan	Squares	Equation	Rubas on Last Square
Plan 1	64	$r = 2^{n-1}$	9.2×10^{18}
Plan 2	16	$r = 3^{n-1}$	14,348,907
Plan 3	12	$r = 4^{n-1}$	4,194,304
Plan 4	64	$r = 20 + 5(n-1)$	335

Getting Costs in Line

Mathematical Goals

- Continue to investigate the role of the growth factor in exponential relationships
- Compare and contrast exponential and linear growth

Launch

Review the terms *exponential growth, exponential relationship,* and *growth factor.*

Describe the last chapter in the saga of the king and the peasant.

To make sure students understand Plan 4, you might ask these questions:

- *How many rubas are on square 1? On square 2?*
- *How many squares does the board contain?*
- *What kind of relationship do you see between the number of the square and the number of rubas? How do you know?*

Ask students who think the peasant should accept the new plan to raise their hands.

Have students work in groups of three or four on the problem.

Materials
- Transparency 1.4 (optional)

Explore

You might want to distribute blank transparencies and have each group record their work for a part of the problem. They can share their work during the summary.

Summarize

In a class discussion, talk about groups' findings for the problem. The important idea to explore here is the distinction between the exponential model (Plan 1) and the linear model (Plan 4).

- *Which plan would you advise the peasant to accept?*
- *Do the plans increase in the same way?*
- *What would the graphs look like if we extended them?*
- *What causes this difference in their patterns of change?*

Discuss the fact that Plan 4 favors the peasant for the first six squares, but Plan 1 is much more favorable thereafter.

Ask students about the equations:

- *What do the numbers and variables mean in the equations for Plans 1 and 4?*

This question offers an opportunity to review equations for exponential and linear relationships.

Have a student add the information for Plan 4 to the class chart.

Materials
- Student notebooks

ACE Assignment Guide for Problem 1.4

Core 25–30
Other *Applications* 24, *Connections* 35–38, 50; unassigned choices from previous problems

Adapted For suggestions about adapting ACE exercises, see the *CMP Special Needs Handbook.*
Connecting to Prior Units 35–38: *Moving Straight Ahead*

Answers to Problem 1.4

A. The growth pattern is not exponential because instead of multiplying the previous number by some constant (as with exponential patterns), you add the constant 5 to the previous number. This pattern makes Plan 4 linear, not exponential.

B. The graph of Plan 4 is a line starting at the point $(1, 20)$. It has a slope of 5, increasing at a rate of 5 rubas per square. The graph of Plan 1 starts at the point $(1, 1)$ and begins to increase much more quickly than Plan 4 after square 6. After this point, the graph of Plan 1 is above the graph of Plan 4.

C. **1.** $r = 20 + 5(n - 1)$ or $r = 15 + 5n$

 2. $r = 20 + 5(n - 1)$ is similar to the equation for Plan 1, $r = 2^{n-1}$, in that it includes the expression $n - 1$. It is different in that it doesn't include an exponent.

 3. The equation for Plan 1, $r = 2^{n-1}$, indicates that 2 is raised to the ever-increasing exponent $n - 1$. The equation for Plan 4, $r = 20 + 5(n - 1)$, shows that 5 is multiplied by the ever-increasing factor $n - 1$. (Note: The linear equation can be simplified to $r = 5n + 15$, in which case the rate of change of 5 is more evident. In more formal language, the change shows up as the base in the exponential equation and as the coefficient in the linear equation.)

D. Square 20: for Plan 1, there will be 524,288 rubas, and for Plan 4 there will be 115 rubas. Square 21: for Plan 1 there will be 1,048,576 rubas (twice as many as on square 20) and for Plan 4 there will be 120 rubas (five more than on square 20).

Investigation 1

Exponential Growth

In this investigation, you will explore *exponential growth* as you cut paper in half over and over and read about a very smart peasant from the ancient kingdom of Montarek. You will compare exponential growth with linear growth. You will also explore exponential patterns in tables, graphs, and equations.

1.1 Making Ballots

Chen, the secretary of the Student Government Association, is making ballots for tonight's meeting. He starts by cutting a sheet of paper in half. He then stacks the two pieces and cuts them in half. He stacks the resulting four pieces and cuts them in half. He repeats this process, creating smaller and smaller pieces of paper.

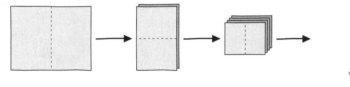

After each cut, Chen counts the ballots and records the results in a table.

Number of Cuts	Number of Ballots
1	2
2	4
3	
4	

Chen wants to predict the number of ballots after any number of cuts.

Investigation 1 Exponential Growth **5**

Notes _____

_____

_____

_____

Problem 1.1 Introducing Exponential Relationships

A. Make a table to show the number of ballots after each of the first five cuts.

B. Look for a pattern in the way the number of ballots changes with each cut. Use your observations to extend your table to show the number of ballots for up to 10 cuts.

C. Suppose Chen could make 20 cuts. How many ballots would he have? How many ballots would he have if he could make 30 cuts?

D. How many cuts would it take to make enough ballots for all 500 students at Chen's school?

ACE Homework starts on page 11.

1.2 Requesting a Reward

When you found the number of ballots after 10, 20, and 30 cuts, you may have multiplied long strings of 2s. Instead of writing long product strings of the same factor, you can use **exponential form.** For example, you can write $2 \times 2 \times 2 \times 2 \times 2$ as 2^5, which is read "2 to the fifth power."

In the expression 2^5, 5 is the **exponent** and 2 is the **base.** When you evaluate 2^5, you get $2^5 = 2 \times 2 \times 2 \times 2 \times 2 = 32$. We say that 32 is the **standard form** for 2^5.

Getting Ready for Problem 1.2

- Write each expression in exponential form.

   a. $2 \times 2 \times 2$ **b.** $5 \times 5 \times 5 \times 5$

   c. $1.5 \cdot 1.5 \cdot 1.5 \cdot 1.5 \cdot 1.5 \cdot 1.5 \cdot 1.5$

- Write each expression in standard form.

   a. 2^7 **b.** 3^3 **c.** 4.2^3

- Most calculators have a ⌃ or ⌃ᵡ key for evaluating exponents. Use your calculator to find the standard form for each expression.

   a. 2^{15} **b.** 3^{10} **c.** 1.5^{20}

- Explain how the meanings of 5^2, 2^5, and 5×2 differ.

Notes

One day in the ancient kingdom of Montarek, a peasant saved the life of the king's daughter. The king was so grateful he told the peasant she could have any reward she desired. The peasant—who was also the kingdom's chess champion—made an unusual request:

"I would like you to place 1 ruba on the first square of my chessboard, 2 rubas on the second square, 4 on the third square, 8 on the fourth square, and so on, until you have covered all 64 squares. Each square should have twice as many rubas as the previous square."

The king replied, "Rubas are the least valuable coin in the kingdom. Surely you can think of a better reward." But the peasant insisted, so the king agreed to her request. *Did the peasant make a wise choice?*

Problem **1.2** **Representing Exponential Relationships**

A. 1. Make a table showing the number of rubas the king will place on squares 1 through 10 of the chessboard.

   2. How does the number of rubas change from one square to the next?

B. Graph the (*number of the square, number of rubas*) data for squares 1 to 10.

C. Write an equation for the relationship between the number of the square *n* and the number of rubas *r*.

D. How does the pattern of change you observed in the table show up in the graph? How does it show up in the equation?

E. Which square will have 2^{30} rubas? Explain.

F. What is the first square on which the king will place at least one million rubas? How many rubas will be on this square?

ACE **Homework starts on page 11.**

Investigation 1 Exponential Growth   **7**

Notes _____

_____

_____

_____

1.3 Making a New Offer

The patterns of change in the number of ballots in Problem 1.1 and in the number of rubas in Problem 1.2 show **exponential growth.** These relationships are called **exponential relationships.** In each case, you can find the value for any square or cut by multiplying the value for the previous square or cut by a fixed number. This fixed number is called the **growth factor.**

- What are the growth factors for the situations in Problems 1.1 and 1.2?

The king told the queen about the reward he had promised the peasant. The queen said, "You have promised her more money than we have in the entire royal treasury! You must convince her to accept a different reward."

After much thought, the king came up with Plan 2. He would make a new board with only 16 squares. He would place 1 ruba on the first square and 3 rubas on the second. He drew a graph to show the number of rubas on the first five squares. He would continue this pattern until all 16 squares were filled.

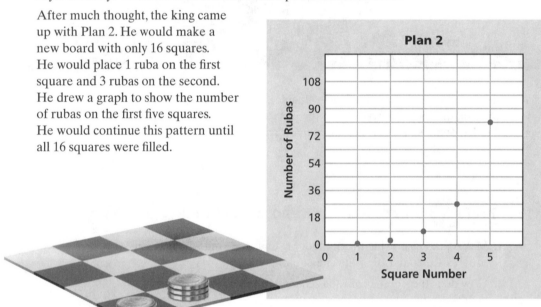

The queen wasn't convinced about the king's new plan, so she devised a third plan. Under Plan 3, the king would make a board with 12 squares. He would place 1 ruba on the first square. He would use the equation $r = 4^{n-1}$ to figure out how many rubas to put on each of the other squares. In the equation, r is the number of rubas on square n.

8   Growing, Growing, Growing

Notes
_____
_____
_____
_____

A. In the table below, Plan 1 is the reward requested by the peasant. Plan 2 is the king's new plan. Plan 3 is the queen's plan. Copy and extend the table to show the number of rubas on squares 1 to 10 for each plan.

Reward Plans

Square Number	Number of Rubas		
	Plan 1	Plan 2	Plan 3
1	1	1	1
2	2	3	4
3	4	■	■
4	■	■	■

B. 1. How are the patterns of change in the number of rubas under Plans 2 and 3 similar to and different from the pattern of change for Plan 1?

2. Are the growth patterns for Plans 2 and 3 exponential relationships? If so, what is the growth factor for each?

C. Write an equation for the relationship between the number of the square n and the number of rubas r for Plan 2.

D. Make a graph of Plan 3 for $n = 1$ to 10. How does your graph compare to the graphs for Plans 1 and 2?

E. The queen's assistant wrote the equation $r = \frac{1}{4}(4^n)$ for Plan 3. This equation is different from the one the queen wrote. Did the assistant make a mistake? Explain.

F. For each plan, how many rubas would be on the final square?

ACE Homework starts on page 11.

Notes _____

_____

_____

_____

1.4 Getting Costs in Line

Before presenting Plans 2 and 3 to the peasant, the king consulted with his financial advisors. They told him that either plan would devastate the royal treasury.

The advisors proposed a fourth plan. Under Plan 4, the king would put 20 rubas on the first square of a chessboard, 25 on the second, 30 on the third, and so on. He would increase the number of rubas by 5 for each square, until all 64 squares were covered.

To help persuade the peasant to accept their plan, the advisors prepared the following table for the first six squares. The king presented the plan to the peasant and gave her a day to consider the offer.

Reward Plans

Square Number	Number of Rubas	
	Plan 1	Plan 4
1	1	20
2	2	25
3	4	30
4	8	35
5	16	40
6	32	45

Do you think the peasant should accept the new plan? Explain.

Problem 1.4 Comparing Growth Patterns

A. Is the growth pattern in Plan 4 an exponential relationship? Explain.

B. Describe the graph of Plan 4 and compare it to the graph of Plan 1.

C. 1. Write an equation for the relationship between the number of the square n and the number of rubas r for Plan 4.

   2. Compare this equation to the equation for Plan 1.

   3. How is the change in the number of rubas from one square to the next shown in the equations for Plan 1 and Plan 4?

D. For Plans 1 and 4, how many rubas would be on square 20? How many rubas would be on square 21?

ACE Homework starts on page 11.

10 Growing, Growing, Growing

Notes _____

_____

_____

_____

Applications

1. Cut a sheet of paper into thirds. Stack the three pieces and cut the stack into thirds. Stack all the pieces and cut the stack into thirds again.

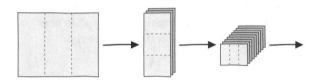

a. Copy and complete this table to show the number of ballots after each of the first five cuts.

Number of Cuts	Number of Ballots
1	3
2	■
3	■
4	■
5	■

b. Suppose you continued this process. How many ballots would you have after 10 cuts? How many would you have after n cuts?

c. How many cuts would it take to make at least one million ballots?

Write each expression in exponential form.

2. $2 \times 2 \times 2 \times 2$

3. $10 \cdot 10 \cdot 10 \cdot 10 \cdot 10 \cdot 10 \cdot 10$

4. $2.5 \times 2.5 \times 2.5 \times 2.5 \times 2.5$

Write each expression in standard form.

5. 2^{10} **6.** 10^2 **7.** 3^9

Investigation 1 Exponential Growth   **11**

STUDENT PAGE

Notes _____

_____

_____

_____

8. You know that $5^2 = 25$. Use this fact to evaluate 5^4.

9. The standard form for 5^{14} is 6,103,515,625. Use this fact to evaluate 5^{15}.

10. Multiple Choice Which expression is equal to one million?

    A. 10^6 **B.** 6^{10} **C.** 100^2 **D.** 2^{100}

11. Use exponents to write an expression for one billion (1,000,000,000).

Decide whether each number is greater or less than one million *without using a calculator*. Try to decide without actually multiplying. Explain how you found your answer. Use a calculator to check whether you are right.

12. 9^6 **13.** 3^{10} **14.** 11^6

For Exercises 15–20, write the number in exponential form using 2, 3, 4, or 5 as the base.

Go Online
PHSchool.com
For: Multiple-Choice Skills Practice
Web Code: apa-3154

15. 125   **16.** 64   **17.** 81

18. 3,125   **19.** 1,024   **20.** 4,096

21. While studying her family's history, Angie discovers records of ancestors 12 generations back. She wonders how many ancestors she has had in the past 12 generations. She starts to make a diagram to help her figure this out. The diagram soon becomes very complex.

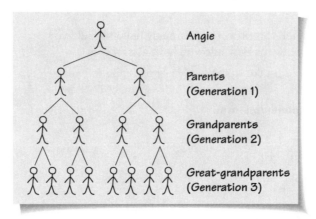

    a. Make a table and a graph showing the number of ancestors in each of the 12 generations.

    b. Write an equation for the number of ancestors a in a given generation n.

    c. What is the total number of ancestors in all 12 generations?

12   Growing, Growing, Growing

STUDENT PAGE

Notes _____

_____

_____

_____

22. Many single-celled organisms reproduce by dividing into two identical cells. Suppose an amoeba (uh MEE buh) splits into two amoebas every half hour.

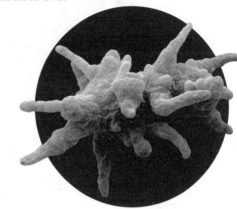

    a. An experiment starts with one amoeba. Make a table showing the number of amoebas at the end of each hour over an 8-hour period.

    b. Write an equation for the number of amoebas a after t hours.

    c. After how many hours will the number of amoebas reach one million?

    d. Make a graph of the (*time, amoebas*) data from part (a).

    e. What similarities do you notice in the pattern of change for the number of amoebas and the patterns of change for other problems in this investigation? What differences do you notice?

23. Zak's wealthy uncle wants to donate money to Zak's school for new computers. He suggests three possible plans for his donations.

Homework
Help Online
PHSchool.com
For: Help with Exercise 23
Web Code: ape-3123

    Plan 1: He will continue the pattern in this table until day 12.

Day	1	2	3	4
Donation	$1	$2	$4	$8

    Plan 2: He will continue the pattern in this table until day 10.

Day	1	2	3	4
Donation	$1	$3	$9	$27

    Plan 3: He will continue the pattern in this table until day 7.

Day	1	2	3	4
Donation	$1	$4	$16	$64

    a. Copy and extend each table to show how much money the school would receive each day.

    b. For each plan, write an equation for the relationship between the day number n and the number of dollars donated d.

    c. Which plan would give the school the greatest total amount of money?

    d. Zak says there is more than one equation for the relationship in Plan 1. He says that $d = 2^{n-1}$ and $d = \frac{1}{2}(2^n)$ both work. Is he correct? Are there two equations for each of the other plans?

Investigation 1 Exponential Growth   **13**

Notes _____

_____

_____

_____

24. Jenna is planning to swim in a charity swim-a-thon. Several relatives said they would sponsor her. Each of their donations is explained.

Grandmother: I will give you $1 if you swim
1 lap, $3 if you swim 2 laps, $5 if you swim 3 laps, $7 if you swim
4 laps, and so on.

Mother: I will give you $1 if you swim 1 lap, $3 if you swim 2 laps,
$9 if you swim 3 laps, $27 if you swim 4 laps, and so on.

Aunt Lori: I will give you $2 if you swim 1 lap, $3.50 if you swim
2 laps, $5 if you swim 3 laps, $6.50 for 4 laps, and so on.

Uncle Jack: I will give you $1 if you swim 1 lap,
$2 if you swim 2 laps, $4 if you swim 3 laps, $8 if you swim 4 laps,
and so on.

a. Decide whether each donation pattern is *exponential*, *linear*, or *neither*.

b. For each relative, write an equation for the total donation d if Jenna swims n laps.

c. For each plan, tell how much money Jenna will raise if she swims 20 laps.

Notes _____

_____

_____

_____

25. The graphs below represent $y = 2^x$ and $y = 2x + 1$.

   a. Tell which equation each graph represents. Explain your reasoning.

   b. The dashed segments show the vertical and horizontal change between points at equal x intervals. For each graph, compare the vertical and horizontal changes between pairs of points. What do you notice?

Graph 1

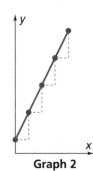

Graph 2

Study the pattern in each table.

   a. Tell whether the relationship between x and y is *linear, exponential,* or *neither.* Explain your reasoning.

   b. If the relationship is linear or exponential, give its equation.

26.

x	0	1	2	3	4	5
y	10	12.5	15	17.5	20	22.5

27.

x	0	1	2	3	4
y	1	6	36	216	1,296

28.

x	0	1	2	3	4	5	6	7	8
y	1	5	3	7	5	8	6	10	8

29.

x	0	1	2	3	4	5	6	7	8
y	2	4	8	16	32	64	128	256	512

30.

x	0	1	2	3	4	5
y	0	1	4	9	16	25

Investigation 1 Exponential Growth   **15**

Notes _____

_____

_____

_____

Connections

31. Refer to Problem 1.1. Suppose a stack of 250 sheets of paper is 1 inch high.

    a. How high would the stack of ballots be after 20 cuts? How high would it be after 30 cuts?

    b. How many cuts would it take to make a stack 1 foot high?

32. In Problem 1.2, suppose a Montarek ruba had the value of a modern U.S. penny. What would be the dollar values of the rubas on squares 10, 20, 30, 40, 50, and 60?

33. A ruba had the same thickness as a modern U.S. penny (about 0.06 inch). Suppose the king had been able to reward the peasant by using Plan 1 (doubling the number of rubas in each square).

    a. What would have been the height of the stack of rubas on square 64?

    b. The average distance from Earth to the moon is about 240,000 miles. Which (if any) of the stacks would have reached the moon?

34. One of the king's advisors suggested this plan: Put 100 rubas on the first square of a chessboard, 125 on the second square, 150 on the third square, and so on, increasing the number of rubas by 25 for each square.

    a. Write an equation for the numbers of rubas r on square n for this plan. Explain the meanings of the numbers and variables in your equation.

    b. Describe the graph of this plan.

    c. What is the total number of rubas on the first 10 squares? What is the total number on the first 20 squares?

For Exercises 35–37, find the slope and y-intercept of the graph of each equation.

35. $y = 3x - 10$ 36. $y = 1.5 - 5.6x$ 37. $y = 15 + \frac{2}{5}x$

38. Write an equation whose line is less steep than the line represented by $y = 15 + \frac{2}{5}x$.

16   Growing, Growing, Growing

Notes _____

_____

_____

_____

39. Sarah used her calculator to keep track of the number of rubas in Problem 1.2. She found that there will be 2,147,483,648 rubas on square 32.

    a. How many rubas will be on square 33? How many will be on square 34? How many will be on square 35?

    b. Which square would have the number of rubas shown here?

       $2{,}147{,}483{,}648 \cdot 2 \cdot 2 \cdot 2 \cdot 2 \cdot 2 \cdot 2 \cdot 2 \cdot 2 \cdot 2$

    c. Use your calculator to do the multiplication in part (b). Do you notice anything strange about the answer your calculator gives? Explain.

    d. Calculators use shorthand notation for showing very large numbers. For example, if you enter 10^12 on your calculator, you may get the result 1E12. This is shorthand for the number 1.0×10^{12}. The number 1.0×10^{12} is written in **scientific notation.** For a number to be in scientific notation, it must be in the form:

       (*a number greater than or equal to 1 but less than 10*) $\times$ (*a power of 10*)

       Write $2{,}147{,}483{,}648 \cdot 2 \cdot 2 \cdot 2 \cdot 2 \cdot 2 \cdot 2 \cdot 2 \cdot 2 \cdot 2$ in scientific notation.

    e. Write the numbers $2^{10}, 2^{20}, 2^{30}$, and 2^{35} in both standard and scientific notation.

    f. Explain how to write a large number in scientific notation.

Write each number in scientific notation.

40. 100,000,000   **41.** 29,678,900,500   **42.** 11,950,500,000,000

Find the largest whole-number value of *n* for which your calculator will display the result in standard notation.

43. 3^n **44.** π^n **45.** 12^n **46.** 237^n

Extensions

47. Consider these two equations:

      Equation 1: $r = 3^n - 1$ **Equation 2:** $r = 3^{n-1}$

    a. For each equation, find r when n is 2.

    b. For each equation, find r when n is 10.

    c. Explain why the equations give different values of r for the same value of n.

Investigation 1 Exponential Growth   **17**

Notes _____

_____

_____

_____

48. This table represents the number of ballots made by repeatedly cutting a sheet of paper in half four times. Assume the pattern continues.

Number of Cuts	Number of Ballots
1	2
2	4
3	8
4	16

   a. Write an equation for the pattern in the table.

   b. Use your equation and the table to determine the value of 2^0.

   c. What do you think b^0 should equal for any number b? For example, what do you think 6^0 and 23^0 should equal? Explain.

49. When the king of Montarek tried to figure out the total number of rubas the peasant would receive under Plan 1, he noticed an interesting pattern.

   a. Extend and complete this table for the first 10 squares.

Reward Plan 1

Square	Number of Rubas on Square	Total Number of Rubas
1	1	1
2	2	3
3	4	7
4	■	■

   b. Describe the pattern of growth in the total number of rubas as the number of the square increases.

   c. Write an equation for the relationship between the number of the square n and the total number of rubas t on the board.

   d. When the total number of rubas reaches 1,000,000, how many squares will have been covered?

   e. Suppose the king had been able to give the peasant the reward she requested. How many rubas would she have received?

50. Refer to Plans 1–4 in Problems 1.2 through 1.4.

   a. Which plan should the king choose? Explain.

   b. Which plan should the peasant choose? Explain.

   c. Write an ending to the story of the king and the peasant.

18   Growing, Growing, Growing

Notes _____

_____

_____

_____

Mathematical Reflections

In this investigation, you explored situations involving exponential growth. You saw how you could recognize patterns of exponential growth in tables, graphs, and equations.

Think about your answers to these questions. Discuss your ideas with other students and your teacher. Then write a summary of your findings in your notebook.

1. Describe an exponential growth pattern. Include key properties such as growth factors.

2. How are exponential growth patterns similar to and different from the linear growth patterns you worked with in earlier units?

Notes _____

_____

_____

_____

Answers   Applications

Investigation 1

ACE Assignment Choices

Differentiated Instruction
Solutions for All Learners

Problem 1.1
Core 1–4
Other *Applications* 5–7; *Connections* 31

Problem 1.2
Core 10–11, 15–21, 39–42
Other *Applications* 8, 9, 12–14, *Connections* 32, 33, 43–46; unassigned choices from previous problems

Problem 1.3
Core 22, 23, 47
Other *Connections* 34; *Extensions* 48, 49; unassigned choices from previous problems

Problem 1.4
Core 25–30
Other *Applications* 24, *Connections* 35–38; *Extensions* 50; unassigned choices from previous problems

Adapted For suggestions about adapting Exercise 22 and other ACE exercises, see the CMP *Special Needs Handbook*
Connecting to Prior Units 34–38: *Moving Straight Ahead*

Applications

1. a.

Number of Cuts	Ballots
1	3
2	9
3	27
4	81
5	243

b. $3^{10} = 59{,}049$; 3^n

c. 13. After 13 cuts, there would be $1{,}594{,}323 = 3^{13}$ ballots, which is over 1 million ballots, but 3^{12} is less than 1 million.

Note to the Teacher Students should be familiar with exponential notation from the grade 6 unit *Prime Time*.

2. 2^4

3. 10^7

4. $(2.5)^5$

5. 1,024

6. 100

7. 19,683

8. Because 5^2 means $5 \cdot 5$ and 5^4 means $5 \cdot 5 \cdot 5 \cdot 5$, 5^4 also equals $5^2 \cdot 5^2 = 25 \cdot 25 = 625$.

9. Because 5^{11} has one more factor of 5 than 5^{10} has, it equals $5^{10} \cdot 5 = 9{,}765{,}625 \cdot 5 = 48{,}828{,}125$.

10. A

11. 10^9

12. 9^6 is less than 1 million; possible explanation: The product of six 9s must be less than the product of six 10s, which is 10^6, or 1 million.

13. 3^{10} is less than 1 million; possible explanation: $3^{10} = 3 \cdot 3 \cdot 3 \cdot 3 \cdot 3 \cdot 3 \cdot 3 \cdot 3 \cdot 3 \cdot 3 = 9 \cdot 9 \cdot 9 \cdot 9 \cdot 9 = 9^5$. So $3^{10} = 9^5$, which is less than 10^6 (1 million).

14. 11^6 is greater than 10^6 or 1 million, because to find 11^6, you multiply 11 by itself six times. The result must be greater than if you multiply 10 by itself 6 times.

15. $5^3 = 125$

16. 2^6 or 4^3

17. 3^4

18. 5^5

19. 2^{10} or 4^5

20. 2^{12} or 4^6

21. a.

Angie's Ancestors

Generation	Ancestors
1	2
2	4
3	8
4	16
5	32
6	64
7	128
8	256
9	512
10	1,024
11	2,048
12	4,096

Angie's Ancestors

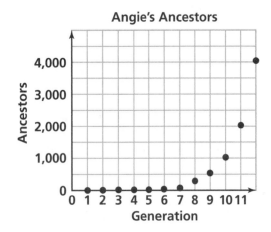

b. $a = 2^n$, where a is the number of ancestors and n is the generation number.

c. 8,190. You can find this by adding $2 + 4 + 8 + \ldots + 4,096 = 8,190$.

Note to the Teacher: See the page 16 for a description of how to use a calculator to find the sum of a sequence.

The ancestor pattern is identical to the pattern in the paper-cutting activity of Problem 1.1 and is very similar to the chessboard pattern in Problem 1.2. The only noticeable difference is that, in Problem 1.2, $n = 0$ doesn't make sense because there is not a square 0. (The graph for the rubas problem in Problem 1.2 is a translation of the graph that applies to both Problem 1.1 and the ancestor problem.)

If you go back 40 generations, the number of ancestors exceeds the number of people who have ever lived!

22. a. Amoeba Reproduction

Time (hr)	Amoebas
0	1
1	4
2	16
3	64
4	256
5	1,024
6	4,096
7	16,384
8	65,536

b. $a = 4^t$

c. 10 hours. At 10 hours, there will be 1,048,576 amoebas present.

d.

Amoeba Reproduction

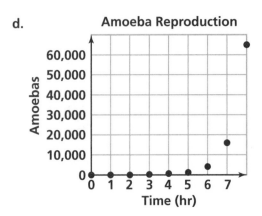

e. The pattern of change in the number of amoebas is similar to the pattern of change in the number of ancestors because it is exponential. The difference between the two patterns is that the number of amoebas increases more rapidly than the number of ancestors because the number of amoebas quadruples at each stage, while the number of ancestors only doubles.

23. a. (Figures 3, 4, and 5)

b. Plan 1: $d = 2^n$
Plan 2: $d = 3^n$
Plan 3: $d = 4^n$

c. Plan 2

24. a. Grandmother's and Aunt Lori's plans are linear and Uncle Jack's and Mother's plans are exponential.

b. Grandmother: $a = 2n - 1$
Mother: $a = 3^{n-1}$
Aunt Lori: $a = 1.5n + 0.50$
Uncle Jack: $a = 2^{n-1}$

c. Grandmother: $39;
Mother: $1,162,261,467;
Aunt Lori: $30.50;
Uncle Jack: $524,288

25. a. Graph 1 represents $y = 2^x$ because it is a curve. Graph 2 represents $y = 2x + 1$ because it is a straight line.

b. In both graphs, the horizontal change is constant. In the graph of $y = 2x + 1$, the vertical change is also constant. In the graph of $y = 2x$, the vertical change increases.

26. a. Linear

b. $y = 2.5x + 10$

27. a. Exponential

b. $y = 6^x$

28. Neither

29. a. Exponential

b. $y = 7(2^x)$

30. Neither (In fact, this is quadratic. Students will study quadratic relationships in the unit *Frogs, Fleas, and Painted Cubes.*)

Figure 3

Plan 1

Day	0	1	2	3	4	5	6	7	8	9	10	11	12
Donation	$1	$2	$4	$8	$16	$32	$64	$128	$256	$512	$1,024	$2,048	$4,096

Figure 4

Plan 2

Day	0	1	2	3	4	5	6	7	8	9	10
Donation	$1	$3	$9	$27	$81	$243	$729	$2,187	$6,561	$19,683	$59,049

Figure 5

Plan 3

Day	0	1	2	3	4	5	6	7
Donation	$1	$4	$16	$64	$256	$1,024	$4,096	$16,384

Connections

31. a. After 20 cuts: $1{,}048{,}576 \div 250 \approx 4{,}194$ in.; about 349.5 ft.; after 30 cuts: $1{,}073{,}741{,}824 \div 250 \approx 4{,}294{,}967$ in.; about 67.8 mi.

b. 12 cuts. A foot-high stack has $250 \times 12 = 3{,}000$ ballots. Because 11 cuts gives 2,048 ballots and 12 cuts gives 4,096 ballots, Chen would have to make at least 12 cuts to get 3,000 ballots.

32. Square 10: $5.12; square 20: $5,242.88; square 30: $5,368,709.12; square 40: $5,497,558,138.88; square 50: about 5.63×10^{12}; square 60: about 5.76×10^{15}

33. a. When $n = 64$, the number of rubas is $2^{64-1} = 9.22 \times 10^{18}$.
The stack would have been about $(9.22 \times 10^{18}) \times 0.06 = 5.53 \times 10^{17}$ in., or 4.61×10^{16} ft, or 8.73×10^{12} mi high.

b. It is $240{,}000$ mi $\cdot$ 5,280 ft/mi $\cdot$ 12 in./ft $\approx 1.52 \cdot 10^{10}$ in. to the moon, so it would take $1.52 \cdot 10^{10} \div 0.06 \approx 2.53 \cdot 10^{11}$ rubas to reach the moon. The stacks on squares 39 ($2.75 \cdot 10^{11}$ rubas) and above will reach the moon.

34. a. $r = 100 + 25(n-1)$ or $r = 25n + 75$

b. The graph will look linear. You might want to ask students to draw the graph.

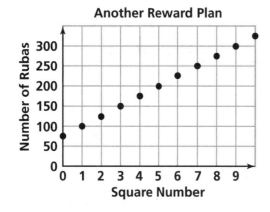

Another Reward Plan

c. 2,125 rubas; 6,750 rubas

35. Slope: 3; y-intercept: -10

36. Slope: -5.6; y-intercept: 1.5

37. Slope: $\frac{2}{5}$; y-intercept: 15

38. Answers will vary. Any equation with a coefficient of less than $\frac{2}{5}$. Possible answers: $y = \frac{1}{5}x + 3$; $y = \frac{1}{6}x + 15$

39. a. Square 33: $2^{32} = 4{,}294{,}967{,}296$
Square 34: $2^{33} = 8{,}589{,}934{,}592$
Square 35: $2^{34} = 17{,}179{,}869{,}184$

b. Square 41. This is because it is the number of rubas on square 32 times nine more factors of 2.

c. The display probably reads 1.09951162778 E12. There is an E in the middle of the number.

d. $1.09951162778 \times 10^{12}$ (There are occasions when the calculator display will not give the last few digits exactly.)

e. $2^{10} = 1.024 \times 10^{3}$; $2^{20} = 1.048576 \times 10^{6}$; $2^{30} = 1.073471824 \times 10^{9}$; $2^{40} = 1.09951162778 \times 10^{12}$; $2^{50} = 1.12589990684 \times 10^{15}$

f. Possible answer: To write a number in scientific notation, place a decimal in the original number to get a number greater than or equal to 1 but less than 10. To compensate for placing the decimal in the original number, multiply the new number by a power of ten that will give you back your original number.

40. 1.0×10^{8}

41. $2.96789005 \times 10^{10}$

42. 1.19505×10^{13}

Values given for Exercises 43–46 are for the standard screen of the TI-83. Different calculators will give different results.

43. 20

44. 20

45. 9

46. 4

Extensions

47. a. Eq. 1: $r = 3^{2} - 1 = 9 - 1 = 8$
Eq. 2: $r = 3^{2-1} = 3^{1} = 3$

b. Eq. 1: $r = 3^{10} - 1 = 59{,}048$
Eq. 2: $r = 3^{10-1} = 3^{9} = 19{,}683$

c. The equations give different values of r because the value of n is used differently. In one equation, 1 is subtracted from n and the result becomes the exponent of 3; in the other, n is used as the exponent of 3, and 1 is subtracted from the result.

Note to the Teacher For $n \geq 0$, the result of Equation 1 will always be greater than that of Equation 2 because the exponent is greater. Subtracting from the greater exponential contribution is almost insignificant.

48. a. $b = 2^n$, where b is the number of ballots made and n is the number of cuts

  b. From the table, 2^0 must equal 1. When you evaluate 2^0 with a calculator, the answer is 1.

  c. The value of any number b raised to a power of 0 is 1.
  Note to the Teacher Talk with students about why this makes sense. Because $b^1 = b$ and because exponents tell us how many factors of the base to use, $b \times b^0 = b^{1+0}$ must be equal to $1 + 0$ factors of b, which is just b; so b^0 should be 1 to make all of the other ideas about exponents work out. Some students might say that for the pattern to continue backwards, 2^0 must equal 1. Explain that mathematicians decided the world of mathematics would make more sense if b^0 were defined to be 1 for $b \neq 0$.

49. a. (Figure 6)

  b. Each entry in the total column is 1 less than the entry in the next individual square column. Another pattern is that we can double the total rubas at a square and add 1 to get the total rubas at the next square.

c. $t = 2^n - 1$
d. The total t will exceed 1,000,000 when 20 squares have been covered: $t = 2^{20} - 1 = 1{,}048{,}575$ rubas.
e. With all 64 squares covered, the total would be $t = 2^{64} - 1 \approx 1.84 \times 10^{19}$ rubas.

50. a–c. Answers will vary.

Possible Answers to Mathematical Reflections

1. One key property of exponential growth patterns is that each time you increase the value of the independent variable by 1, you multiply the value of the dependent variable by the same constant number, the growth factor. Another key property of exponential growth patterns is that the numbers begin to grow very quickly. The graphs of exponential growth patterns are increasing curves.

2. With exponential growth patterns, you *multiply* the y-value by a constant each time the x-value increases by 1. With linear growth patterns, you *add or subtract* a constant to the y-value each time the x-value increases by 1. Also, the graphs of linear patterns are straight lines, while graphs of exponential growth patterns are curves.

Figure 6

Reward Plan 1

Square	Number of Rubas on Square	Total Number of Rubas
1	1	1
2	2	3
3	4	7
4	8	15
5	16	31
6	32	63
7	64	127
8	128	255
9	256	511
10	512	1,023

Mathematical and Problem-Solving Goals

- Recognize exponential growth in verbal descriptions, tables, graphs, and equations
- Determine and interpret the *y*-intercept (initial value) for an exponential relationship
- Determine the growth factor based on a verbal description, table, graph, or equation for an exponential relationship
- Write an equation for an exponential relationship from its graph
- Solve problems involving exponents and exponential growth

Summary of Problems

Problem 2.1   **Killer Plant Strikes Lake Victoria**

Students read about a real situation in which a nonnative plant spread rapidly and began to cover a lake. Students then solve a problem about a similar situation. In the problem, the area of the plant doubles each month, and the starting value is greater than 1.

Problem 2.2   **Growing Mold**

Students are given an equation for a real-world exponential growth relationship. They find and interpret the *y*-intercept and growth factor, and use the equation to answer questions about the relationship.

Problem 2.3   **Studying Snake Populations**

Exponential data is presented in the form of a graph. Students find and interpret the *y*-intercept and growth factor and use this information to write an equation. Students use the graph or equation to answer questions about the situation.

	Suggested Pacing	Materials for Students	Materials for Teachers	ACE Assignments
All	$3\frac{1}{2}$ days	Graph paper, graphing calculators, student notebooks	Blank transparencies (optional), overhead graphing calculator (optional)	
2.1	1 day		Transparency 2.1 (optional)	1–4, 15–21, 31–33
2.2	1 day			5–8, 22, 23
2.3	1 day		Transparency 2.3 (optional)	9–14, 24–30
MR	$\frac{1}{2}$ day			

Killer Plant Strikes Lake Victoria

Goals

- Recognize exponential growth in verbal descriptions of situations

- Determine and interpret the y-intercept (initial value) for an exponential relationship

- Determine the growth factor based on a verbal description of an exponential relationship

- Solve problems involving exponents and exponential growth

Launch 2.1

Begin by discussing the situation and questions in the Getting Ready. Problem 1.3 in Investigation 1 presented two forms of the equation for the queen's reward plan, so the ideas in the Getting Ready should not be completely new to students.

Suggested Questions Ask:

- *Are both equations correct? Explain.* (Both equations are correct. We can check by comparing tables or graphs.)

- *What is the value of* r *if* n $= 1$? ($\frac{1}{2}(2^n) = \frac{1}{2}(2^1) = 1$, so $2^{n-1} = 2^0 = 1$)

- *What is the y-intercept for this relationship?* (The y-intercept is $\frac{1}{2}$. This is clearer from the $r = \frac{1}{2}(2^n)$ form. Some students will use the fact that $2^0 = 1$ to find $\frac{1}{2}(2^0) = \frac{1}{2}$. Others will work backward and use the fact that each time n decreases by 1, r is halved. Because the value of r for $n = 1$ is 1, the value of r for $n = 0$ must be $\frac{1}{2}$.)

Make sure students have a way of checking that the forms are equivalent, perhaps by generating a table or a graph. You may need to remind students of the meaning of y-intercept. Just as with linear equations, the y-intercept is the y-value when $x = 0$ (or in this case, the r value when $n = 0$).

Point out that the y-intercept has no meaning in this situation. It would be the number of rubas on square 0, which does not make sense.

Tell the real story about the water hyacinth taking over Lake Victoria.

Suggested Questions Ask:

- *The article says the plant doubles in size every 5 to 15 days. Does this mean the growth factor is 2?* (It depends on what you consider to be a "unit" of time. Say, the plant area doubles every 10 days. The growth factor is the number the y-value is multiplied by each time the x-value increases by 1 unit, for example, 1 day, 1 month, or 1 year. If you considered a 10-day period to be 1 unit of time, then the growth factor would be 2.)

Tell students to consider the area of 769 square miles to be the initial value, or the value at time 0. Have students help you make a table to show the growth pattern.

Water Hyacinth Growth

Days	Area Covered (sq. mi)
0	769
10	1,578
20	3,156
30	6,312
40	12,624
50	25,248

Now tell the class that Ghost Lake has a problem similar to the one on Lake Victoria. Discuss the first paragraph of Problem 2.1, which gives the details.

Suggested Questions Ask:

- *Is the area of the plant growing exponentially? How do you know?*

- *How is this problem similar to the problems you solved in Investigation 1?* (A quantity is being multiplied by a constant factor at each stage. For this problem, the growth factor is 2, as it was in the ballot-cutting problem and in Reward Plan 1.)

- *How is this problem different from previous problems?* (The initial value is 1,000 when the independent variable, in this case time, is 0. In the ballot-cutting problem, the initial value is 1 when the independent variable, the number of cuts, is 0. In the reward problems, the initial value is 1 when the independent variable, the square number, is 1.)

Explain that we want to represent the growth of the plant starting today, when the area is 1,000 square feet.

- *The initial value, 1,000 square feet, is the y-intercept for this relationship. Can anybody explain why?* (It is the value when the time is 0, before any months have passed.)

Let the class work in pairs on this problem.

Explore 2.1

If students are having trouble writing an equation, suggest that they make a table for the first few months.

Suggested Questions You might ask questions such as the following:

- *What is the starting value, or y-intercept?*

- *What is the growth factor?*

- *What information do you need to write an equation?*

If students are still having difficulty, refer them to the equation $r = \frac{1}{2}(2^n)$ for Reward Plan 1, which was discussed in the Getting Ready.

- *What does the $\frac{1}{2}$ in the ruba equation represent?* (the y-intercept)

- *What does the 2 in the ruba equation represent?* (the growth factor)

- *How could you write an equation in a similar form for the Ghost Lake plant growth?* (Use 1,000 instead of $\frac{1}{2}$ for the y-intercept. Use 2 for the growth factor.)

Suggest that students test their equation for a couple of months' values to make sure it works.

Some students may also need prompting to choose appropriate scales for the y-axis of the graph.

You might pass out large sheets of paper or blank transparencies for students to display their equations and graphs for the summary.

Summarize 2.1

Call on a couple of students to write their equations on the overhead and to explain what the numbers and variables mean.

Suggested Questions Ask:

- *How would the equation change if the initial area covered was 1,500 square feet?* [The equation would be $a = 1,500(2^n)$, where n is the number of months.]

- *How would the equation change if the area covered tripled every month?* [The equation would be $a = 1,000(3^n)$, where n is the number of months.]

- *Use your equation to find the area of the lake that is covered with the plant after 11 months.* (177,147,000 sq. ft)

- *How did you find the number of months it will take the plant to completely cover the lake?* (Some students will use a table, some will use the graph, and some will guess and check, using the equation and their calculator.)

Going Further

- *Find the daily growth factor for the Lake Victoria situation if the area doubles every 10 days.* (It is approximately 1.072. Students can get close by guessing and checking.)

2.1 Killer Plant Strikes Lake Victoria

Mathematical Goals

- Recognize exponential growth in verbal descriptions of situations
- Determine and interpret the *y*-intercept (initial value) for an exponential relationship
- Determine the growth factor based on a verbal description of an exponential relationship
- Solve problems involving exponents and exponential growth

Launch

Begin by discussing the questions in the Getting Ready. Make sure students have a way of checking that the two equations are equivalent. Discuss 2^0. Then discuss the *y*-intercept.

Tell the story about the water hyacinth taking over Lake Victoria.

- *The article says the plant doubles in size every 5 to 15 days. Does this mean the growth factor is 2?*

Make a table showing the water hyacinth's growth and have students look at the pattern.

Tell the class that Ghost Lake has a similar problem. Discuss the first paragraph of Problem 2.1.

- *Is the area of the plant growing exponentially? How do you know?*
- *How is this problem similar to the problems you solved in Investigation 1?*
- *How is this problem different from previous problems?*

Explain that we want to represent the growth of the plant starting today, when the area is 1,000 square feet.

- *The initial value, 1,000 square feet, is the* y-*intercept for this relationship. Can anybody explain why?*

Let the class work in pairs on this problem.

Materials

- Transparency 2.1
- Blank transparencies (optional)
- Graphing calculators
- Graph paper

Explore

If students are having trouble writing an equation, suggest they make a table for the first few months.

- *What is the starting value or* y-*intercept?*
- *What is the growth factor?*
- *What information do you need to write an equation?*

If students are still having difficulty, refer them to the equation $r = \frac{1}{2}(2^n)$ for Reward Plan 1.

- *What does the $\frac{1}{2}$ in the ruba equation represent?*
- *What does the 2 in the ruba equation represent?*
- *How could you write an equation in a similar form for the Ghost Lake plant growth?*

Summarize

Call on a couple of students to write their equations on the overhead and to explain what the numbers and variables in the equation mean.

- *How would the equation change if the initial area covered was 1,500 square feet?*
- *How would the equation change if the area covered tripled every month?*
- *Use your equation to find the area of the lake that is covered with the plant after 11 months.*
- *How did you find the number of months it will take the plant to completely cover the lake?*

Going Further

- *Find the daily growth factor for the Lake Victoria situation if the area doubles every 10 days.*

Materials
- Student notebooks

ACE Assignment Guide for Problem 2.1

 Differentiated Instruction
Solutions for All Learners

Core 1, 2, 4, 15–16, 21
Other *Applications* 3, *Connections* 17–20, *Extensions* 31–33

Adapted For suggestions about adapting Exercise 3 and other ACE exercises, see the *CMP Special Needs Handbook*.
Connecting to Prior Units 21: *Prime Time*

Answers to Problem 2.1

A. 1. $a = 1{,}000(2^n)$ (Variable names may vary.)

  2. a is the surface area of the lake covered after n months. 1,000 is the area in ft^2 covered now (at time 0). The growth factor is 2; it represents the doubling of the area each month.

  3. Possible answer: All of the equations in Investigation 1 were of the form $y =$ some number raised to an exponent, such as $y = 2^n$ or $y = 3^{n-1}$, and there was no number in front of the 2 or 3. In this equation, $a = 1{,}000(2^n)$, there is a number in front of the 2.

  Some students will observe that this problem is more like the ballots than like the ruba problems, with a starting point at $x = 0$ instead of at $x = 1$.

B. 1.

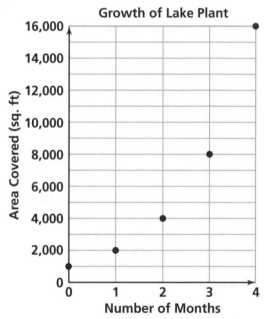

Growth of Lake Plant

  2. This graph has a y-intercept of $(0, 1{,}000)$, while the ballot problem has a y-intercept of $(0, 1)$. The ruba problems' graphs all started at $(1, 1)$. In the ruba problems, the y-intercept had no meaning in the story because there is no such thing as square 0.

C. After 12 months, $1{,}000(2^{12}) = 4{,}096{,}000 \text{ ft}^2$ will be covered.

D. It will take between 14 and 15 months for the plant to cover all $25{,}000{,}000 \text{ ft}^2$ because $1{,}000(2)^{14} = 16{,}384{,}000$ and $1{,}000(2)^{15} = 32{,}768{,}000$.

2.2 Growing Mold

Goals

- Recognize an exponential relationship from an equation

- Determine the growth factor and y-intercept based on an equation for an exponential relationship

- Solve problems involving exponents and exponential growth

In this activity, students explore the exponential growth of mold. An equation for the growth pattern is given. Students find the initial amount of mold and the growth factor from the equation, and use the equation to answer specific questions about the situation.

You might wish to have your class conduct an experiment in which they grow mold, collect data on the mold's growth, and then analyze that data. See the directions below.

If the class begins the mold-growing experiment at the start of Problem 2.2, they should have enough data by the end of the unit to analyze the pattern of growth in the mold.

Directions for Mold-Growing Experiment Follow these steps to begin the experiment, or consult a science teacher in your building for advice on setting up the experiment.

- Cut a piece of transparent quarter-centimeter grid paper to fit the bottom of an 8- or 9-inch cake pan.

- Glue the paper to the bottom of the pan.

- Prepare a mixture of dry beef or chicken bouillon, gelatin, and water.

- Cover the bottom of the pan with a thin layer of the mixture.

- Put a very small amount of mold taken from bread or yogurt into the pan.

- Cover the pan with plastic wrap and secure it tightly with a rubber band.

- Place the pan in a dark place with a fairly uniform room temperature.

Beginning with day 1, have a group of students count the number of squares covered by mold each day. The amount of mold is equal to the area, or the number of squares, covered. Have students record the data in a table. When much of the pan is covered with mold, they can graph the data, determine an approximate growth factor, and write an equation.

Launch 2.2

Discuss with students the information in the student edition about moldy food. Having a piece of moldy bread or cheese on display makes a great attention grabber.

Suggested Question Ask:

- *How much mold is there at the end of day 1? At the end of day 2? At the end of day 3?*

- *Do you see any similarities between the pattern of change in this situation and the patterns of change in some of the problems in the last investigation and in Problem 2.1? Explain.* (The area covered by the mold increases by repeated multiplication. This is similar to the patterns seen in many of the reward plans from Investigation 1 and to the pattern of plant growth in Problem 2.1. It is also similar to Problem 2.1 in that both problems have an initial value greater than 1 and both involve an area being covered by something—either a plant or mold.)

Have students work on the problem in pairs.

Explore 2.2

This problem is similar to Problem 2.1, but it describes an exponential relationship with an equation, rather than with a verbal description.

When students evaluate the equation for a specific d value, make sure they raise only the base to the exponent, and not both the base and the initial value. For example, when computing $50(3^5)$, watch for students who find 50×3 and then raise the product, 150, to the exponent of 5.

This is not correct. Remind students to follow the order of operations: Evaluate exponents first and then multiply. Most graphing calculators use the correct order of operations. For example, if the expression 50 $\boxed{\times}$ 3 $\boxed{\wedge}$ 5 is entered, the calculator will give the correct result.

Summarize 2.2

Suggested Questions Ask questions such as the following to provoke discussion:

- *How does the mold grow from one day to the next?*

- *Is the mold growth similar to other growth situations you have studied? Explain.*

- *What does each part of your equation tell you about the growth of the mold?*

- *Suppose you started with 25 mm² of mold and it grew in the same way that it did in the problem. How would the equation change? How would the graph change?*

Discuss the standard form for an exponential equation introduced in Question E: $y = a(b^x)$. Help students see how this equation is similar to and different from the slope-intercept form of a linear equation.

- *In the linear equation, $y = mx + b$, which letter represents the y-intercept?* (b)

- *In the exponential equation, which letter represents the y-intercept?* (a)

- *Why do you think we add the y-intercept in a linear equation, but we multiply by it in an exponential equation?* (You find the y-intercept by substituting 0 for x. In a linear equation, $y = mx + b$, you get $y = m(0) + b = b$. So, you are left with the added term. Therefore, the added term must be the y-intercept. When you find the y-intercept for an exponential equation, $y = a(b^x)$, you get $y = a(b^0) = a(1) = a$. So, you are left with the term you multiply the power by. This term must be the y-intercept.

- *In the linear equation, what tells us how quickly the dependent variable is changing as the value of the independent variable increases in increments of 1?* (the slope, m)

- *In the exponential equation, what tells us how quickly the dependent variable is changing as the value of the independent variable increases in increments of 1?* (the base, b)

- *What other similarities and differences do you notice between linear and exponential equations?*

Check for Understanding
Repeat the last set of questions with specific examples such as these:

$$y = -3x + 4 \qquad y = 1.5x$$
$$y = 3^x \qquad y = 10(5^x)$$

Growing Mold

Mathematical Goals

- Recognize an exponential relationship from an equation
- Determine the growth factor and *y*-intercept based on an equation for an exponential relationship
- Solve problems involving exponents and exponential growth

Launch

Discuss with students the information in the student edition about moldy food.

- *Do you see any similarities between the pattern of change in this situation and the patterns of change in some of the problems in the last investigation and in Problem 2.1? Explain.*

Have students work on the problem in pairs.

Materials
- Graphing calculators

Explore

When students evaluate the equation for a specific *d* value, make sure they raise only the base to the exponent. For example, when computing $50(3^5)$, watch for students who multiply 50×3 and then raise the product, 150, to the exponent of 5. This is not correct. Remind students to follow the order of operations: Evaluate exponents first and then multiply.

Summarize

- *How does the mold grow from one day to the next?*
- *Is the mold growth similar to other growth situations you have studied? Explain.*
- *What does each part of your equation tell you about the growth of the mold?*
- *Suppose you started with 25 mm^2 of mold and it grew in the same way it did in the problem. How would the equation change?*
- *How would the graph change?*

Discuss the standard form of an exponential equation: $y = a(b^x)$. Help students see how this is similar to and different from the slope-intercept form of a linear equation.

- *In the linear equation,* y = mx + b, *which letter represents the* y-*intercept?*
- *In the exponential equation, which letter represents the* y-intercept?
- *Why do you think we add the* y-intercept *in a linear equation, but we multiply by it in an exponential equation?*

Materials
- Student notebooks

continued on next page

- *In the linear equation, what tells us how quickly the dependent variable is changing as the value of the independent variable increases in increments of 1?*

- *In the exponential equation, what tells us how quickly the dependent variable is changing as the value of the independent variable increases in increments of 1?*

- *What other similarities and differences do you notice between linear and exponential equations?*

Check for Understanding

Repeat the last set of questions with specific examples of linear and exponential equations, such as $y = -3x + 4; y = 1.5x;$ $y = 3^x;$ and $y = 10(5^x)$.

ACE Assignment Guide for Problem 2.2

Core 5, 6, 8
Other *Applications* 7, *Connections* 22, 23; unassigned choices from previous problems

Adapted For suggestions about adapting ACE exercises, see the *CMP Special Needs Handbook*.
Connecting to Prior Units 22: *Moving Straight Ahead;* 23: *Stretching and Shrinking*

Answers to Problem 2.2

A. 50 mm^2

B. 3

C. $50(3)^5 = 12{,}150$ mm^2

D. Between day 4 and day 5. On day 4, the area was 6,250 mm^2, and on day 5, the area was 12,150 mm^2.

E. 1. The value of b is 3. This represents the growth factor.

   2. The value of a is 50. This represents the initial amount of mold.

Studying Snake Populations

Goals

- Recognize exponential growth in graphs
- Determine and interpret the y-intercept of an exponential relationship
- Determine the growth factor based on a graph of an exponential relationship
- Write an equation for an exponential relationship from its graph
- Solve problems involving exponents and exponential growth

In this problem, students continue to look at the y-intercept and growth factor, but this time they investigate data displayed in a graph.

Launch 2.3

Put the graph of the snake population on the overhead. Give a brief description of the problem. Students can work on this problem in pairs.

Explore 2.3

Suggested Questions It is difficult to read the y-intercept from the graph. You can ask the following to guide student thinking:

- *Which points are easy to read?* [(2, 25), (3, 125) and (4, 625)]

- *What is the growth pattern for these 3 years?* (The growth factor is 5.)

- *If we assume this same growth pattern for years 0 to* n, *what is the population in year 1? What is the population in year 0?*

Students may need to put the data in a table and then reason backward to reach year 1, then year 0. Dividing 25 by 5, the population in year 1 is 5. Dividing 5 by 5, the population in year 0 is 1.

- *What is the* y-intercept? (0, 1)

Students should now be able to write the equation $p = 1(5^n)$, or just $p = 5^n$. But look for other ways students may arrive at the equation. Some students may write the equation in a different form. (See Summarize 2.3 below.)

Summarize 2.3

Ask the class to share the ways they found their equations. Some students may have used (2, 25) as a starting point and written $p = 25(5^{n-2})$. This is also correct. You can ask students to check a few points to verify that the two equations are equivalent. You can come back to these two equations after students learn the properties of exponents in Investigation 5. Then, they will be able to show the equivalence symbolically: $25(5^{n-2}) = 5^2 \cdot 5^{n-2} = 5^{2+n-2} = 5^n$

Check for Understanding

Do one of the following activities:

1. On a large sheet of paper, have each group or pair of students write an exponential equation for the growth of a population and describe the variables. As each group holds up its poster, ask the rest of the class:

- *What is the growth factor?*

- *What is the initial population?*

- *How large is the population after 4 years?*

- *How long will it take the population to reach a certain number?*

After a couple of presentations, say:

- *Compare the growth of this population to some of the previous examples we have seen.*

2. Have students look at the growth of these populations.

Year	Population A	Population B
0	600	10
1	603	30
2	606	90
3	609	270
4	612	810

Ask:

- *Is either of these an exponential relationship? Is either a linear relationship?*

- *Will Population A always be greater than Population B? Explain.*

Studying Snake Populations

Mathematical Goals

- Recognize exponential growth in graphs
- Determine and interpret the *y*-intercept of an exponential relationship
- Determine the growth factor based on a graph of an exponential relationship
- Write an equation for an exponential relationship from its graph
- Solve problems involving exponents and exponential growth

Launch

Put the graph of the snake population on the overhead. Give a brief description of the problem.

Students can work on this problem in pairs.

Materials
- Transparency 2.3
- Graphing calculators

Explore

Students may have trouble reading the *y*-intercept from the graph. You can ask the following questions to guide their thinking:

- *Which points are easy to read?*
- *What is the growth pattern for these 3 years?*
- *If we assume this same growth pattern for years 0 to* n, *what is the population in year 1?*
- *What is the population in year 0?*

Students may need to put the data in a table and then reason backward to reach year 1, then year 0.

- *What is the* y-intercept?

Students should now be able to write the equation $p = 1(5)^n$, or just $p = 5^n$. But look for other ways that students may arrive at the equation. Some students may write the equation in a different form.

Summarize

Ask the class to share the ways they found their equations. Some students may write $p = 25(5^{n-2})$. Ask the class to check a few points to show that the two equations are equivalent. You can come back to these two equations after the students learn the properties of exponents in Investigation 5.

Materials
- Student notebooks

continued on next page

Summarize
continued

Check for Understanding

Do one of the following:

- On a large sheet of paper, have each group write an exponential equation for the growth of a population and describe the variables. Ask other students questions about the growth factor, initial population, the population after a certain time period, and the amount of time it will take to reach a certain number.

- Have students discuss and compare the growth of the number in this table.

Year	Population A	Population B
0	600	10
1	603	30
2	606	90
3	609	270
4	612	810

ACE Assignment Guide for Problem 2.3

Core 9–13, 24–27
Other *Applications* 14; *Connections* 28–30; unassigned choices from previous problems

Adapted For suggestions about adapting ACE exercises, see the *CMP Special Needs Handbook*.
Connecting to Prior Units 24–27: *Moving Straight Ahead, Thinking With Mathematical Models;* 28, 29: *Stretching and Shrinking;* 30: *Bits and Pieces I*

Answers to Problem 2.3

A. The growth factor is 5 because $(2, 25)$, $(3, 125)$, and $(4, 625)$ are on the graph and the y-value for each of these points is 5 times the previous y-value.

B. 1. The population in year 2 is 25, in year 3 is 125, and in year 4 is 625.

2. Working backward, you divide the population for each year by 5 to get the population for the previous year. So, the population for year 1 would be $25 \div 5 = 5$ snakes.

3. You can find the y-intercept by working backward and dividing the population for year 1 by 5. In this case, the y-intercept is $(0, 1)$.

Note to the Teacher A y-intercept of 1 would mean that the population started with one (presumably pregnant) snake. If students raise this issue, you may want to ask them how they would alter the graph so it makes more sense in this context.

C. $p = 5^t$, or $p = 1(5^t)$, where p represents the snake population after t years

D. Between year 4 and year 5 because $5^4 = 625$ and $5^5 = 3,125$

**The student edition pages for this
investigation begin on the next page.**

Notes _____
_____
_____
_____

Examining Growth Patterns

Now that you have learned to recognize exponential growth, you are ready to take a closer look at the tables, graphs, and equations of exponential relationships. You will explore this question:

How are the starting value and growth factor for an exponential relationship reflected in the table, graph, and equation?

Getting Ready for Problem

Students at West Junior High came up with two equations to represent the reward in Plan 1 of Investigation 1. Some students wrote $r = 2^{n-1}$ and others wrote $r = \frac{1}{2}(2^n)$. In both equations, r represents the number of rubas on square n.

- Are both equations correct? Explain.
- What is the value of r if $n = 1$? Does this make sense?
- What is the y-intercept for this relationship?

2.1 Killer Plant Strikes Lake Victoria

Exponential growth occurs in many real-life situations. For example, consider this story from 1998:

> **Water hyacinths, which experts say double in area every 5 to 15 days, are expanding across Africa's giant Lake Victoria. The foreign plant has taken over more than 769 square miles of the lake and is growing exponentially.**

"Killer Weed Strikes Lake Victoria" from *Christian Science Monitor*. January 12, 1998, Vol. 90, No. 32, p. 1.

Notes

Plants like the water hyacinth that grow and spread rapidly can affect native plants and fish. This in turn can affect the livelihood of fishermen. To understand how such plants grow, you will look at a similar situation.

Problem 2.1 y-Intercepts Other Than 1

Ghost Lake is a popular site for fishermen, campers, and boaters. In recent years, a certain water plant has been growing on the lake at an alarming rate. The surface area of Ghost Lake is 25,000,000 square feet. At present, 1,000 square feet are covered by the plant. The Department of Natural Resources estimates that the area is doubling every month.

A. 1. Write an equation that represents the growth pattern of the plant on Ghost Lake.

2. Explain what information the variables and numbers in your equation represent.

3. Compare this equation with the equations in Investigation 1.

B. 1. Make a graph of the equation.

2. How does this graph compare with the graphs of the exponential relationships in Investigation 1?

C. How much of the lake's surface will be covered with the water plant by the end of a year?

D. In how many months will the plant completely cover the surface of the lake?

ACE Homework starts on page 24.

Notes _____

_____

_____

_____

2.2 Growing Mold

Mold can spread rapidly. For example, the area covered by mold on a loaf of bread left out in warm weather grows exponentially.

Problem 2.2 Interpreting Exponential Equations

Students at Magnolia Middle School conducted an experiment. They set out a shallow pan containing a mixture of chicken bouillon (BOOL yahn), gelatin, and water. Each day, the students recorded the area of the mold in square millimeters.

The students wrote the exponential equation $m = 50(3^d)$ to model the growth of the mold. In this equation, m is the area of the mold in square millimeters after d days.

A. What is the area of the mold at the start of the experiment?

B. What is the growth factor?

C. What is the area of the mold after 5 days?

D. On which day will the area of the mold reach 6,400 mm^2?

E. An exponential equation can be written in the form $y = a(b^x)$, where a and b are constant values.

   1. What value does b have in the mold equation? What does this value represent?

   2. What value does a have in the mold equation? What does this value represent?

ACE Homework starts on page 24.

22   Growing, Growing, Growing

Notes

2.3 Studying Snake Populations

The graph shows the growth of a garter snake population after it was introduced to a new area. The population is growing exponentially.

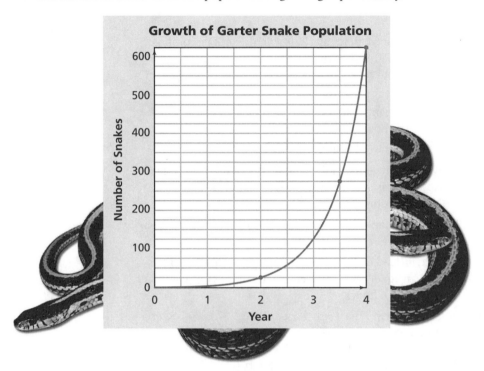

Growth of Garter Snake Population

Problem 2.3 Interpreting Exponential Graphs

A. Explain how to find the growth factor for the population.

B. 1. Find the snake population for years 2, 3, and 4.

    2. Use the pattern in your answers from part (1) to estimate the population in year 1. Explain.

    3. Explain how you can find the y-intercept for the graph.

C. Write an equation relating time t in years and population p. Explain what information the numbers in the equation represent.

D. In what year is the population likely to reach 1,500?

ACE Homework starts on page 24.

Notes _____

_____

_____

_____

Applications

1. If you don't brush your teeth regularly, it won't take long for large colonies of bacteria to grow in your mouth. Suppose a single bacterium lands on your tooth and starts multiplying by a factor of 4 every hour.

   a. Write an equation that describes the number of bacteria b in the new colony after n hours.

   b. How many bacteria will be in the colony after 7 hours?

   c. How many bacteria will be in the colony after 8 hours? Explain how you can find this answer by using the answer from part (b) instead of the equation.

   d. After how many hours will there be at least 1,000,000 bacteria in the colony?

   e. Suppose that, instead of 1 bacterium, 50 bacteria land in your mouth. Write an equation that describes the number of bacteria b in this colony after n hours.

   f. Under the conditions of part (e), there will be 3,276,800 bacteria in this new colony after 8 hours. How many bacteria will there be after 9 hours and after 10 hours? Explain how you can find these answers without using the equation from part (e).

2. Loon Lake has a "killer plant" problem similar to Ghost Lake in Problem 2.1. Currently, 5,000 square feet of the lake is covered with the plant. The area covered is growing by a factor of 1.5 each year.

   a. Copy and complete the table to show the area covered by the plant for the next 5 years.

   b. The surface area of the lake is approximately 200,000 square feet. How long will it take before the lake is completely covered?

Growth of Loon Lake Plant

Year	Area Covered (sq. ft)
0	5,000
1	■
2	■
3	■
4	■
5	■

Notes _____

_____

_____

_____

3. Leaping Leonora just signed a contract with a women's basketball team. The contract guarantees her $20,000 the first year, $40,000 the second year, $80,000 the third year, $160,000 the fourth year, and so on, for 10 years.

   a. Make a table showing Leonora's salary each year of this contract.

   b. What total amount will Leonora earn over the 10 years?

   c. Describe the growth pattern in Leonora's salary.

   d. Write an equation for Leonora's salary s for any year n of her contract.

4. As a biology project, Talisha is studying the growth of a beetle population. She starts her experiment with 5 beetles. The next month she counts 15 beetles.

Homework
Help **O**nline
PHSchool.com
For: Help with Exercise 4
Web Code: ape-3204

   a. Suppose the beetle population is growing linearly. How many beetles can Talisha expect to find after 2, 3, and 4 months?

   b. Suppose the beetle population is growing exponentially. How many beetles can Talisha expect to find after 2, 3, and 4 months?

   c. Write an equation for the number of beetles b after m months if the beetle population is growing linearly. Explain what information the variables and numbers represent.

   d. Write an equation for the number of beetles b after m months if the beetle population is growing exponentially. Explain what information the variables and numbers represent.

   e. How long will it take the beetle population to reach 200 if it is growing linearly?

   f. How long will it take the beetle population to reach 200 if it is growing exponentially?

Investigation 2 Examining Growth Patterns   **25**

STUDENT PAGE

Notes _____

_____

_____

_____

5. Fruit flies are often used in genetic experiments because they reproduce very quickly. In 12 days, a pair of fruit flies can mature and produce a new generation. The table below shows the number of fruit flies in three generations of a laboratory colony.

    a. What is the growth factor for this fruit-fly population? Explain how you found your answer.

Growth of Fruit-Fly Population

Generations	0	1	2	3
Number of Fruit Flies	2	120	7,200	432,000

    b. Suppose this growth pattern continues. How many fruit flies will be in the fifth generation?

    c. Write an equation for the population p of generation g.

    d. After how many generations will the population exceed one billion?

6. A population of mice has a growth factor of 3. After 1 month, there are 36 mice. After 2 months, there are 108 mice.

    a. How many mice were in the population initially (at 0 months)?

    b. Write an equation for the population after any number of months. Explain what information the numbers and variables in your equation represent.

7. Fido did not have fleas when his owners took him to the kennel. The number of fleas on Fido after he returned from the kennel grew according to the equation $f = 8(3^n)$, where f is the number of fleas and n is the number of weeks since he returned from the kennel. (Fido left the kennel at week 0.)

    a. How many fleas did Fido pick up at the kennel?

    b. What is the growth factor for the number of fleas?

    c. How many fleas will Fido have after 10 weeks if he is not treated?

STUDENT PAGE

Notes _____

_____

_____

_____

8. Consider the equation $y = 150(2^x)$.

   a. Make a table of x and y-values for whole-number x-values from 0 to 5.

   b. What do the numbers 150 and 2 in the equation tell you about the relationship?

For Exercises 9–12, find the growth factor and the y-intercept of the equation's graph.

9. $y = 300(3^x)$

10. $y = 300(3)^x$

11. $y = 6{,}500(2)^x$

12. $y = 2(7)^x$

Go Online
PHSchool.com
For: Multiple-Choice Skills
Practice
Web Code: apa-3254

13. The following graph represents the population growth of a certain kind of lizard.

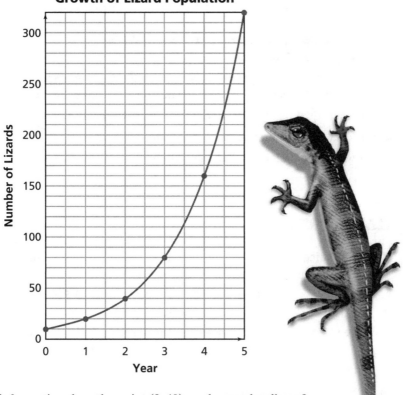

Growth of Lizard Population

Number of Lizards (y-axis)
Year (x-axis)

   a. What information does the point $(2, 40)$ on the graph tell you?

   b. What information does the point $(1, 20)$ on the graph tell you?

   c. When will the population exceed 100 lizards?

   d. Explain how you can use the graph to find the growth factor for the population.

Investigation 2 Examining Growth Patterns   **27**

Notes _____

_____

_____

_____

14. The following graphs show the population growth for two species.

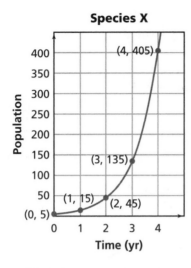

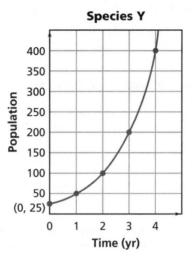

a. Find the growth factors for the two species. Which species is growing faster? Explain.

b. What are the y-intercepts for the graphs of Species X and Species Y? Explain what these y-intercepts tell you about the populations.

c. Write an equation that describes the growth of Species X.

d. Write an equation that describes the growth of Species Y.

e. For which equation is $(5, 1215)$ a solution?

Connections

15. Multiple Choice Choose the answer that best approximates 3^{20} in scientific notation.

A. 3.5×10^{-9} **B.** 8×10^3 **C.** 3×10^9 **D.** 3.5×10^9

16. Multiple Choice Choose the answer that is closest to 2.575×10^6.

F. 2^{18} **G.** 12^6 **H.** 6^{12} **J.** 11^9

17. Approximate 5^{11} in scientific notation.

For Exercises 18–20, decide whether each number is less than or greater than one million *without using a calculator*. Explain your reasoning.

18. 3^6 **19.** 9^5 **20.** 12^6

Notes _____

_____

_____

_____

21. The prime factorization of 54 is $3 \times 3 \times 3 \times 2$. This can be written using exponents as $3^3 \times 2$. Write the prime factorization of each number using exponents.

    a. 45   **b.** 144   **c.** 2,024

22. Consider these equations.

    Equation 1: $y = 10 - 5x$ **Equation 2:** $y = (10)5^x$

    a. What is the y-intercept of each equation?

    b. For each equation, explain how you could use a table to find how the y-values change as the x-values increase. Describe the change.

    c. Explain how you could use the equations to find how the y-values change as the x-values increase.

    d. For each equation, explain how you could use a graph to find how the y-values change as the x-values increase.

23. Maria enlarges a 2-cm-by-3-cm rectangle by a factor of 2 to get a 4-cm-by-6-cm rectangle. She then enlarges the 4-cm-by-6-cm rectangle by a factor of 2. She continues this process, enlarging each new rectangle by a factor of 2.

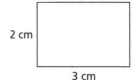

2 cm

3 cm

    a. Copy and complete the table to show the dimensions, perimeter, and area of the rectangle after each enlargement.

Rectangle Changes

Enlargement	Dimensions (cm)	Perimeter (cm)	Area (cm²)
0 (original)	2 by 3	▨	▨
1	4 by 6	▨	▨
2	▨	▨	▨
3	▨	▨	▨
4	▨	▨	▨
5	▨	▨	▨

    b. Is the pattern of growth for the perimeter *linear, exponential,* or *neither*? Explain.

    c. Is the pattern of growth for the area *linear, exponential,* or *neither*? Explain.

    d. Write an equation for the perimeter P after n enlargements.

    e. Write an equation for the area A after n enlargements.

    f. How would your answers to parts (a)–(e) change if the copier were set to enlarge by a factor of 3?

STUDENT PAGE

Notes _____

_____

_____

_____

Write an equation for each line. Identify the slope and y-intercept.

24.
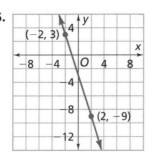

25.
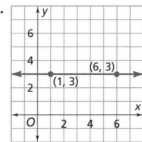

26.
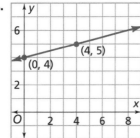

27.
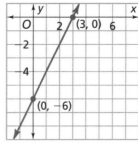

Kele enlarged the figure below by a scale factor of 2. Ahmad enlarged the figure 250%. Use this information for Exercises 28 and 29.

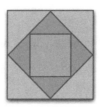

28. Who made the larger image?

29. **Multiple Choice** Which scale factor would give an image whose size is between those of Ahmad's image and Kele's image?

   A. $\frac{2}{5}$ **B.** $\frac{3}{5}$ **C.** $\frac{9}{4}$ **D.** $\frac{10}{4}$

Notes _____

_____

_____

_____

30. Companies sometimes describe part-time jobs by comparing them to full-time jobs. For example, a job that requires working half the number of hours of a full-time job is described as a $\frac{1}{2}$-time job or a 50%-time job. ACME, Inc. has three part-time job openings:

- A $\frac{5}{6}$-time job as a gadget inspector

- A 75%-time job as a widget designer

- A 0.875-time job as a gizmo seller

Order these jobs from the one requiring the most time to the one requiring the least time.

Extensions

31. a. Make a table and a graph for the exponential equation $y = 1^x$.

  b. How are the patterns in the table and the graph of $y = 1^x$ similar to patterns you have observed for other exponential relationships? How are they different?

32. You can find the equation for an exponential relationship if you know two points on its graph. Find the equation of the exponential relationship whose graph passes through each pair of points. Explain.

  a. $(1, 6)$ and $(2, 12)$ **b.** $(2, 90)$ and $(4, 810)$

33. Leaping Leonora from Exercise 3 also considered an offer from another team. They promised her $1 million a year for the next 25 years. The same team offered Dribbling Dawn $1 the first year, $2 the second year, $4 the third year, $8 the fourth year, and so on for 25 years.

  a. Suppose Leonora and Dawn had both accepted the offers and played for 20 years. At the end of 20 years, who would have received more money?

  b. Tell which player would have received more after 21 years, 22 years, 23 years, and 25 years.

Notes _____

_____

_____

_____

Mathematical Reflections 2

In this investigation, you studied quantities that grew exponentially. You looked at how the values changed from one stage to the next, and you wrote equations to find the value at any stage.

Think about your answers to these questions. Discuss your ideas with other students and your teacher. Then write a summary of your findings in your notebook.

1. **a.** Explain how you can use a table, a graph, and an equation to find the y-intercept and growth factor for an exponential relationship.

   b. Explain how you can use the y-intercept and growth factor to write an equation for an exponential relationship.

2. **a.** In the equation $y = a(b^x)$, explain what the values of a and b represent in the exponential relationship.

   b. How is a represented in a graph of $y = a(b^x)$?

   c. How is b represented in a graph of $y = a(b^x)$?

Notes _____

_____

_____

_____

Answers   Applications

Investigation

ACE
Assignment Choices

Differentiated Instruction
Solutions for All Learners

Problem 2.1
Core 1, 2, 4, 15–16, 21
Other *Applications* 3, *Connections* 17–20, *Extensions* 31–33

Problem 2.2
Core 5, 6, 8
Other *Applications* 7, *Connections* 22, 23; unassigned choices from previous problems

Problem 2.3
Core 9–13, 24–27
Other *Applications* 14; *Connections* 28–30; unassigned choices from previous problems

Adapted For suggestions about adapting Exercise 3 and other ACE exercises, see the *CMP Special Needs Handbook*.
Connecting to Prior Units 21: *Prime Time*; 22, 24–27: *Moving Straight Ahead*; 23, 28, 29: *Stretching and Shrinking*; 30: *Bits and Pieces I*

Applications

1. a. $b = 4^n$

   b. $4^7 = 16,384$ bacteria

   c. 65,536; this can be found by computing $16,384 \cdot 4$ because $4^8 = 4^7 \times 4$.

   d. 10 hours. There will be at least 1 million bacteria in the colony after 9 hr and before 10 hr, as shown by $4^9 = 262,144$ and $4^{10} = 1,048,576$. (Note: This is essentially solving the equation $1,000,000 = 4^n$. Students can solve this problem in a variety of ways. They might guess and check values of n in 4^n. They might make a chart. They might enter the equation into a calculator and look at the table. They might trace a calculator graph, although setting an appropriate graphing window for exponential equations can be challenging.)

   e. $b = 50(4^n)$

   f. There will be 13,107,200 bacteria after 9 hr and 52,428,800 after 10 hr. We can find these by multiplying the number of bacteria at hour 8 by 4, and then multiplying that number by 4.

2. a.

Growth of Loon Lake Plant

Year	Area Covered (sq. ft)
0	5,000
1	7,500
2	11,250
3	16,875
4	25,312.5
5	37,968.75

   b. 10 yr (more closely, about 9.098 yr)

3. a. Leaping Leanora's Salary

Year	Salary
1	$20,000
2	$40,000
3	$80,000
4	$160,000
5	$320,000
6	$640,000
7	1,280,000
8	$2,560,000
9	$5,120,000
10	$10,240,000

   b. $20,460,000. (Note: Students can find this by adding the amounts in the table or by using their calculators to find the sum of the sequence of $S = 10,000(2^n)$ from $n = 1$ to 10. See page 16 for information on how to do this.)

c. The growth pattern is doubling from year to year.

d. $s = 20{,}000(2^{n-1})$ or $s = 10{,}000(2^n)$

4. a. 25 beetles; 35 beetles; 45 beetles

b. 45 beetles; 135 beetles; 405 beetles

c. $b = 5 + 10m$, where b is the number of beetles and m is the number of months

d. $b = 5(3^m)$ or $b = 15(3^{m-1})$, where b is the number of beetles and m is the number of months

e. 19.5 months. Solve $200 = 5 + 10m$.

f. Between 3 and 4 mo. There are 135 beetles after 3 mo and 405 beetles after 4 mo. (**Note:** Students won't be able to solve the exponential equation algebraically. They can find an approximate solution by scrolling through a calculator table for the equation, using appropriate increments. Or, students might graph the equation and trace its graph.)

5. a. 60; the number of fruit flies in any generation divided by the number in the previous generation is 60.

b. 1,555,200,000; $432{,}000 \times 60 \times 60 = 1.5552 \times 10^9$

c. $p = 2(60^g)$

d. 4

6. a. 12 mice. There were 36 mice after 1 mo and the growth factor is 3. So, at 0 mo, there were $36 \div 3 = 12$ mice.

b. $p = 12(3^n)$. 12 is the original population, 3 is the growth factor, p is the population, n is the number of months. [Or, $p = 36(3^{n-1})$, where 36 is the population after 1 mo.]

7. a. 8 fleas

b. 3

c. $8(3^{10}) = 472{,}392$ fleas

Note to the Teacher Point out to students that this answer demonstrates that exponential growth equations have limits as models of real-life phenomena. Although something might start out increasing in a nearly exponential way, the predictive validity of the model will eventually break down.

8. a.

x	y
0	150
1	300
2	600
3	1,200
4	2,400
5	4,800

b. The starting population, or initial value, is 150, and the growth factor is 2.

9. Growth factor: 3; y-intercept: 300

10. Growth factor: 3; y-intercept: 300

11. Growth factor: 2; y-intercept: 6,500

12. Growth factor: 7; y-intercept: 2

13. a. After 2 yr, the lizard population was 40.

b. After 1 yr, the lizard population was 20.

c. Between years 3 and 4.

d. Divide the population for one year by the population for the previous year. For example, divide the population for year 3, which is 80, by the population for year 2, which is 40: $80 \div 40 = 2$.

14. a. The growth factor for Species X is 3 because the y-value for each point is 3 times the previous y-value. The growth factor for Species Y is 2 because the y-value for each point is 2 times the previous y-value.

b. The y-intercept is $(0, 5)$, so the starting population for Species X is 5.

c. The y-intercept is $(0, 25)$, so the starting population for Species Y is 25.

d. $y = 5(3^x)$

e. $y = 25(2^x)$

Connections

15. D

16. G

17. 4.88×10^7

18. Less than; 1 million is 10^6 and $3 < 10$. Therefore, $3^6 < 10^6$.

19. Less than; 1 million is 10^6 and $9 < 10$. Therefore, $9^5 < 9^6 < 10^6$.

20. Greater than; 1 million is 10^6 and $10 < 12$. Therefore, $10^6 < 12^6$.

21. a. $3^2 \times 5$

   b. $2^4 \times 3^2$

   c. $2^3 \times 11 \times 23$

22. a. The y-intercept is $(0, 10)$ for each equation.

   b. If you make a table of (x, y) values for Equation 1 for consecutive x-values, you will see that the y-values decrease by 5, so the rate of change is -5. In the table for Equation 2, the values increase. If you subtract successive y-values, you get differences of 40, 200, 1,000, and so on. So the rate of change is increasing. (Students will learn in Investigation 3 that the growth rate is 400%.) (Note: Students may describe the pattern of change for Equation 2 multiplicatively, saying that each y-value is 5 times the previous y-value. You could ask these students to describe the change additively, which will get at the increasing rate of change described above.)

   c. In Equation 1, the rate of change (the slope) is the -5 in front of the x. In the Equation 2, the rate of change is harder to see. It is easier to see in a table. However, the growth factor of 5 can be seen in the equation as the number raised to the exponent. (Note: Students will be introduced to rate of change of exponential equations in Investigation 3, so this problem is just to get them to think about patterns of change for linear and exponential functions.)

   d. Look at the vertical distance between points for each horizontal change of 1 unit. In the graph of Equation 1, the vertical distance between any two points is 5. In the graph of Equation 2, the vertical distance increases, indicating that the y-values are increasing at a faster and faster rate. Students may also describe this multiplicatively at this time.

23. a. (Figure 1)

   b. Exponential; each perimeter is multiplied by 2 to obtain the next perimeter.

   c. Exponential; each area is multiplied by 4 to obtain the next area. (Note: Because both width and length increase by a factor of 2, area increases by a factor of 4.)

   d. $P = 10(2^n)$

   e. $A = 6(4^n)$ or $A = 3(2^n) \times 2(2^n)$

   f. Perimeter and area would still increase exponentially, but the related equations would be $P = 10(3^n)$ and $A = 6(9^n)$.

24. $y = \frac{1}{4}x + 4$; slope is $\frac{1}{4}$, y-intercept is $(0, 4)$

25. $y = 2x - 6$; slope is 2, y-intercept is $(0, -6)$

26. $y = -3x - 3$; slope is -3, y-intercept is $(0, -3)$

27. $y = 3$; slope is 0, y-intercept is $(0, 3)$

28. Ahmad. Expressed as a percent, Kele's scale factor is 200%, which is less than 250%.

29. C

30. Gizmo seller, gadget inspector, widget designer

Figure 1

Enlargement	Dimensions (cm)	Perimeter (cm)	Area (cm²)
0 (original)	2 by 3	10	6
1	4 by 6	20	24
2	8 by 12	40	96
3	16 by 24	80	384
4	32 by 48	160	1,536
5	64 by 96	320	6,144

Extensions

31. a.

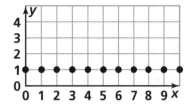

x	y
0	1
1	1
2	1
3	1
4	1

b. The equation $y = 1^x$ looks like other exponential equations, but the pattern in the table—in which every value of 1^x is 1—and in the straight-line graph looks like a linear relationship.

32. a. $y = 3(2)^x$; the growth factor can be found by dividing the y-values: $12 \div 6 = 2$. The y-intercept can be found by dividing the y-value for $x = 1$, which is 6, by the growth factor of 2. So the y-intercept is $(0, 3)$.

b. $y = 10(3)^x$; the growth factor can be found by dividing the y-values: $270 \div 90 = 3$. The y-intercept can be found by dividing the y-value for $x = 1$, which is 30, by the growth factor of 3. So the y-intercept is $(0, 10)$.

33. a. Dawn. At the end of 20 years, Leonora would have $\$1,000,000(20) = \$20,000,000$, and Dawn would have $2^{20} - 1 = \$1,048,575$. Students will probably sum up the values for each year to find Dawn's total: $\$1 + \$2 + \ldots + \$2^{19} = \$1,048,575$. (Note: Dawn receives 2^{n-1} dollars in salary, where n is the year number, and her total for the n years is $2^n - 1$.)

b. Leonora will continue to have a greater salary through year 25, when Dawn will overtake her with $\$33,554,431$ to Leonora's $\$25,000,000$.

Note to the Teacher: You may want to discuss with students a realistic time span for players in professional basketball. It is unusual for players to remain in high demand for 20 years or more. Salaries may even decrease after time.

Possible Answers to Mathematical Reflections

1. a. Using the table, the y-intercept is the point where $x = 0$. If the y-intercept is not given in the table, you can use the growth factor to find it. To find the growth factor, divide a y-value by the previous y-value. Then, start with a y-value and divide by this growth factor, moving backward in the table until you find the y-value for the point with x-coordinate 0. Using the equation $y = a(b^x)$, the y-intercept is a and the growth factor is b. Using the graph, the y-intercept is the point where the graph crosses the y-axis. The growth factor can be found by taking two points on the graph with x-values 1 unit apart, such as $(2, 4)$ and $(3, 8)$ and then dividing the second y-value by the first y-value.

b. If a is the y-intercept and b is the growth factor, then write the equation $y = a(b^x)$.

2. a. a is the y-intercept (the value when $x = 0$), and b is the growth factor.

b. a is the y-intercept.

c. In the graph of $y = a(b^x)$, the b is how much one y-value is multiplied by to get the next y-value. A greater value of b will increase the rate of growth, resulting in a steeper graph at each x-value.

Investigation 3 — Growth Factors and Growth Rates

Mathematical and Problem-Solving Goals

- Determine a non-whole number growth factor using information in a table or a graph
- Determine the growth rate, or percent change
- Use sample population data to write an equation to model population growth
- Investigate the growth of an investment with a given growth rate (percent increase)
- Relate growth rates and growth factors
- Review and extend understanding of percent
- Understand the role of initial value (*y*-intercept) in compound growth

Summary of Problems

Problem 3.1 Reproducing Rabbits

This problem is set in the context of a historical account of a rapidly multiplying rabbit population in Australia. Students use population data given in table form to write an equation to model population growth. The growth factor in this situation is *not* a whole number. Students also find the *doubling time* for a population.

Problem 3.2 Investing for the Future

Students examine patterns of change due to compound growth. Students learn the connection between *growth rate* (or percent change) and growth factor.

Problem 3.3 Making a Difference

Students study the effects of the initial value (*y*-intercept) on the growth patterns of three different savings plans.

	Suggested Pacing	Materials for Students	Materials for Teachers	ACE Assignments
All	$3\frac{1}{2}$ days	Graph paper, graphing calculators		
3.1	1 day		Transparency 3.1 (optional)	1–8, 24–30
3.2	1 day			9–20, 31, 32, 40–45
3.3	1 day			21–23, 33–39, 46, 47
MR	$\frac{1}{2}$ day			

Goals

- Determine a non-whole number growth factor using information in a table or a graph

- Use sample population data to write an equation to model population growth

This problem is set in the context of a historical account of a rapidly multiplying rabbit population in Australia. In the problems students have studied in this unit so far, the exponential growth factor was a whole number, either given in the problem story or evident from the pattern in the data. When the growth factor is not a whole number—as it is in this problem—the pattern is not as obvious, and it will be important to explore ratios of successive terms. However, the strategy for finding the growth factor is the same as in previous problems—divide successive y-values. The language of decimals and percents is commonly used in situations involving fractional growth factors to describe both the growth factor and its effects.

During the launch or summary you may want to use the graphing calculator to demonstrate how to make a STAT plot of the data. (See page 15 for a description of how to enter data pairs and make a plot.) Making a STAT plot is a visual way to ascertain the exponential nature of the pattern. If time permits, let students enter the data into their calculators. For these data, window settings of x-values from 0 to 5 with a scale of 1 and y-values from 0 to 1,100 with a scale of 100 work well.

Launch 3.1

Discuss with students the story of the rabbits that were introduced to Australia by English settlers. Direct their attention to the table of data in the student edition, or project the table on Transparency 3.1.

Suggested Questions Ask:

- *Does the relationship between time and rabbit population appear to be linear, exponential, or neither?*

Because the growth factor is not a whole number, the exponential nature of the relationship may not be immediately apparent to students. If they guess that the relationship is linear, ask:

- *By how much did the rabbit population increase in each year shown?* (By 80, 145, 258, and then 467 rabbits)

- *Is that a constant rate of change?* (No)

- *Why is this pattern exponential?* (Collect a few answers.)

The relationship is, in fact, exponential. However, unlike the other exponential relationships they have studied, the growth factor is not a whole number. Students will determine the growth factor as they work on the problem. Have students work on the problem in pairs.

Explore 3.1

To find the overall growth factor, students will need to find the growth factor for consecutive years and decide on a typical, or average, value.

Suggested Questions As you circulate, you might ask students questions to guide them in finding the year-to-year growth factors and in determining an overall growth factor.

- *How can you determine the growth factor from one year to the next?* (Divide the number of rabbits in any year by the number in the preceding year. In other words, find the ratio of one year's population to the previous year's population.)

- *What is the growth factor from the initial year (year 0) to year 1?* ($180 \div 100$, or 1.80)

- *What is the growth factor from year 1 to year 2?* ($325 \div 180$, or about 1.81)

- *Why do you think these ratios are not equal?* (The data are experimental. Factors such as food availability and weather conditions would affect the growth of the population from year to year.)

- *How can you find an overall growth factor for these data?* (Students might suggest using the mean, median, or mode of the year-to-year growth factors. Or, they might simply approximate the growth factor at 1.80. Any of these methods is viable.)

To answer part (4) of Question A, students are likely to use a guess-and-check approach or to extend the table. Students can also enter the equation $y = 100(1.8)^x$ on a graphing calculator and scroll through a table or trace a graph. They can adjust the calculator settings to get a more precise answer.

Ask some groups to make a graph of the data on chart paper or a transparency to present during the summary.

For Question B, you might suggest that some students make a table for the first 4 years to help them make sense of the equation. Ask students about their understanding of the "doubling time."

- *How can you find the doubling time for the population?* (Using a table or graph, choose a population value and then find the population value that is twice the value you chose. The difference in the time values for these two population values is the doubling time.)

Summarize 3.1

Suggested Questions Ask:

- *When we look at a table of population data like this one, how can we determine whether the data represent a linear relationship?*

- *How can we determine whether the data represent an exponential relationship?*

Students should be able to explain that if the time values increase by a constant amount, then the relationship is linear if the difference between successive population values is constant, and the relationship is exponential if the ratio of successive population values is constant. This is a review, but these ideas are fundamental. Students need many opportunities to think about and articulate their understanding of linear and exponential patterns.

Suggested Questions Ask:

- *How did you determine the growth factor for these data?*

Because this is the first time students have encountered an exponential equation with a base

that is not a whole number, you might talk with them about this explicitly. Although this may seem counterintuitive to students at first, there is no reason that the base should be a whole number.

Quickly sketch the graph relating to the equation $p = 100(1.8)^n$ or ask the class to describe 3 or 4 important points and have them make the sketch.

Suggested Questions Tell students you want to figure out how long it took the rabbit population to double from 100 to 200.

- *Find the point corresponding to a population of 200.*

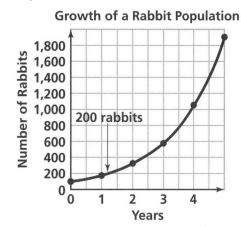

Growth of a Rabbit Population

- *About how many years did it take for the initial population to double?*

From the graph or the table, students can see that it took between 1 and 2 years for the population to double. Discuss how students could find a more exact time. For example, the graph shows that the doubling occurred closer to year 1 than to year 2. Students can use their calculators to check the population for time values such as 1.1 and 1.2 to find a time value that gives a population close to 200.

- *Pick another point. How many years does it take the population to double from this point?* (Between 1 and 2 more years)

The doubling time is the same no matter what population we start with. (Note: This can be shown algebraically. If s is the starting population, then the doubling time is the value of t in the equation $2s = s(1.8)^t$. Dividing both sides by s (since $s \neq 0$) gives $2 = (1.8)^t$. From this second, simplified equation, it is clear that the initial population is not important.)

Doubling time is revisited in Question B. Students do not need to do algebraic calculations to find the doubling time. They can use a table or graph or guess and check. Doubling time is not an essential idea at this stage, but many students find it interesting. It also provides an opportunity to make sense of exponential functions.

Suggested Questions Ask students to evaluate the accuracy of the exponential model in making long-range predictions.

- *In part (3) of Question A, what was your estimate for the number of rabbits in the population after 50 years?* (About 5.80×10^{14} rabbits)

- *Does this seem realistic?*

This is nearly 600 trillion rabbits, which seems highly unlikely. This question raises the point that mathematical models are often not useful for long-range predictions.

Check for Understanding

- *Suppose the growth factor for a population of cats is 1.7 per year and the starting population is 50 cats. What is an equation for the population growth?* [$p = 50(1.7^t)$]

- *When will the population double?* (At the end of the first year, the population will be 85. At the end of the second year, the population will be about 145. Therefore, the population doubles sometime during the second year. By guessing and checking, or by generating a table on their calculators, students could make a more precise estimate of about 1.3 yr.)

Reproducing Rabbits

Mathematical Goals

- Determine a non-whole-number growth factor using information in a table or a graph
- Use sample population data to write an equation to model population growth

Launch

Discuss with students the story of the rabbits that were introduced to Australia by English settlers. Direct their attention to the table of data.

- *Does the relationship between time and rabbit population appear to be linear, exponential, or neither?*

If they guess that the relationship is linear, ask:

- *By how much did the rabbit population increase in each year shown?*
- *Is that a constant rate of change?*
- *Why is this pattern exponential?*

Have students work on the problem in pairs.

Materials
- Transparency 3.1 (optional)

Explore

As you circulate, you might ask students questions to guide them in finding the year-to-year growth factors and in determining an overall growth factor.

- *How can you determine the growth factor from one year to the next?*
- *What is the growth factor from the initial year (year 0) to year 1?*
- *What is the growth factor from year 1 to year 2?*
- *Why do you think these ratios are not equal?*
- *How can you find an overall growth factor for these data?*

For Question B, you might suggest that some students make a table for the first 4 years to help them make sense of the equation.

Summarize

- *When we look at a table of population data like this one, how can we determine whether the data represent a linear relationship?*
- *How can we determine whether they represent an exponential relationship?*

This is a review, but these ideas are fundamental.

- *How did you determine the growth factor for these data?*

Because this is the first time students have encountered an exponential equation with a base that is not a whole number, you might talk with them about this explicitly.

Materials
- Student notebooks

continued on next page

Sketch the graph relating to the equation $P = 100(1.8^n)$.

- *Find the point corresponding to a population of 200.*

- *About how many years did it take for the initial population to double?*

From the graph or the table, students can see that it took between 1 and 2 years for the population to double. Discuss how students could find a more exact time. Have students find the doubling time from a different starting population.

Doubling time is revisited in Question B.

After a discussion of the growth factor in the data, ask students to evaluate the predictive accuracy of the exponential model. Discuss the fact that mathematical models are often not useful for long-range predictions.

ACE Assignment Guide for Problem 3.1

Differentiated Instruction
Solutions for All Learners

Core 1, 2, 4, 24–30
Other *Applications* 3, 5–8; unassigned choices from previous problems

Adapted For suggestions about adapting Exercise 1 and other ACE exercises, see the *CMP Special Needs Handbook*.
Connecting to Prior Units 24–26: *Bits and Pieces III*

Answers to Problem 3.1

A. 1. About 1.80; possible explanation: I divided each population value by the previous value and then took the average. The average of $\frac{180}{100}, \frac{325}{180}, \frac{583}{325}$, and $\frac{1,050}{583}$ is approximately 1.80.

2. $p = 100(1.8)^n$; 100 represents the initial population of rabbits and 1.8 represents the growth factor.

3. After 10 yr, there would have been $100(1.8)^{10} \approx 35,704$ rabbits.

After 25 yr, there would have been $100(1.8)^{25} \approx 240,886,592$ rabbits.

After 50 yr, there would have been about $100(1.8)^{50} \approx 5.80 \times 10^{14}$ rabbits.

4. About 16 years. Students may use a table or a graph to get a more precise answer. It takes about 15.7 yr, or 15 yr and 8 mo.

B. 1. 1.2.

2. 15 million

3. About 4 yr (3.8 yr)

4. About 26 million; about 4 yr

5. About 93 million; about 4 yr

6. The doubling times are all the same. It appears that the doubling time does not depend on the starting population.

Investing for the Future

Goals

- Investigate the growth of an investment with a given growth rate (percent increase)

- Relate growth rates and growth factors

- Review and extend understanding of percent

   In this problem, students study *compound growth*. Compound growth applied to the value of an asset is an example of exponential growth. Students look at the growth in the value of a stamp collection for 6% and 4% annual rates of growth. They use these rates to find the growth factors, which are 1.06 and 1.04, respectively.

Launch 3.2

Suggested Questions Use the rabbit population situation in Problem 3.1 to introduce the concept of *growth rate*. Carefully model the calculation for students.

- *In Problem 3.1, the initial rabbit population is 100, and the yearly growth factor is 1.8, so there are 180 rabbits at the end of year 1. What is the increase in the number of rabbits? (80 rabbits)*

- *What percent change in the original population does this represent?*
  (% change $= \frac{\text{change in pop.}}{\text{previous pop.}} = 80 \div 100 =$ 0.8 or 80%)

- *How can this percent change be used to calculate the approximate population at the end of year 2?* (180 × 0.80 = 144. This increase is added to 180; 180 + 144 = 324.)

- *How can we write this as one calculation?* (Because 180 + 0.80 × 180 = 180(1 + 0.80), we can write this as 180(1.80). Note that 1.8 is the growth factor.)

   Tell students that the percent change is called the *growth rate*. Explain that in some exponential growth situations, the growth rate is given instead of the growth factor. (Note: In Problems 3.2 and 3.3, the percent change is an increase. In the next investigation, students solve problems in which the percent change is a decrease.)

   Discuss the story of Sam's stamp collection. You may find it helpful to calculate the increase in the value of the collection after each of the first 2 years on a transparency or the board. This will help students to clarify their understanding of percent change. You can also take this opportunity to introduce the term *compound growth*. (This term is formally introduced in Problem 3.3.)

Suggested Questions

- *When we calculate the increase for the second year, do we base it on the original $2,500 value or on the value at the end of the first year?* (on the value at the end of the first year; the change is from one year to the next year)

- *Why is the increase in value in the second year greater than the increase in value in the first year?* (because the 6% increase is applied to the increased value of $2,650 at the end of year 1, not to the original value of $2,500)

   Help the class to understand that this idea is the reason this pattern of change is called compound growth.

- *In this problem, you will create tables to find the growth factor for the value of the stamps between successive years. How would you find the growth factor for the values between two years?* (Divide the value in one year by the value in the previous year.)

- *Will you get the same factor between any two successive years?* (Yes, if the growth is exponential. Students may reply that they don't have enough information to answer this question. Some may say yes, the factor will be constant because the percent increase is constant.)

   Have students work on the problem in pairs.

Explore 3.2

As you circulate, be sure each student is calculating the value of the stamps and the growth factor correctly. You may want to have one or two pairs put their responses on blank transparencies for sharing during the summary discussion of the problem.

Some students may need help in generating the table using the percent increase. Use questions similar to those given at the start of the launch.

This is a good review of the use of percents. ACE Exercises 24–26, which were assigned with Problem 3.1, should have given students a chance to think about percents again before this problem.

Summarize 3.2

Have pairs share their strategies for determining the values in the tables and their answers to the questions. Record the data on the board or overhead.

The data can be generated by performing repeated multiplication by hand or with a calculator. (See page 14 for a description of how to use a calculator to perform recursive multiplication.)

Suggested Questions Relate the growth factor to the percent increase.

- *What is the growth factor from year 1 to year 2?* (1.06)

- *What is the growth factor from year 2 to year 3?* (1.06)

- *What is the growth factor from year 4 to year 5?* (1.06)

Write each growth factor on the table between the appropriate years. Students should be comfortable dividing the value for one year by the value for the previous year to find the growth factor. You want them to understand that if the pattern in the table is exponential, this ratio, or growth factor, will be the same (or approximately the same) for any two successive years. In other words, the growth factor will be constant.

Suggested Questions Ask:

- *How is this relationship similar to others you have investigated in this unit?* (You multiply each value by the growth factor to get the next value.)

- *If the growth factor is constant for consecutive values of x (or years, in this case), what kind of relationship is this?* (exponential)

You could make a quick sketch of the graph to show that it has an exponential shape. Plot additional points to make the exponential pattern clear.

The intent of Question B is to provide more help to students to see how the concepts of percent increase and growth factor are related. Extend the question by asking:

- *What is the growth factor for a yearly increase of 7%?* (1.07)

- *What is the growth factor for a yearly increase of 70%?* (1.70 or 1.7)

- *If you know the growth rate, or percent increase, how can you find the growth factor? Why?* [Write the growth rate as a decimal, and then add 1. To see why, look at an example: If the growth rate is 7%, then to get from the amount A one year to the amount the following year, you calculate $A + A \times 0.07$. Using the distributive property, this is $A(1.07)$, so the growth factor is 1.07.]

- *If you know the growth factor how can you find the growth rate? Why?* [Subtract 1 from the growth factor, and then write the result as a percent. To see why, look at an example: if the growth factor is 1.07, then to get from the amount A one year to the amount the following year, you calculate $A(1.07)$. This is the same as $A(1 + 0.07)$, or $A + (7\% \text{ of } A)$. The increase is $(7\% \text{ of } A)$, so the percent increase, or growth rate, is 7%.]

Use the questions in parts C and D to assess students' understanding of the relationship between growth rate and growth factor.

Some students may be interested in the Rule of 72 in the *Did You Know?* box before Problem 3.2. Make sure students understand that this rule does not give exact answers. However, it is a very useful for making estimates and is often used in practice, particularly for growth rates between 2% and 14%. For growth rates over 20%, the estimate errs significantly on the small side.

Suggested Questions Explain that the Rule of 72 can be used in other contexts as well.

- *The world population is currently about 6.4 billion, and the growth rate is 3%. If this rate continues, about how many years will it take the population to double?* (Using the Rule of 72, it will take $72 \div 3 \approx 24$ years.)

- *Do you think this rate of growth could continue indefinitely?* (Answers will vary. It is unlikely that this growth rate could continue indefinitely.)

Investing for the Future

Mathematical Goals

- Investigate the growth of an investment with a given growth rate (percent increase)
- Relate growth rates and growth factors
- Review and extend understanding of percent

Launch

Use the rabbit population situation in Problem 3.1 to introduce the concept of *growth rate*.

- *In Problem 3.1, the initial rabbit population is 100, and the yearly growth factor is 1.8, so there are 180 rabbits at the end of year 1. What is the increase in the number of rabbits?*

- *What percent change does this represent?*

- *How can this percent change be used to calculate the population at the end of year 2?*

- *How can we write this as one calculation?*

Tell students that the percent increase is called the *growth rate*. Explain that in some exponential growth situations, the growth rate is given instead of the growth factor.

Discuss the story of Sam's stamp collection. You may find it helpful to calculate the increase in the value of the collection after each of the first 2 years on a transparency or the board. You can also take this opportunity to introduce the term *compound growth*.

- *When we calculate the increase for the second year, do we base it on the original $2,500 value or on the value at the end of the first year?*

- *Why is the increase in value in the second year greater than the increase in value in the first year?*

Help the class to understand that this idea is the reason that this pattern of change is called compound growth.

Have students work on the problem in pairs.

Materials
- Graphing calculators
- Graph paper

Vocabulary
- compound growth
- growth rate

Explore

Be sure students are calculating the values and the growth factor correctly. Have one or two pairs put their responses on blank transparencies for sharing during the summary.

Some students may need help in generating the table using the percent increase.

Have pairs share their strategies. Record the data on the board.

Relate the growth factor to the percent increase.

- *What is the growth factor from year 1 to year 2? From year 2 to year 3? From year 4 to year 5?*

Write each growth factor on the table between the appropriate years.

- *How is this relationship similar to others you have investigated in this unit?*

- *If the growth factor is constant for consecutive values of* x *(or years, in this case), what kind of relationship is this?*

Make a quick sketch of the graph. Extend Question B by asking:

- *What is the growth factor for a yearly increase of 7%?*

- *What is the growth factor for a yearly increase of 70%?*

Use the questions in parts C and D to assess students' understanding of the relationship between growth rate and growth factor.

ACE Assignment Guide for Problem 3.2

Differentiated Instruction
Solutions for All Learners

Core 9–15, 18, 20
Other *Applications* 16, 17, 19; *Connections* 31, 32; *Extensions* 40–45; unassigned choices from previous problems

Adapted For suggestions about adapting ACE exercises, see the *CMP Special Needs Handbook*.
Connecting to Prior Units 32: *Bits and Pieces III*

Answers to Problem 3.2

A. 1. Sam's Stamp Collection at 6%

Year	Value
0	$2,500
1	$2,650
2	$2,809
3	$2,977.54
4	$3,156.19
5	$3,345.56

2. Yes. This is exponential growth with a growth factor of 1.06.

3. $v = 2,500(1.06)^n$

B. 1. Sam's Stamp Collection at 4%

Year	Value
0	$2,500
1	$2,600
2	$2,704
3	$2,812.16
4	$2,924.65
5	$3,041.63

2. 1.04

3. $v = 2,500(1.04)^n$

C. 1. a. 1.05
   b. 1.15
   c. 1.3
   d. 1.75
   e. 2
   f. 2.5

2. Possible answer: Change the growth rate to a decimal and add 1. (Be sure students know why this works.)

D. 1. a. 50%
   b. 25%
   c. 10%

2. Possible answer: Change the growth factor to a percent and subtract 100%. (Be sure students know why this works.)

Making a Difference

Goals

- Investigate the growth of an investment with a given growth rate (percent increase)

- Understand the concept of compound growth

- Relate growth rates and growth factors

- Understand the role of initial value (*y*-intercept) in compound growth

- Review and extend understanding of percent

Problems 3.2 and 3.3 work in conjunction to help students explore the ideas of compound growth and growth rate. In Problem 3.2, students focused on finding the growth factor in a situation involving compound growth. In this problem, they use growth rates and different starting values to write equations for three different savings plans set up by a grandmother for her grandchildren.

Launch 3.3

Review the idea of compound growth, or introduce it if you didn't do so in Problem 3.2.

Tell the story about the two sisters' college funds.

Suggested Question Ask the class to predict the effects of the different initial values.

- *The two funds have the same growth rate, but different starting values. How do you think this will affect the growth pattern?* (Collect some suggestions. Some students may think the growth factor will change.)

Have students work in pairs.

Explore 3.3

Circulate as students work, and assess who is having difficulty with the concept of growth rate. Exploring this concept provides an opportunity for students to strengthen the understanding of exponential growth patterns and the equations that represent them.

Summarize 3.3

Discuss the problem, paying particular attention to whether students understand how to use the given information to write an equation. By this time, students should be very familiar with exponential growth patterns in tables, and should recognize that the ratio between any two successive values is a constant. They should also understand how the initial value affects the value over time and that the initial value has no effect on the rate of growth. The growth factor is determined only by the yearly rate of increase in value.

Suggested Questions Ask:

- *When comparing the values of the investment over the 10 years, what differences did you notice?* (Kayle's investment seems to grow more quickly because she starts with more money.)

- *Can someone explain how to use the growth factor and the initial value to write an equation for an exponential relationship?*

The value for any year is the initial value multiplied by the growth factor raised to a variable power that represents the number of years that have passed.

$$value = initial\ value(growth\ factor)^{year}$$

Discuss Question D. This gives you a chance to check students' understanding of the mathematics that underpin the equation.

Check for Understanding

- *For a growth factor of 1.10, what is the growth rate, or percent increase?* (Because $1.10 = 1 + 0.10$, the growth rate is 10%. Be sure students understand why this rule works.)

- *Suppose you have a stamp collection worth $880 and a stamp-collecting expert tells you the value will increase by about 3% per year. What equation will tell you the value after t years?* [$v = 880(1.03^t)$] *What is the growth factor for this situation?* (1.03; Be sure students understand how to figure this out.)

- *What would be the equation if the initial value were $1,760 and the projected increase were 1% per year?* [$v = 1,760(1.01^t)$]

Making a Difference

Mathematical Goals

- Investigate the growth of an investment with a given growth rate (percent increase)
- Understand the concept of compound growth
- Relate growth rates and growth factors
- Understand the role of initial value (*y*-intercept) in compound growth
- Review and extend understanding of percent

Launch

Review the idea of compound growth, or introduce it if you didn't do so in Problem 3.2.

Tell the story about the two sisters' college funds.

- *The two funds have the same growth rate, but different starting values. How do you think this will affect the growth pattern?*

Have students work in pairs.

Materials
- Graphing calculators
- Graph paper

Explore

Circulate as students work, and assess who is having difficulty with the concept of growth rate. Exploring this concept provides an opportunity for students to strengthen the understanding of exponential growth patterns and the equations that represent them.

Summarize

Discuss the problem, paying particular attention to whether students understand how to use the given information to write an equation.

- *When comparing the values of the investment over the 10 years, what differences did you notice?*
- *Can someone explain how to use the growth factor and the initial value to write an equation for an exponential relationship?*

Discuss Question D. This gives you a chance to check students' understanding of the mathematics that underpin the equation.

Check for Understanding

- *For a growth factor of 1.10, what is the growth rate, or percent increase?*
- *Suppose you have a stamp collection worth $880 and a stamp-collecting expert tells you the value will increase by about 3% per year. What equation will tell you the value after* t *years? What is the growth factor for this situation?*
- *What would be the equation if the initial value were $1,760 and the projected increase were 1% per year?*

Materials
- Student notebooks

ACE Assignment Guide for Problem 3.3

Differentiated Instruction
Solutions for All Learners

Core 21, 22, 23
Other *Connections* 33–39; *Extensions* 46, 47; unassigned choices from previous problems

Adapted For suggestions about adapting ACE exercises, see the *CMP Special Needs Handbook.*
Connecting to Prior Units 34: *Bits and Pieces III;* 33, 38: *Stretching and Shrinking;* 35: *Moving Straight Ahead;* 37: *Comparing and Scaling;* 39: *Bits and Pieces I*

Answers to Problem 3.3

A. Cassie: $a = 1{,}250(1.04^t)$
Kayle: $a = 2{,}500(1.04^t)$, where a is the amount in the fund and t is the time in years since the money was invested

B. 1.

Value of College Funds

Year	Casie's Fund	Kayle's Fund
0	$1,250	$2,500
1	$1,300	$2,600
2	$1,352	$2,704
3	$1,406.08	$2,812.16
4	$1,462.32	$2,924.65
5	$1,520.82	$3,041.63
6	$1,581.65	$3,163.30
7	$1,644.91	$3,289.83
8	$1,710.71	$3,421.42
9	$1,779.14	$3,558.28
10	$1,850.31	$3,700.61

C. 1. Kayle's increase is double Cassie's increase every year. The minor discrepancies are rounding errors. This does not reflect a difference in the growth factor, but a difference in the initial value.

2. The initial value of the fund does not affect the growth factor.

3. The final value of Kayle's fund will be double that of Cassie's, just as the initial investment was double.

D. 1. The initial value was $2,000, the growth factor is 1.05, the growth rate is 5%, and it is a four-year investment.

2. In one more year, the fund will be worth $2{,}000 \cdot 1.05^5 = \$2{,}552.56$.

Growth Factors and Growth Rates

In the previous investigation, you studied exponential growth of plants, mold, and a snake population. In each case, once you knew the growth factor and the starting value, you could make predictions. The growth factors in these examples were whole numbers. In this investigation, you will study examples of exponential growth with fractional growth factors.

3.1 Reproducing Rabbits

In 1859, a small number of rabbits were introduced to Australia by English settlers. The rabbits had no natural predators in Australia, so they reproduced rapidly and became a serious problem, eating grasses intended for sheep and cattle.

Did You Know?

In the mid-1990s, there were more than 300 million rabbits in Australia. The damage they caused cost Australian agriculture $600 million per year. There have been many attempts to curb Australia's rabbit population. In 1995, a deadly rabbit disease was deliberately spread, reducing the rabbit population by about half. However, because rabbits are developing immunity to the disease, the effects of this measure may not last.

Investigation 3 Growth Factors and Growth Rates **33**

Notes _____

_____

_____

_____

Problem 3.1 Fractional Growth Factors

If biologists had counted the rabbits in Australia in the years after they were introduced, they might have collected data like these:

Growth of Rabbit Population

Time (yr)	Population
0	100
1	180
2	325
3	583
4	1,050

A. The table shows the rabbit population growing exponentially.

   1. What is the growth factor? Explain how you found your answer.

   2. Assume this growth pattern continued. Write an equation for the rabbit population p for any year n after the rabbits are first counted. Explain what the numbers in your equation represent.

   3. How many rabbits will there be after 10 years? How many will there be after 25 years? After 50 years?

   4. In how many years will the rabbit population exceed one million?

B. Suppose that, during a different time period, the rabbit population could be predicted by the equation $p = 15(1.2^n)$, where p is the population in millions, and n is the number of years.

   1. What is the growth factor?

   2. What was the initial population?

   3. In how many years will the population double from the initial population?

   4. What will the population be after 3 years? After how many more years will the population at 3 years double?

   5. What will the population be after 10 years? After how many more years will the population at 10 years double?

   6. How do the doubling times for parts (3)–(5) compare? Do you think the doubling time will be the same for this relationship no matter where you start to count?

ACE Homework starts on page 38.

STUDENT PAGE

Notes

_____

_____

_____

_____

Investing for the Future

The yearly growth factor for one of the rabbit populations in Problem 3.1 is about 1.8. Suppose the population data fit the equation $P = 100(1.8)^n$ exactly. Then its table would look like the one below.

Rabbit Population Growth

n	P
0	100
1	$100 \times 1.8 = 180$
2	$180 \times 1.8 = 324$
3	$324 \times 1.8 = 583.2$
4	$583.2 \times 1.8 = 1049.76$

The growth factor of 1.8 is the number by which the population for year n is multiplied to get the population for the next year, $n + 1$.

You can think of the growth factor in terms of a percent change. To find the percent change, compare the difference in population for two consecutive years, n and $n + 1$, with the population of year n.

- From year 0 to year 1, the percent change is $\frac{180 - 100}{100} = \frac{80}{100} = 80\%$. The population of 100 rabbits in year 0 *increased* by 80%, resulting in 100 rabbits $\times$ 80% = 80 additional rabbits.

- From year 1 to year 2 the percent change is $\frac{324 - 180}{180} = \frac{144}{180} = 80\%$. The population of 180 rabbits in year 1 *increased* by 80%, resulting in 180 rabbits $\times$ 80% = 144 additional rabbits.

The percent increase is called the **growth rate.** In some growth situations, the growth rate is given instead of the growth factor. For example, changes in the value of investments are often expressed as percents.

Did You Know?

Some investors use a rule of thumb called the "Rule of 72" to approximate how long it will take the value of an investment to double. To use this rule, simply divide 72 by the annual interest rate. For example, an investment at an 8% interest rate will take approximately 72 ÷ 8, or 9, years to double. At a 10% interest rate, the value of an investment will double approximately every 7.2 years. This rule doesn't give you exact doubling times, only approximations.

Investigation 3 Growth Factors and Growth Rates **35**

STUDENT PAGE

Notes

When Sam was in seventh grade, his aunt gave him a stamp collection worth $2,500. Sam considered selling the collection, but his aunt told him that, if he saved it, it would increase in value.

A. Sam saved the collection, and its value increased by 6% each year for several years in a row.

  1. Make a table showing the value of the collection each year for the five years after Sam's aunt gave it to him.

  2. Look at the pattern of growth from one year to the next. Is the value growing exponentially?

  3. Write an equation for the value v of the collection after n years.

B. Suppose the value of the stamps increased by 4% each year instead of by 6%.

  1. Make a table showing the value of the collection each year for the five years after Sam's aunt gave it to him.

  2. What is the growth factor from one year to the next?

  3. Write an equation that represents the value of the stamp collection for any year.

C. 1. Find the growth factor associated with each growth rate.

  a. 5%   **b.** 15%   **c.** 30%

  d. 75%   **e.** 100%   **f.** 150%

  2. How you can find the growth factor if you know the growth rate?

D. 1. Find the growth rate associated with each growth factor.

  a. 1.5   **b.** 1.25   **c.** 1.1

  2. How can you find the growth rate if you know the growth factor?

ACE Homework starts on page 38.

STUDENT PAGE

Notes _____

_____

_____

_____

3.3 Making a Difference

In Problem 3.2, the value of Sam's stamp collection increased by the same percent each year. However, each year, this percent was applied to the previous year's value. So, for example, the increase from year 1 to year 2 is 6% of $2,650, not 6% of the original $2,500. This type of change is called **compound growth.**

In the next problem, you will continue to explore compound growth. You will consider the effects of both the initial value and the growth factor on the value of an investment.

Problem 3.3 Connecting Growth Rate and Growth Factor

Cassie's grandmother started college funds for her two granddaughters. She gave $1,250 to Cassie and $2,500 to Cassie's older sister, Kayle. Each fund was invested in a 10-year bond that pays 4% interest a year.

A. For each fund, write an equation to show the relationship between the number of years and the amount of money in the fund.

B. Make a table to show the amount in each fund for 0 to 10 years.

C. 1. How does the initial value of the fund affect the yearly value increases?

   2. How does the initial value affect the growth factor?

   3. How does the initial value affect the final value?

D. A year later, Cassie's grandmother started a fund for Cassie's younger brother, Matt. Cassie made this calculation to predict the value of Matt's fund several years from now:

$$\text{Value} = \$2,000 \times 1.05 \times 1.05 \times 1.05 \times 1.05$$

   1. What initial value, growth rate, growth factor, and number of years is Cassie assuming?

   2. If the value continues to increase at this rate, how much would the fund be worth in one more year?

ACE **Homework starts on page 38.**

STUDENT PAGE

Notes _____

_____

_____

_____

Applications

1. In parts of the United States, wolves are being reintroduced to wilderness areas where they had become extinct. Suppose 20 wolves are released in northern Michigan, and the yearly growth factor for this population is expected to be 1.2.

   a. Make a table showing the projected number of wolves at the end of each of the first 6 years.

   b. Write an equation that models the growth of the wolf population.

   c. How long will it take for the new wolf population to exceed 100?

2. a. The table shows that the elk population in a state forest is growing exponentially. What is the growth factor? Explain.

   Growth of Elk Population

Time (yr)	Population
0	30
1	57
2	108
3	206
4	391
5	743

   b. Suppose this growth pattern continues. How many elk will there be after 10 years? How many elk will there be after 15 years?

   c. Write an equation you could use to predict the elk population p for any year n after the elk were first counted.

   d. In how many years will the population exceed one million?

Notes _____

_____

_____

_____

3. Suppose there are 100 trout in a lake and the yearly growth factor for the population is 1.5. How long will it take for the number of trout to double?

4. Suppose there are 500,000 squirrels in a forest and the growth factor for the population is 1.6 per year. Write an equation you could use to find the squirrel population p in n years.

5. Multiple Choice The equation $p = 200(1.1)^t$ models the growth of a population. The variable p is the population in millions and t is the time in years. How long will it take this population to double?

A. 4 to 5 years   **B.** 5 to 6 years   **C.** 6 to 7 years   **D.** 7 to 8 years

In Exercises 6 and 7, the equation models the growth of a population, where p is the population in millions and t is the time in years. Tell how much time it would take the population to double.

6. $p = 135(1.7)^t$ **7.** $p = 1{,}000(1.2)^t$

8. a. Fill in the table for each equation.

$y = 50(2.2)^x$

x	0	1	2	3	4	5
y	▪	▪	▪	▪	▪	▪

$y = 350(1.7)^x$

x	0	1	2	3	4	5
y	▪	▪	▪	▪	▪	▪

b. What is the growth factor for each equation?

c. Predict whether the graphs of these equations will ever cross.

d. Estimate any points at which you think the graphs will cross.

9. Maya's grandfather opened a savings account for her when she was born. He opened the account with $100 and did not add or take out any money after that. The money in the account grows at a rate of 4% per year.

For: Help with Exercise 9
Web Code: ape-3309

a. Make a table to show the amount in the account from the time Maya was born until she turned 10.

b. What is the growth factor for the account?

c. Write an equation for the value of the account after any number of years.

STUDENT PAGE

Notes _____

_____

_____

_____

Find the growth rate associated with the given growth factor.

10. 1.4 **11.** 1.9 **12.** 1.75

Go Online
PHSchool.com
For: Multiple-Choice Skills
Practice
Web Code: apa-3354

For Exercises 13–15, find the growth factor associated with the given growth rate.

13. 45% **14.** 90% **15.** 31%

16. Suppose the price of an item increases by 25% per year. What is the growth factor for the price from year to year?

17. Currently, 1,000 students attend Greenville Middle School. The school can accommodate 1,300 students. The school board estimates that the student population will grow by 5% per year for the next several years.

  a. In how many years will the population outgrow the present building?

  b. Suppose the school limits its growth to 50 students per year. How many years will it take for the population to outgrow the school?

18. Suppose that, for several years, the number of radios sold in the United States increased by 3% each year.

  a. Suppose one million radios sold in the first year of this time period. About how many radios sold in each of the next 6 years?

  b. Suppose only 100,000 radios sold in the first year. About how many radios sold in each of the next 6 years?

19. Suppose a movie ticket costs about $7, and inflation causes ticket prices to increase by 4.5% a year for the next several years.

  a. At this rate, how much will a ticket cost 5 years from now?

  b. How much will a ticket cost 10 years from now?

  c. How much will a ticket cost 30 years from now?

40 Growing, Growing, Growing

STUDENT PAGE

Notes _____

_____

_____

_____

20. Find the growth rate (percent growth) for a relationship with the equation $y = 30(2^x)$.

21. Multiple Choice Ms. Diaz wants to invest $500 in a savings bond. At which bank would her investment grow the most over 8 years?

   F. Bank 1: 7% interest for 8 years.

   G. Bank 2: 2% interest for the first 4 years and 12% interest for the next four years.

   H. Bank 3: 12% interest for the first 4 years and 2% interest for the next four years.

   J. All three result in the same growth.

22. Oscar made the following calculation to predict the value of his baseball card collection several years from now:

$$\text{Value} = \$130 \times 1.07 \times 1.07 \times 1.07 \times 1.07 \times 1.07$$

   a. What initial value, growth rate, growth factor, and number of years is Oscar assuming?

   b. If the value continues to increase at this rate, how much would the collection be worth in three more years?

23. Carlos, Latanya, and Mila work in a biology laboratory. Each of them is responsible for a population of mice.

   ● The growth factor for Carlos's population of mice is $\frac{8}{7}$.

   ● The growth factor for Latanya's population of mice is 3.

   ● The growth factor for Mila's population of mice is 125%.

   a. Whose mice are reproducing fastest?

   b. Whose mice are reproducing slowest?

Notes _____

_____

_____

_____

Connections

Calculate each percent.

24. 120% of $3,000   **25.** 150% of $200   **26.** 133% of $2,500

For Exercises 27–30, tell whether the sequence of numbers could represent an exponential growth pattern. Explain your reasoning. If the pattern is exponential, give the growth factor.

27. 1   1.1   1.21   1.331   1.4641   1.61051   1.771561

28. 3   5 $8\frac{1}{3}$ $13\frac{8}{9}$ $23\frac{4}{27}$

29. 3 $4\frac{2}{3}$ $6\frac{1}{3}$ 8 $9\frac{2}{3}$ $11\frac{1}{3}$

30. 2   6.4   20.5   66   210

31. The graph shows the growth in the number of wireless subscribers in the United States from 1994 to 2004.

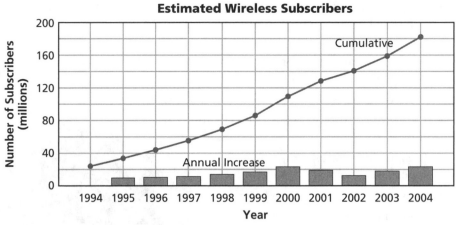

Estimated Wireless Subscribers

Source: CTIA-The Wireless Association™

a. What do the bars in the graph represent?

b. What does the curve represent?

c. Describe the pattern of change in the total number of subscribers from 1994 to 2004. Could the pattern be exponential? Explain.

d. The number of subscribers in 2001 was 128,375,000 and in 2002 the number was 140,455,000. Do these numbers fit the pattern you described in part (c)? Explain.

Notes _____

_____

_____

_____

32. A worker currently receives a yearly salary of $20,000.

    a. Find the dollar values of a 3%, 4%, and 6% raise for this worker.

    b. Find the worker's new annual salary for each raise in part (a).

    c. You can find the new salary after a 3% raise in two ways:

        $20,000 + 3% of ($20,000) *or* 103% of $20,000

    Explain why these two methods give the same result.

33. Arturo enlarges this drawing to 110% of this size. Make a copy of the drawing on grid paper and use it as you answer the following questions.

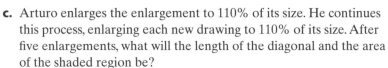

    a. What is the length of the diagonal in the original drawing? What is the area of the shaded region?

    b. What is the length of the diagonal in the enlarged drawing? What is the area of the shaded region?

    c. Arturo enlarges the enlargement to 110% of its size. He continues this process, enlarging each new drawing to 110% of its size. After five enlargements, what will the length of the diagonal and the area of the shaded region be?

    d. Is each enlargement similar to the original figure? Explain. (**Hint:** Compare the ratio of the length to the width for each enlargement with the ratio of the length to the width for the original.)

34. Kwan cuts lawns every summer to make money. One of her customers offers to give her a 3% raise next summer and a 4% raise the summer after that.

Kwan says she would prefer to get a 4% raise next summer and a 3% raise the summer after that. She claims she will earn more money this way. Is she correct? Explain.

Notes _____

_____

_____

_____

35. After graduating from high school, Kim accepts a job with a package delivery service, earning $9 per hour.

  a. How much will Kim earn in a year if she works 40 hours per week for 50 weeks and gets 2 weeks of paid vacation time?

  b. Write an equation showing the relationship between the number of weeks Kim works w and the amount she earns a.

  c. Kim writes the following equation: $9{,}000 = 360w$. What question is she trying to answer? What is the answer to that question?

  d. Suppose Kim works for the company for 10 years, receiving a 3% raise each year. Make a table showing how her annual income grows over this time period.

  e. When Kim was hired, her manager told her that instead of a 3% annual raise, she could choose to receive a $600 raise each year. How do the two raise plans compare over a 10-year period? Which plan do you think is better? Explain your answer.

36. Which represents faster growth, a growth factor of 2.5 or a growth rate of 25%?

37. Order these scale factors from least to greatest.

130% $\frac{3}{2}$ 2   1.475

38. Christopher made a drawing that measures $8\frac{1}{2}$ by 11 inches. He needs to reduce it so it will fit into a space that measures $7\frac{1}{2}$ by 10 inches. What scale factor should he use to get a similar drawing that is small enough to fit? (Do not worry about getting it to fit perfectly.)

39. a. Match each growth rate from List 1 with the equivalent growth factor in List 2 if possible.

  List 1: 20%, 120%, 50%, 200%, 400%, 2%

  List 2: 1.5,   5,   1.2,   2.2,   4,   2,   1.02

  b. Order the growth rates from List 1 from least to greatest.

  c. Order the growth factors from List 2 from least to greatest.

Notes _____

_____

_____

_____

Extensions

40. In Russia, shortly after the breakup of the Soviet Union, the yearly growth factor for inflation was 26. What growth rate (percent increase) is associated with this growth factor? We call this percent increase the *inflation rate*.

41. In 1990, the population of the United States was about 250 million and was growing exponentially at a rate of about 1% per year.

  a. At this growth rate, what will the population of the United States be in the year 2010?

  b. At this rate, how long will it take the population to double?

  c. Do you think the predictions in parts (a) and (b) are accurate? Explain.

  d. The population in 2000 was about 282 million. How accurate was the growth rate?

42. Use the table to answer parts (a)–(d).

  a. One model of world population growth assumes the population grows exponentially. Based on the data in this table, what would be a reasonable growth factor for this model?

  b. Use your growth factor from part (a) to write an equation for the growth of the population at 5-year intervals beginning in 1955.

  c. Use your equation from part (b) to estimate the year in which the population was double the 1955 population.

  d. Use your equation to predict when the population will be double the 2000 population.

World Population Growth

Year	Population (billions)
1955	2.76
1960	3.02
1965	3.33
1970	3.69
1975	4.07
1980	4.43
1985	4.83
1990	5.26
1995	5.67
2000	6.07

Write an exponential growth equation that matches each description.

43. A population is initially 300. After 1 year, the population is 360.

44. A population has a yearly growth factor of 1.2. After 3 years, the population is 1,000.

45. The growth rate for an investment is 3% per year. After 2 years, the value of the investment is $2,560.

Notes _____

_____

_____

_____

46. Suppose your calculator did not have an exponent key. You could find 1.5^{12} by entering:

$1.5 \times 1.5 \times 1.5 \times 1.5 \times 1.5 \times 1.5 \times 1.5 \times 1.5 \times 1.5 \times 1.5 \times 1.5 \times 1.5$

a. How could you evaluate 1.5^{12} with fewer keystrokes?

b. What is the fewest number of times you could press ☒ to evaluate 1.5^{12}?

47. Mr. Watson sold his boat for $10,000. He wants to invest the money.

a. How much money will he have after 1 year if he invests the $10,000 in an account that pays 4% interest per year?

b. Mr. Watson sees an advertisement for another type of savings account:

"4% interest per year compounded quarterly."

He asks the bank teller what "compounded quarterly" means. She explains that instead of giving him 4% of $10,000 at the end of one year, the bank will give him 1% at the end of each 3-month period (each quarter of a year).

Growth of $10,000 Investment at 4% Interest Compounded Quarterly

Time (mo)	Money in Account
0	$10,000
3	$10,100
6	$10,201
9	$10,303.01

If Mr. Watson invests his money at this bank, how much will be in his account at the end of one year?

c. Mr. Watson sees an advertisement for a different bank that offers 4% interest per year *compounded monthly*. (This means he will get $\frac{1}{12}$ of 4% interest every month.) How much money will he have at the end of the year if he invests his money at this bank?

d. Which account would have the most money at the end of one year? Explain.

Notes _____

_____

_____

_____

Mathematical Reflections 3

In this investigation, you explored exponential growth situations in which the growth factor was not a whole number. In some of these situations, the growth was described by giving the percent growth, or growth rate.

Think about your answers to these questions. Discuss your ideas with other students and your teacher. Then write a summary of your findings in your notebook.

1. Suppose you know the initial value for a population and the yearly growth rate.

    a. How can you determine the population several years from now?

    b. How is a growth rate related to the growth factor for the population?

2. Suppose you know the initial value for a population and the yearly growth factor.

    a. How can you determine the population several years from now?

    b. How can you determine the yearly growth rate?

3. Suppose you know the equation that represents the exponential relationship between the population size p and the number of years n. How can you determine the doubling time for the population?

Notes _____

_____

_____

_____

Answers Applications

Investigation

ACE
Assignment Choices

Differentiated Instruction
Solutions for All Learners

Problem 3.1

Core 1, 2, 4, 24–30
Other *Applications* 3, 5–8; unassigned choices from previous problems

Problem 3.2

Core 9–15, 18, 20
Other *Applications* 16, 17, 19; *Connections* 31, 32; *Extensions* 40–45; unassigned choices from previous problems

Problem 3.3

Core 21, 22, 23
Other *Connections* 33–39; *Extensions* 46, 47; unassigned choices from previous problems

Adapted For suggestions about adapting Exercise 1 and other ACE exercises, see the *CMP Special Needs Handbook*.
Connecting to Prior Units 24–26, 32, 34: *Bits and Pieces III*; 33, 38: *Stretching and Shrinking*, 35: *Moving Straight Ahead*; 37: *Comparing and Scaling*; 39: *Bits and Pieces I*

Applications

1. a. Growth of Wolf Population

Year	Wolf Population
0	20
1	24
2	29
3	35
4	41
5	50
6	60

b. $p = 20(1.2^t)$, where p is the population and t is the number of years

c. About 9 yr

2. a. 1.9. Possible explanation:
$\frac{57}{30} \approx \frac{108}{57} \approx \frac{206}{108} \approx \frac{391}{206} \approx \frac{793}{391} \approx 1.9$

b. After 10 yr, there would be $30 \times (1.9^{10}) \approx 18{,}393$ elk. After 15 yr, there would be $30 \times (1.9^{15}) \approx 455{,}434$ elk.

c. $p = 30(1.9^n)$

d. After 16 yr, there will be 865,324 elk. After 17 yr, there will be 1,644,116 elk. This means that between year 16 and year 17 the population will reach 1 million. Some industrious students might find by guess-and-check that the population exceeds 1 million after 16.225 yr, or approximately 16 yr and 3 mo.

3. Between 1 and 2 years. $100(1.5) = 150$, and $100(1.5)^2 = 225$. Students may want to use a graph, a table, or guess-and-check to find a more precise answer: 1.71 yr.

4. $p = 500{,}000(1.6^n)$. (Note: This isn't a good model as n gets large. In fact, in less than 500 years, it predicts there will be more squirrels than atoms in the universe.)

5. D

6. 1.3 yr. (Note: Students are likely to estimate the doubling time.)

7. 3.8 yr. (Note: Students are likely to estimate the doubling time.)

8. a.

$y = 50(2.2)^x$

x	y
0	50
1	110
2	242
3	532.4
4	1,171.3
5	2,576.8

$y = 350(1.7)^x$

x	y
0	350
1	595
2	1,011.5
3	1,719.6
4	2,923.2
5	4,969.5

b. In the first equation, the growth factor is 2.2. In the second, the growth factor is 1.7.

c. Yes; although the y-intercept of the first graph is lower, the graph is increasing at a faster rate.

d. The graphs will cross between $x = 7$ and $x = 8$. Some students might check carefully and find that the graphs cross at around $x = 7.547$.

9. a.

Maya's Savings Account

Age	Value
0	$100
1	$104
2	$108.16
3	$112.49
4	$116.99
5	$121.67
6	$126.53
7	$131.59
8	$136.86
9	$142.33
10	$148.02

b. 1.04

c. $a = 100(1.04)^n$, where a is the amount of money in the account and n is Maya's age

10. 40%

11. 90%

12. 75%

13. 1.45

14. 1.9

15. 1.31

16. 1.25

17. a. 6 yr. The projected population at that point is 1,340.

b. 6 yr. The projected population at that time is 1,300. (Note: The linear equation $p = 1,000 + 50x$ models the problem, where p is the population in year x. Solving $1,300 = 1,000 + 50x$ shows that the population will outgrow the facilities in 6 yr. The two growth models can also be compared by looking at tables for

$y = 1,000(1.05)^x$ and $y = 1,000 + 50x$. This is particularly easy if a calculator is used to generate the tables. You might ask students to continue to scroll beyond the values for the first 6 yr and see what they discover. Beyond that time, the exponential assumption will produce greater year-to-year growth.)

18. a.

Year	Radios Sold
1	1,000,000
2	1,030,000
3	1,060,900
4	1,092,727
5	1,125,509
6	1,159,274
7	1,194,052

b.

Year	Radios Sold
1	100,000
2	103,000
3	106,090
4	109,273
5	112,551
6	115,927
7	119,405

19. a. About $8.72 [Note: The related equation is $p = 7(1.045^t)$ where p is the price of the ticket and t is the time in years; when $t = 5$, p is about $8.72.]

b. About $10.87

c. About $26.22 [Note: Students may round the prices in parts (a)–(c) to $8.75, $10.75, and $26.25 (or $26), arguing that movie theaters don't generally charge prices like $8.72 or $10.87.]

20. 100%

21. F. This results in 72% total growth over the 8 years. G and H each give a total growth of 70%.

22. a. Initial value: $130; growth rate: 7%; growth factor: 1.07; number of years: 5

b. $223.36

23. Latanya's mice are reproducing most quickly. Carlos's mice are reproducing most slowly. Expressed as percents, the growth factors are Carlos: 114%; Mila: 125%; and Latanya: 300%.

Connections

24. $3,600

25. $300

26. $3,325

27. This pattern represents exponential growth because each value is the previous value times a growth factor of 1.1.

28. This pattern represents exponential growth because each value is the previous value times a growth factor of $\frac{5}{3}$.

29. This pattern does not represent exponential growth because there is no constant by which each value is multiplied to find the next value. The pattern is, in fact, linear with an addition of $\frac{5}{3}$ for each term.

30. Answers may vary. A student could argue that the growth factor is approximately 3.2 and be correct. If this were "real world" data, most people (for most purposes) would consider this exponential growth. Another student might say that since there is variation in the growth factor between 3.18 and 3.22, this does not represent exponential growth.

31. a. The bars represent the number of new subscribers for each year.

b. The curve represents the total number of subscribers each year.

c. Answers will vary. It is difficult to read exact data from this graph. Although the graph appears to be exponential, it does not demonstrate pure exponential growth. The number of subscribers in 1995 was about 3.4 million, and in 1996, it was about 4.4 million, representing a growth factor of approximately 1.29. Between 1997 and 1998, the growth was from about 5.5 million to about 6.9 million, a growth factor of 1.25.

d. The growth between these two years is only about 10%—a growth factor of about 1.10. This is significantly smaller than the growth factor in the preceding years.

32. a. 3% raise: $600; 4% raise: $800; 6% raise: $1,200

b. 3% raise: $20,600; 4% raise: $20,800; 6% raise: $21,200

c. Possible answer: 103% = 100% + 3%, so 103% of $20,000 is the same as 100% of $20,000 plus 3% of $20,000. This is the same as $20,000 + (3% of $20,000). Or, because 103% = 1.03, we can reason as follows: 103% of $20,000 = 1.03($20,000) = 1($20,000) + 0.03($20,000) = $20,000 + 0.03($20,000) = $20,000 + (3% of $20,000)

33. a. 5 cm; 6 cm^2.

b. 5.5 cm; 7.26 cm^2. [Note: As each linear dimension increases by a factor of 1.1—a 10% increase—the area increases by $(1.1)^2 = 1.21$.]

c. After five enlargements, the length of the diagonal will be about 8.05 cm, and the area of the shaded region will be about 15.56 cm^2.

d. Yes, they are similar: $\frac{3}{4} = \frac{3.3}{4.4} = \frac{3.63}{4.84}$.

34. She is correct. If the amount the customer pays her this summer is s, then under her plan, she will earn $(1.04)s$ the second summer and $(1.03)(1.04)s$ the third summer, for a total of $s + (1.04)s + (1.03)(1.04)s$. Under the customer's plan, her total will be $s + (1.03)s + (1.04)(1.03)s$. Her earnings the third summer will be the same under both plans, but because she will make more money the second summer, her total earnings will be greater under her plan.

35. a. $9.00 \times 40 \times 52 = $18,720.

b. $a = 360w$ (Note: Some students may include the paid vacation time and write the equation $a = 360w + 720$.)

c. She is trying to figure out how many weeks she needs to work to earn $9,000. The answer is 25 weeks.

d.

Kim's Salary

Year	Annual Income
1	$18,720
2	$19,282
3	$19,860
4	$20,456
5	$21,070
6	$21,702
7	$22,353
8	$23,023
9	$23,714
10	$24,425

e. For the first 6 years, the $600-per-year raise plan is better. Under the $600-per-year plan, Kim would earn $21,720 in year 6 and $22,320 in year 7. In year 7, the salary for the 3% raise plan would be $22,353 and from then on would result in greater yearly salaries than the $600-per-year raise plan. The plan Kim chooses would depend on how many years she anticipates working for this company. (Note: Graphing the equations may not help students answer this question; for x-values from 0 to 10, both graphs look linear because the exponential growth is very slow for the first 10 years.)

36. 2.5

37. 130%, 1.475, $\frac{3}{2}$, 2

38. Answers may vary. Anything less than or equal to 88% (the scale factor that takes $8\frac{1}{2}$ to $7\frac{1}{2}$) will work.

39. a. Matches: 20% and 1.2; 120% and 2.2; 50% and 1.5; 400% and 5; 2% and 1.02. No match: 200%, 4, 2.

b. 2%, 20%, 50%, 120%, 200%, 400%

c. 1.02, 1.2, 1.5, 2, 2.2, 4, 5

Extensions

40. 2,500%. Because the growth factor is 26, the growth rate is 26 – 1, or 25, expressed as a percent, which is 2,500%.

41. a. Using these assumptions, in 2010, the population would be about 305 million.

b. About 70 yr

c. Answers will vary. Students may compare their answers to current information on the U.S. population. Seventy years is a very long time for a model to remain a good predictor. The fact that a 1% rate of increase translates into 2,500,000 additional people the first year and a greater number in each successive year might surprise some students.

d. The actual growth rate for this time period was greater than that predicted by the model in this problem.

42. a. Averaging the ratios gives a growth factor of 1.1.

$$\left(\frac{3.02}{2.76} + \frac{3.33}{3.02} + \frac{3.69}{3.33} + \frac{4.07}{3.69} + \frac{4.43}{4.07} + \frac{4.83}{4.43} + \frac{5.26}{4.83} + \frac{5.67}{5.26} + \frac{6.07}{5.67}\right) \div 9 \approx 1.1$$

b. $p = 2.76(1.1)^x$, where x is the number of 5-year intervals

c. $p = 2.76(1.1)^8 \approx 5.92$ billion, so the population will double the 1955 population sometime between 1990 and 1995 (the eighth 5-year period).

d. When $x = 16$, $p = 2.76(1.1)^{16} \approx 12.68$ billion, so the population will double the 2000 population sometime between 2030 and 2035 (the sixteenth 5-year period). (Note: Doubling time is independent of the starting population.)

43. $p = 300(1.2)^t$, where p is population and t is the year

44. $p = 579(1.2)^t$, where p is population and t is the year

45. $v = 2,413(1.03)^t$, where v is the value of the investment and t is the year

46. a. Possible answer: You could evaluate $(((1.5)^2)^2)^3$; in other words, multiply $1.5 \times 1.5 = 2.25$, then $2.25 \times 2.25 = 5.0625$, and then $5.0625 \times 5.0625 \times 5.0625 = 129.75$.

b. You have to press the ⊠ key 4 times to get the answer in the method outlined above.

47. a. $10,400

b. $10,406.04

c. $10,407.42. (**Note:** This is the exact answer using a growth factor of $1.00\overline{3} = 1 + \frac{1}{12}(0.04)$. However, students may round and use a growth factor of 1.003. This gives an answer of $10,366.00, which is significantly less. In compound growth situations, rounding leads to significantly different answers over time.)

d. He will earn more if he chooses the account for which interest is compounded monthly. The more often the interest is compounded, the faster the investment grows.

Possible Answers to Mathematical Reflections

1. a. You can convert the growth rate to a growth factor by adding 100% and changing the result to a decimal. Then, you can use an equation of the form $p = a \times b^t$, where b is the growth factor and a is the size of the original population. You can also compute the population from one time to the next by finding the percent increase and adding it to the previous value to get the next successive value. If the growth rate is 4% and population after n yr is P, then the value after $n + 1$ yr is $P + 0.04P$ or $P(1.04)$.

b. A growth rate is the percent growth. If you convert the growth rate to a decimal and add 1, you will get the growth factor. For example, a growth rate of 4% corresponds to a growth factor of 1.04.

2. a. You can use the equation $p = a \times b^t$, where b is the growth factor and a is the size of the original population. You can also generate the population for each year recursively, by multiplying the population for each year by the growth factor to get the population for the next year.

b. Figure out the percent change from one year to the next. If you convert the growth factor to a percent and subtract 100%, you will get the growth rate. For example, a growth factor of 1.04 corresponds to a growth rate of 4%.

Investigation 4 Exponential Decay

Mathematical and Problem-Solving Goals

- Use knowledge of exponential relationships to make tables and graphs and to write equations for exponential decay patterns

- Analyze and solve problems involving exponents and exponential decay

- Recognize patterns of exponential decay in tables, graphs, and equations

- Use information in a table or graph of an exponential relationship to write an equation

- Analyze an exponential decay relationship that is represented by an equation and use the equation to make a table and graph

Summary of Problems

Problem 4.1 Making Smaller Ballots

Students revisit the paper-cutting activity of Investigation 1 with a new question in mind: How does the area of a ballot change with each successive cut?

Problem 4.2 Fighting Fleas

This problem focuses on the decreasing amount of active medicine in an animal's blood in the hours following the initial dose.

Problem 4.3 Cooling Water

Students conduct an experiment to determine the rate at which a cup of water cools, a phenomenon that can be closely modeled by exponential decay.

	Suggested Pacing	Materials for Students	Materials for Teachers	ACE Assignments
All	$4\frac{1}{2}$ days	Graphing calculators, student notebooks		
4.1	1 day	Inch or 1/4-inch grid paper, scissors (1 pair of scissors per pair of students)	Transparency 4.1 (optional), 8-inch square of inch grid paper for demonstration, scissors	1, 2, 8
4.2	1 day		Transparency 4.2 (optional)	3–5, 9–11, 13
4.3	2 days	Very hot water, cups for holding hot liquid (1 per group), thermometer (1 per group), watches or clocks with second hands (1 per group), CBLs (1 per group; optional), graph paper	Thermometer for measuring the room temperature	6, 7, 12
MR	$\frac{1}{2}$ day			

Making Smaller Ballots

Goals

- Use knowledge of exponential relationships to make tables and graphs and to write equations for exponential decay patterns

- Analyze and solve problems involving exponents and exponential decay

Students' experiences with exponential change in the previous investigations all involved exponential growth. In this problem, they revisit the ballot-cutting activity to study the pattern of decreasing exponential change in the area of a ballot after each cut.

Launch 4.1

Remind students that in the ballot-cutting activity in Investigation 1, they looked at how the number of ballots changes with each cut. Explain that they are going to revisit that activity, but this time, they will look at how the area of a ballot changes with each cut. Demonstrate, starting with an 8-inch square of inch grid paper.

Suggested Questions Hold up your square of grid paper.

- *This sheet of paper has an area of 64 square inches. When I make the first cut, what happens to the area of a ballot?* (It becomes half the original area, or 32 in.^{2})

- *What will be the area of each ballot after the second cut?* (16 in.^{2})

- *What would a ballot look like if I made 10 cuts?* (It would be very small.)

- *Do you think it would be large enough for you to write your name on it?* (no)

- *Will I ever have a ballot with an area of 0?* (No; although the area will become smaller and smaller, it will theoretically never reach 0.)

Have students work in pairs.

Explore 4.1

Distribute a sheet of quarter-inch or inch grid paper and scissors to each pair. Students will also need grid paper for their graphs.

Have the class cut 8-inch squares from the grid paper. Each pair should then cut their paper square into ballots as directed, complete the table, and answer Questions B–E. (Students need only actually cut the paper for the first two or three cuts.)

Have some students put graphs on a transparent grid for the summary.

Summarize 4.1

Suggested Questions Ask students to share what they discovered in the problem.

- *What happens to the area of a ballot with each successive cut?* (It is half the previous area, or the previous area divided by 2.)

- *Does this pattern remain consistent as you make more cuts?* (yes)

- *Do the data in your table look like data from other situations you have encountered?* (In some ways, no; the values are decreasing. In previous situations, the values increased. In other ways, yes; each value can be determined by multiplying the previous value by a constant number.)

- *How can you determine the area of a ballot from the area of the previous ballot?* (Multiply it by $\frac{1}{2}$, or 0.5.)

- *Let's start at the beginning and generate the table using the constant factor $\frac{1}{2}$. If I know the area of the original ballot is 64 square inches, how do I get the area of a ballot after one cut?* (Multiply 64 by $\frac{1}{2}$.)

● *What is the area after two cuts?* (32 in.^{2})

Cuts	Area Calculation	Area (in.^{2})
0	64	64
1	$64 \times \frac{1}{2}$	32
2	$64 \times \frac{1}{2} \times \frac{1}{2}$	16
3	$64 \times \frac{1}{2} \times \frac{1}{2} \times \frac{1}{2}$	8

● *Suppose I could continue cutting. How could I find the area of a ballot after 50 cuts?* [Multiply 64 by a string of 50 factors of $\frac{1}{2}$; or, calculate $64(\frac{1}{2})^{50}$.]

● *What is the area of a ballot after* n *cuts?* [$64(\frac{1}{2})^n$ in.^{2}]

● *Explain how you got your equation in Question C.*

● *What does the graph of this situation look like?*

● *How is the graph similar to and different from the graphs in the previous problems?*

Students should realize that the graph is not a straight line because this is not a linear relationship. It has a curved shape similar to a graph of exponential growth, but it is decreasing rather than increasing.

Check for Understanding

Ask questions that connect the various representations of the relationship.

● Pick a pair of values from the table and ask students to explain what these values mean in terms of the context, the equation, and the graph.

● Have students explain how the variables and numbers in the equation relate to the context of the situation, the table, and the graph.

● Have students discuss how the pattern and features of the graph are related to the equation, situation, and table.

Then ask the following question:

● *When will the area be about 0.01 square inches? Explain your reasoning.*

Making Smaller Ballots

PACING 1 day

Mathematical Goals

- Use knowledge of exponential relationships to make tables and graphs and to write equations for exponential decay patterns
- Analyze and solve problems involving exponents and exponential decay

Launch

Remind students of the ballot-cutting activity. Explain that this time they will look at how the area of a ballot changes with each cut. Demonstrate, starting with an 8-inch square of inch grid paper.

- *This sheet of paper has an area of 64 square inches. When I make the first cut, what happens to the area of a ballot?*
- *What will be the area of each ballot after the second cut?*
- *What would a ballot look like if I made 10 cuts?*
- *Do you think it would be large enough for you to write your name on it?*
- *Will I ever have a ballot with an area of 0?*

Have students work in pairs on the problem.

Materials

- 8-inch square of inch grid paper for demonstration
- Inch or quarter-inch grid paper for students
- Scissors (1 pair per pair of students)

Explore

Distribute a sheet of quarter-inch or inch grid paper and scissors to each pair. Students will also need grid paper for their graphs.

Have the class cut 8-inch squares from the grid paper. Each pair should then cut their paper square into ballots as directed, complete the table, and answer Questions B–E. (Students need only actually cut the paper for the first two or three cuts.)

Have some students put graphs on a transparent grid for the summary.

Summarize

Ask students to share what they discovered in the problem.

- *What happens to the area of a ballot with each successive cut?*
- *Does this pattern remain consistent as you make more cuts?*
- *Do the data in your table look like data from other situations you have encountered?*
- *How can you determine the area of a ballot from the area of the previous ballot?*
- *Let's start at the beginning and generate the table using the constant factor $\frac{1}{2}$. If I know the area of the original ballot is 64 square inches, how do I get the area of a ballot after one cut?*
- *What is the area after two cuts?*

Materials

- Student notebooks

continued on next page

- *What is the area of a ballot after n cuts?*
- *Explain how you got your equation in Question C.*
- *What does the graph of this situation look like?*
- *How is the graph similar to and different from the graphs in the previous problems?*

Students should realize that the graph is not a straight line because this is not a linear relationship. It has a curved shape similar to a graph of exponential growth, but it is decreasing rather than increasing.

Check for Understanding

Ask questions that connect the various representations of the relationship. Then, ask:

- *When will the area be about 0.01 square inches? Explain your reasoning.*

ACE Assignment Guide for Problem 4.1

Differentiated Instruction
Solutions for All Learners

Core 1, 2, 8
Other Unassigned choices from previous problems

Adapted For suggestions about adapting Exercise 1 and other ACE exercises, see the *CMP Special Needs Handbook*.

Answers to Problem 4.1

A.

Number of Cuts	Area (in.²)
0	64
1	32
2	16
3	8
4	4
5	2
6	1
7	0.5
8	0.25
9	0.125
10	0.0625

B. Each cut makes the area of a ballot half the previous area.

C. $A = 64(\frac{1}{2})^n$

D.

Area of Ballot

E. The pattern is different from the exponential growth patterns in that the numbers decrease instead of increase. It is similar in that each value (area) can be derived from the preceding value. Some students might notice that each value is obtained by dividing the previous value by 2, and some may notice that each value is obtained by multiplying the previous value by $\frac{1}{2}$.

Fighting Fleas

Goals

- Recognize patterns of exponential decay in tables, graphs, and equations

- Use information in a table or graph of an exponential relationship to write an equation

- Analyze an exponential decay relationship that is represented by an equation and use the equation to make a table and graph

- Analyze and solve problems involving exponents and exponential decay

For animals and human beings alike, many chemicals introduced into the bloodstream break down, or metabolize, in patterns that are modeled well by exponential decay. In this problem, students analyze the breakdown of a preventative flea medicine in a dog's blood, as represented in a table and a graph. Students find the decay factor associated with the data, use it to write an equation, and then consider the role of the initial dose and its effect on the equation. They are then given the initial dose and *decay rate* for a similar situation, and use this information to make a table and write an equation. They also investigate the connection between decay rate and decay factor.

Launch 4.2

You could start by writing an equation for the pattern in Problem 4.1, $A = 64(\frac{1}{2})^n$. Then introduce the terms *exponential decay* and *decay factor*. Discuss the similarities and differences between exponential decay patterns and exponential growth patterns.

- In both exponential growth and exponential decay, each y-value is found by multiplying the previous y-value by a constant factor (assuming the x-values change by a constant amount).

- In exponential growth, the constant factor (the growth factor) is greater than 1. In exponential decay, the constant factor (the decay factor) is between 0 and 1.

Suggested Questions

- *What was the decay factor in the ballot-area situation in Problem 4.1?* $(\frac{1}{2})$

- *How was this represented in the table? In the graph? In the equation?*

Talk with the class about the context of a flea medicine being administered to a dog and subsequently breaking down in the dog's blood.

Suggested Questions

- *According to the table, how much medicine was in the dog's blood initially?* (400 mg)

- *How much active medicine remained after 1 hour?* (100 mg) *After 2 hours?* (25 mg)

- *How would you describe the pattern of decline in the amount of active medicine in the dog's blood?* (The medicine breaks down quickly at first, and then more slowly.)

Have students work in pairs. They can move into groups of four to discuss their findings.

Explore 4.2

As you circulate, verify that students are finding a decay factor by dividing the milligrams of medicine remaining in the dog's blood in any hour by the milligrams remaining in the *previous* hour. Because the decay factor is less than 1, some students may be tempted to divide by the number for the *next* hour to get a number greater than 1. Students may need help understanding the 20% decay rate in Question B.

Summarize 4.2

Suggested Questions Compare the equation students wrote in this problem to the equation for ballot area in Problem 4.1.

- *Let's examine the equations for the ballot-area problem and this problem,* $A = 64(0.5^n)$ *and* $m = 400(0.25^h)$.

- *How do these equations compare?* (In the first equation, the decay factor is 0.5, or $\frac{1}{2}$ and, in the second, it is 0.25, or $\frac{1}{4}$. So, the area of a ballot is half the previous area, and the amount of active medicine in the blood each hour is $\frac{1}{4}$ the previous amount. The initial values are different. For the ballot problem, the sheet of paper had an initial area of 64 in.^{2} For this problem, the initial dose of medicine was 400 mg.)

For Question B, you may want to sketch the graph of the data and compare it to the graph of the ballot data from Problem 4.1. See Figure 1.

- *How do these graphs compare?* (Both graphs display data points in an exponential decay pattern. However, in the graph of the medicine in the dog's blood, the points are connected by a smooth curve. The ballot graph descends much more quickly, then levels out.)

- *Why does it make sense to connect the points in the active-medicine graph but not in the ballot-area graph?* (The points in the active-medicine graph can be connected because the amount of medicine in the blood changes continuously. In the ballot model, the area

does not change between cuts, so only whole-number values for the number of cuts make sense. The active-medicine graph represents a continuous relationship between time and amount of active medicine in the blood; the ballot-area graph represents a discrete relationship between number of cuts and area of a ballot.)

Be sure to discuss the equation for the situation in Question B, focusing on the decay factor and its relationship to the decay rate. Students may find it confusing that because 20%, or $\frac{1}{5}$, of the active medicine is used each hour, 80%, or $\frac{4}{5}$, remains. However, this is the key to understanding the exponential decay nature of the situation.

Suggested Questions

- *Is the decay factor greater than 1 or less than 1?* (less than 1)

- *If 20% of the medicine is used each hour, what percent remains active in the blood each hour?* (80% of the amount at the start of the hour)

- *What is the fractional equivalent of that percent?* ($\frac{8}{10}$, or $\frac{4}{5}$)

- *So, what is the decay factor in this situation?* ($\frac{4}{5}$, or 0.8)

Figure 1

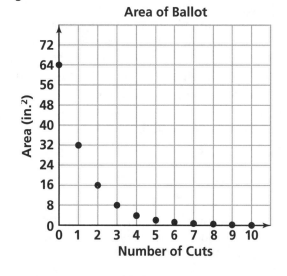

Area of Ballot

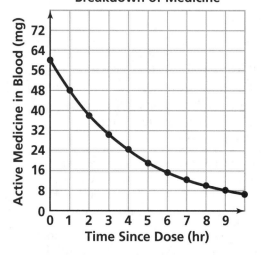

Breakdown of Medicine

Fighting Fleas

Mathematical Goals

- Recognize patterns of exponential decay in tables, graphs, and equations
- Use information in a table or graph of an exponential relationship to write an equation
- Analyze an exponential decay relationship that is represented by an equation and use the equation to make a table and graph
- Analyze and solve problems involving exponents and exponential decay

Launch

Introduce the terms *exponential decay* and *decay factor*.

Talk with the class about the context of a flea medicine being administered to a dog and subsequently breaking down in the dog's blood.

- *According to the table, how much medicine was in the dog's blood initially?*
- *How much active medicine remained after 1 hour? After 2 hours?*
- *How would you describe the pattern of decline in the amount of active medicine in the dog's blood?*

Have students work in pairs. They can move into groups of four to discuss their findings.

Materials
- Transparency 4.2

Vocabulary
- decay factor
- exponential decay

Explore

As you circulate, verify that students are finding a decay factor by dividing the milligrams of medicine remaining in the dog's blood in any hour by the milligrams remaining in the *previous* hour. Because the decay factor is less than 1, some students may be tempted to divide by the number for the *next* hour to get a number greater than 1.

Summarize

Compare the equation students wrote in this problem to the equation from the ballot-area model in Problem 4.1.

- *Let's examine the equations for the ballot-area problem and this problem: $A = 64(0.5^n)$ and $m = 400(0.25^h)$. How do these equations compare?*

For Question B, you might want to sketch the graph of the data and compare it to the graph of the ballot data from Problem 4.1.

- *How do these graphs compare?*
- *Why does it make sense to connect the points in the active-medicine graph but not in the ballot-area graph?*

Materials
- Student notebooks

Vocabulary
- decay rate

continued on next page

Be sure to discuss the equation for the situation in Question B, focusing on the decay factor and its relationship to the rate of decay.

- *Is the decay factor greater than 1 or less than 1?*
- *If 20% of the medicine is used each hour, what percent remains active in the blood each hour?*
- *What is the fractional equivalent of that percent?*
- *So, what is the decay factor in this situation?*

ACE Assignment Guide for Problem 4.2

Core 3–5
Other *Connections* 9–11; *Extension* 13; unassigned choices from previous problems

Adapted For suggestions about adapting ACE exercises, see the *CMP Special Needs Handbook*.
Connecting to Prior Units 9: *Moving Straight Ahead*; 10: *Bits and Pieces II*; 11: *Covering and Surrounding, Stretching and Shrinking*

Answers to Problem 4.2

A. 1. The amount of active medicine in the dog's blood each hour is one fourth the amount from the previous hour.

2. $m = 60\left(\frac{1}{4}\right)^h$

3. This graph has the same shape as the graph in Problem 4.1, but it has a greater initial value and the y-values decrease more quickly.

B. 1.

Breakdown of Medicine

Time Since Dose (hr)	Active Medicine in Blood (mg)
0	60
1	48
2	38.4
3	30.72
4	24.58
5	19.66
6	15.73

2. Janelle's equation gives the same quantities as the table. This is because when 20% of the active medicine is used, 80% remains. Therefore, the decay factor is 80%, or 0.8, and the equation is $m = 60(0.8)^h$.

3. The decay factor is the number by which one value is multiplied to get the next value. With a rate of decay of 20%, the medicine in the blood decreases from, for example, 60 mg to 48 mg. To get this, you have to multiply 60 by 0.8, not by 0.2.

To find the amount remaining, you take away the amount that has decayed. In other words, you multiply the initial amount by 20% and then subtract the answer from the initial amount. This is the same as multiplying by 80%. For example:

$60 \times 0.20 = 12$ (the amount of decay), so
$60 - 12 = 48$ (the amount remaining), or
$60 \times 0.80 = 48$

Some students may be able to understand the following argument:
$$\begin{aligned} 60 - 12 &= 60 - (60 \times 0.20) \\ &= 60(1 - 0.20) \\ &= 60(0.8) \end{aligned}$$

Goals

- Recognize an exponential decay pattern in a table and graph of experimental data

- Write an exponential decay equation to model experimental data

- Analyze and solve problems involving exponents and exponential decay

In this hands-on activity, students conduct an experiment and gather data about the temperature of a cup of hot water as it cools over time. The data they generate and then analyze will turn out to exhibit an exponential decay pattern.

This problem will require two class periods because the data gathering will occupy an entire period. If students conduct the experiment in small groups, group members could divide the tasks. One student could read the water temperature, a second could watch the time, a third could make the table, and a fourth could make the graph.

Between temperature readings, students can work on ACE exercises. The trick is to keep them busy but not so busy that they forget to record the temperature at the correct intervals. You might set a timer to go off at regular intervals, reminding groups to stop and record the temperature.

One thermometer for measuring the room temperature will suffice for the entire class.

An alternative approach is to have one or two groups gather data while the rest of the class works on another task. Everyone could then make a graph from the collected data, estimate the decay factor, and answer the questions.

Gathering the data will require an entire class period. Students will need time during the following class period to compile their data, find the differences between the water and room temperatures, and determine the decay factor for the cooling of the water. Alternatively, they could do these tasks at home and discuss their results in their groups the next day.

If the whole-class approach is taken, the data tables, graphs, and equations would make a good bulletin board display.

A CBL (Computer-Based Laboratory) can be used to collect the temperature data. If you have one CBL, you could demonstrate this for the whole class. If you have several, you might let the groups use the CBLs themselves after you have given them instructions.

Students construct two graphs from the data they collect in this problem. The graph of the (*time, water temperature*) data will appear exponential, but the value that it eventually approaches is not 0, as has been the case in the exponential decay relationships students have studied so far. Instead, the water temperature eventually approaches room temperature. To adjust the graph so it behaves like those for which students know how to write equations, the room temperature must be subtracted from each water temperature. In effect, this translates the graph down the y-axis so the graph approaches the x-axis rather than the room temperature.

Students will probably not completely understand this important technique through this one exposure. In later science classes, they will likely revisit this cooling experiment and be able to make more sense of it. At this time, it is enough to expect every student to construct the two graphs; to observe that they both appear to be exponential; and to notice how they are different. In addition, students need to understand why they are different: They are seeing the effect of subtracting a constant value from each data value.

Launch 4.3

Introduce the experiment by discussing the questions in the opening paragraph. Describe how the experiment is to be conducted, emphasizing that both the water temperature and the room temperature are to be recorded. Students will later analyze the differences between these two temperature readings.

Students can work on this problem in groups of four.

Some students will be able to complete the problem by estimating the decay factor and writing an equation for the difference data, but some may need help with these tasks. The main goal of this problem is to give students a hands-on experience in gathering data that produce an exponential graph and table and to let them proceed as far as they can toward writing the equation. With help, all students will have an equation, but they may not be able to write one of their own.

Summarize 4.3

As a class, compare the collected data and the graphs for each group. Ask how students found the decay factor. Write the ratios, which will vary, in the table on the overhead or at the board.

Suggested Questions

- *To write an equation in the form* y = a(b^x), *we need the values of* a *and* b. *What is the value of* a *in this situation?*

- *What information does it represent in this experiment?* (It is the starting temperature, or the temperature at time 0.)

- *How did you find the decay factor for the cooling water?* (by finding the ratios between successive temperature differences and averaging them)

- *How does the decay factor affect the equation?* (It is the value of *b,* the base.)

- *What things might affect the cooling rate you found?* (the room temperature, the shape and material of the cup, the accuracy of the temperature readings, and so on)

- *If you wanted to get different cooling rates, how could you vary the experiment?* (by stirring the liquid, by using a different liquid, by using a different container, and so on)

As a class, choose one group's decay factor and starting value. Use these values to write an equation and sketch its graph. Discuss the relationship of the graph of the equation to the graph of the group's experimental data. Students should notice that they are not identical. Review with the class the idea that mathematical models are a generalized view of the actual data.

Check for Understanding

- *Using the class equation, about how long will it take for the water temperature to reach room temperature?*

Answers to this question will vary. Theoretically, because this is an exponential relationship, the temperature will never reach room temperature. The graph of the (*time, temperature difference*) equation might help students understand this idea. In this graph, the temperature will have reached room temperature when the temperature difference reaches 0.

Cooling Water

Mathematical Goals

- Recognize an exponential decay pattern in a table and graph of experimental data
- Write an exponential decay equation to model experimental data
- Analyze and solve problems involving exponents and exponential decay

Launch

Discuss the questions in the opening paragraph. Describe how the experiment is to be conducted, emphasizing that both the water temperature and the room temperature are to be recorded. Students will later analyze the differences between these two temperature readings.

Students can work on this problem in groups of four.

Materials
- Very hot water
- Cups for holding hot liquid (1 per group)
- Watches or clock with second hand (1 per group)
- CBLs (1 per group, optional)
- Graphing calculators
- Graph paper
- Thermometer for measuring room temperature

Explore

Students may need help estimating the decay factor and writing an equation for the difference data. The goal is to give students experience in gathering data that produce an exponential graph and table and to let them go as far as they can toward writing the equation. With help, all students will have an equation, but they may not be able to do a similar task on their own.

Summarize

Compare the collected data and the graphs. Ask how students found the decay factor. Write the ratios in the table on the overhead or at the board.

Materials
- Student notebooks

- *To write an equation in the standard form, $y = a(b^x)$, we need the values of a and b. What is the value of a in this situation?*
- *What information does it represent in this experiment?*
- *How did you find the decay factor for the cooling water?*
- *How does the decay factor affect the equation?*
- *What things might affect the cooling rate you found?*
- *If you wanted to get different cooling rates, how could you vary the experiment?*

As a class, choose one group's decay factor and starting value, write an equation, and sketch its graph. Discuss the relationship of the graph of the equation to the graph of the group's experimental data. Students should notice that they are not identical. Review with the class the idea that mathematical models are a generalized view of the actual data.

Check for Understanding

- *Using the class equation, about how long will it take for the water temperature to reach room temperature?*

ACE Assignment Guide
for Problem 4.3

Core 6, 7
Other *Connections* 12; unassigned choices from previous problems

Adapted For suggestions about adapting ACE exercises, see the *CMP Special Needs Handbook.*
Connecting to Prior Units 12: *Bits and Pieces I*

Answers to Problem 4.3

The following answers are based on the following data, which was obtained from one class.

Time (min)	Water Temp. (°C)	Room Temp. (°C)	Temp. Diff. (°C)
0	89	27	62
5	71	27	44
10	59	27	32
15	52	27	25
20	47	27	20
25	43	27	16
30	40	27	13
35	37	27	10
40	35	27	8
45	33	27	6
50	32	27	5
55	31	27	4
60	30	27	3

A. 1.

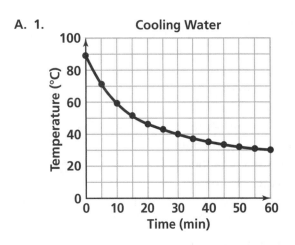

2. The temperature dropped quickly in the first 10 min; near the end of the hour, the change became minimal. The graph has the greatest change in the first 5 min and the least change at the end of the time period.

B. 1. See the preceding table.

2.

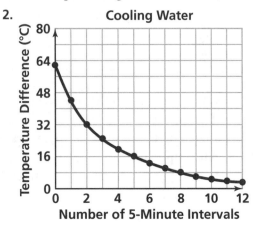

3. The time-versus-temperature-difference graph has the same pattern as the time-versus-water-temperature graph. The greatest change is in the first 5 min, and the least change is near the end of the time period.

4. The decay factor can be estimated by averaging the ratios between temperature differences: $(0.71 + 0.73 + 0.78 + 0.80 + 0.80 + 0.81 + 0.77 + 0.80 + 0.75 + 0.83 + 0.80 + 0.75) \div 12 \approx 0.78$.

5. $d = 62(0.78^n)$, where d is the temperature difference after n 5-min intervals

C. 1. The water temperature would eventually be the same as the room temperature, so the difference would become 0°C. The graph would eventually flatten out along the x-axis.

2. Possible answers: Type of liquid; starting temperature; room temperature; material, size, and shape of the cup; movement of air across the liquid; whether the liquid was stirred

3. Possible answers: Inaccurate timing of the readings, inaccurate reading of the thermometer, rounding, a faulty thermometer

**The student edition pages for this
investigation begin on the next page.**

Notes _____
_____
_____
_____

Exponential Decay

The exponential patterns you have studied so far have all involved quantities that increase. In this investigation, you will explore quantities that decrease, or *decay*, exponentially as time passes.

4.1 Making Smaller Ballots

In Problem 1.1, you read about the ballots Chen, the secretary of the Student Government Association, is making for a meeting. Recall that Chen cuts a sheet of paper in half, stacks the two pieces and cuts them in half, stacks the resulting four pieces and cuts them in half, and so on.

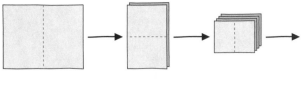

You investigated the pattern in the number of ballots created by each cut. In this problem, you will look at the pattern in the areas of the ballots.

BALLOTS

STUDENT PAGE

Notes _____

_____

_____

_____

A. The paper Chen starts with has an area of 64 square inches. Copy and complete the table to show the area of a ballot after each of the first 10 cuts.

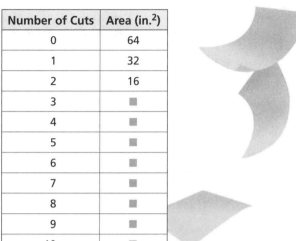

Number of Cuts	Area (in.²)
0	64
1	32
2	16
3	■
4	■
5	■
6	■
7	■
8	■
9	■
10	■

B. How does the area of a ballot change with each cut?

C. Write an equation for the area A of a ballot after any cut n.

D. Make a graph of the data.

E. How is the pattern of change in the area different from the exponential growth patterns you studied? How is it similar?

ACE Homework starts on page 53.

4.2 Fighting Fleas

Exponential patterns like the one in Problem 4.1, in which a quantity decreases at each stage, show **exponential decay.** The factor the quantity is multiplied by at each stage is called the **decay factor.** A decay factor is always less than 1 but greater than 0. In Problem 4.1, the decay factor is $\frac{1}{2}$.

Notes _____

_____

_____

_____

After an animal receives a preventive flea medicine, the medicine breaks down in the animal's bloodstream. With each hour, there is less medicine in the blood. The table and graph show the amount of medicine in a dog's bloodstream each hour for 6 hours after receiving a 400-milligram dose.

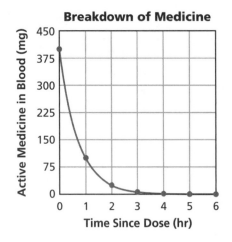

Breakdown of Medicine

Time Since Dose (hr)	Active Medicine in Blood (mg)
0	400
1	100
2	25
3	6.25
4	1.5625
5	0.3907
6	0.0977

Problem 4.2 Representing Exponential Decay

A. Study the pattern of change in the graph and the table.

   1. How does the amount of active medicine in the dog's blood change from one hour to the next?

   2. Write an equation to model the relationship between the number of hours h since the dose is given and the milligrams of active medicine m.

   3. How is the graph for this problem similar to the graph you made in Problem 4.1? How is it different?

B. 1. A different flea medicine breaks down at a rate of 20% per hour. This means that as each hour passes, 20% of the active medicine is used. The initial dose is 60 milligrams. Extend and complete this table to show the amount of active medicine in an animal's blood at the end of each hour for 6 hours.

Breakdown of Medicine

Time Since Dose (hr)	Active Medicine in Blood (mg)
0	60
1	■
2	■
⋮	⋮
6	■

Notes
_____
_____
_____
_____

2. For the medicine in part (1), Janelle wrote the equation $m = 60(0.8)^h$ to show the amount of active medicine m after h hours. Compare the quantities of active medicine in your table with the quantities given by Janelle's equation. Explain any similarities or differences.

3. Dwayne was confused by the terms **decay rate** and *decay factor.* He said that because the rate of decay is 20%, the decay factor should be 0.2, and the equation should be $m = 60(0.2^h)$. How would you explain to Dwayne why a rate of decay of 20% is equivalent to a decay factor of 0.8?

ACE Homework starts on page 53.

4.3 Cooling Water

Sometimes a cup of hot cocoa or tea is too hot to drink at first, so you must wait for it to cool.

What pattern of change would you expect to find in the temperature of a hot drink as time passes?

*What shape would you expect for a graph of (*time, drink temperature*) data?*

This experiment will help you explore these questions.

Equipment:

- very hot water, a thermometer, a cup or mug for hot drinks, and a watch or clock

Directions:

- Record the air temperature.
- Fill the cup with the hot water.
- In a table, record the water temperature and the room temperature in 5-minute intervals throughout your class period.

Hot Water Cooling

Time (min)	Water Temperature	Room Temperature
0	■	■
5	■	■
10	■	■
■	■	■
■	■	■

Investigation 4 Exponential Decay **51**

Notes _____

_____

_____

_____

A. 1. Make a graph of your (*time, water temperature*) data.

   2. Describe the pattern of change in the data. When did the water temperature change most rapidly? When did it change most slowly?

B. 1. Add a column to your table. In this column, record the difference between the water temperature and the air temperature for each time value.

   2. Make a graph of the (*time, temperature difference*) data. Compare this graph with the graph you made in Question A.

   3. Describe the pattern of change in the (*time, temperature difference*) data. When did the temperature difference change most rapidly? When did it change most slowly?

   4. Estimate the decay factor for the relationship between temperature difference and time in this experiment.

   5. Find an equation for the (*time, temperature difference*) data. Your equation should allow you to predict the temperature difference at the end of any 5-minute interval.

C. 1. What do you think the graph of the (*time, temperature difference*) data would look like if you had continued the experiment for several more hours?

   2. What factors might affect the rate at which a cup of hot liquid cools?

   3. What factors might introduce errors in the data you collect?

D. Compare the two graphs in Questions A and B with the graphs in Problems 4.1 and 4.2. What similarities and differences do you observe?

ACE Homework starts on page 53.

Notes

_____

_____

_____

_____

Applications

1. Latisha has a 24-inch string of licorice (LIK uh rish) to share with her friends. As each friend asks her for a piece, Latisha gives him or her half of what she has left. She doesn't eat any of the licorice herself.

   a. Make a table showing the length of licorice Latisha has left each time she gives a piece away.

   b. Make a graph of the data from part (a).

   c. Suppose that, instead of half the licorice that is left each time, Latisha gives each friend 4 inches of licorice. Make a table and a graph for this situation.

   d. Compare the tables and the graphs for the two situations. Explain the similarities and the differences.

2. Chen, from Problem 4.1, finds that his ballots are very small after only a few cuts. He decides to start with a larger sheet of paper. The new paper has an area of 324 in². Copy and complete this table to show the area of each ballot after each of the first 10 cuts.

Number of Cuts	Area (in.²)
0	324
1	162
2	81
3	■
4	■
5	■
6	■
7	■
8	■
9	■
10	■

   a. Write an equation for the area A of a ballot after any cut n.

   b. With the smaller sheet of paper, the area of a ballot is 1 in² after 6 cuts. How many cuts does it take to get ballots this small, starting with the larger sheet?

   c. Chen wants to be able to make 12 cuts before getting ballots with an area of 1 in². How large does his starting piece of paper need to be?

Investigation 4 Exponential Decay   **53**

Notes _____

_____

_____

_____

3. Penicillin decays exponentially in the human body. Suppose you receive a 300-milligram dose of penicillin to combat strep throat. About 180 milligrams will remain active in your blood after 1 day.

Homework
Help Online
PHSchool.com
For: Help with Exercise 3
Web Code: ape-3303

   a. Assume the amount of penicillin active in your blood decreases exponentially. Make a table showing the amount of active penicillin in your blood for 7 days after a 300-milligram dose.

   b. Write an equation for the relationship between the number of days d since you took the penicillin and the amount of the medicine m remaining active in your blood.

   c. What would be the equation if you had taken a 400-milligram dose?

In Exercises 4 and 5, tell whether the equation represents exponential decay or exponential growth. Explain your reasoning.

Go Online
PHSchool.com
For: Multiple-Choice Skills
Practice
Web Code: apa-3354

4. $y = 0.8(2.1)^x$ **5.** $y = 20(0.5)^x$

6. The graph below shows an exponential decay relationship.

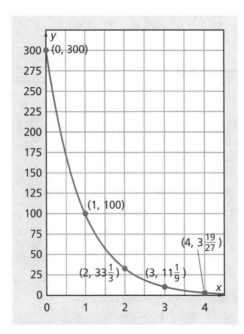

   a. Find the decay factor and the y-intercept.

   b. What is the equation for the graph?

STUDENT PAGE

Notes _____

_____

_____

_____

7. Hot coffee is poured into a cup and allowed to cool. The difference between coffee temperature and room temperature is recorded every minute for 10 minutes.

Cooling Coffee

Time (min)	0	1	2	3	4	5	6	7	8	9	10
Temperature Difference (°C)	80	72	65	58	52	47	43	38	34	31	28

a. Plot the (*time, temperature difference*) data. Explain what the patterns in the table and the graph tell you about the rate at which the coffee cools.

b. Approximate the decay factor for this relationship.

c. Write an equation for the relationship between time and temperature difference.

d. About how long will it take the coffee to cool to room temperature? Explain.

Connections

8. Scientific notation is useful for writing very large numbers. Write each of the following numbers in scientific notation.

  a. There are about 33,400,000,000,000,000,000,000 molecules in 1 gram of water.

  b. There are about 25,000,000,000,000 red blood cells in the human body.

  c. Earth is about 93,000,000 miles (150,000,000 km) from the sun.

  d. According to the Big Bang Theory, our universe began with an explosion 18,000,000,000 years ago, generating temperatures of 100,000,000,000° Celsius.

9. Consider these equations:

  $$y = 0.75^x \qquad y = 0.25^x \qquad y = -0.5x + 1$$

  a. Sketch graphs of all three equations on one set of axes.

  b. What points, if any, do the three graphs have in common?

  c. In which graph does y decrease the fastest as x increases?

  d. How can you use your graphs to figure out which of the equations is not an example of exponential decay?

  e. How can you use the equations to figure out which is not an example of exponential decay?

Notes _____

_____

_____

_____

10. A cricket is on the 0 point of a number line, hopping toward 1. She covers half the distance from her current location to 1 with each hop. So, she will be at $\frac{1}{2}$ after one hop, $\frac{3}{4}$ after two hops, and so on.

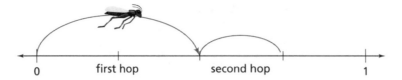

0   first hop   second hop   1

   a. Make a table showing the cricket's location for the first 10 hops.

   b. Where will the cricket be after n hops?

   c. Will the cricket ever get to 1? Explain.

11. The pizza in the ad for Mr. Costa's restaurant has a diameter of 5 inches.

   a. What are the circumference and area of the pizza?

   b. Mr. Costa reduces his ad to 90% of its original size. He then reduces the reduced ad to 90% of its size. He repeats this process five times. Extend and complete the table to show the diameter, circumference, and area of the pizza after each reduction.

Advertisement Pizza Sizes

Reduction Number	Diameter (in.)	Circumference (in.)	Area (in.²)
0	5	■	■
1	■	■	■

   c. Write equations for the diameter, circumference, and area of the pizza after n reductions.

   d. How would your equations change if Mr. Costa had used a reduction setting of 75%?

   e. Express the decay factors from part (d) as fractions.

   f. Mr. Costa claims that when he uses the 90% reduction setting on the copier, he is reducing the size of the drawing by 10%. Is Mr. Costa correct? Explain.

Notes _____

_____

_____

_____

12. Answer parts (a) and (b) without using your calculator.

   a. Which decay factor represents faster decay, 0.8 or 0.9?

   b. Order the following from least to greatest:

   0.9^4 $\qquad$ 0.9^2 $\qquad$ 90% $\qquad$ $\dfrac{2}{10}$ $\qquad$ $\dfrac{2}{9}$ $\qquad$ 0.8^4 $\qquad$ 0.84

Extensions

13. Freshly cut lumber, known as *green lumber*, contains water. If green lumber is used to build a house, it may crack, shrink, and warp as it dries. To avoid these problems, lumber is dried in a kiln that circulates air to remove moisture from the wood. Suppose that, in 1 week, a kiln removes $\frac{1}{3}$ of the moisture from a stack of lumber.

   a. What fraction of the moisture remains in the lumber after 5 weeks in a kiln?

   b. What fraction of the moisture has been removed from the lumber after 5 weeks?

   c. Write an equation for the fraction of moisture m remaining in the lumber after w weeks.

   d. Write an equation for the fraction of moisture m that has been removed from the lumber after w weeks.

   e. Graph your equations from parts (c) and (d) on the same set of axes. Describe how the graphs are related.

   f. A different kiln removes $\frac{1}{4}$ of the moisture from a stack of lumber each week. Write equations for the fraction of moisture remaining and the fraction of moisture removed after w weeks.

   g. Graph your two equations from part (f) on the same set of axes. Describe how the graphs are related. How do they compare to the graphs from part (e)?

   h. Green lumber is about 40% water by weight. The moisture content of lumber used to build houses is typically 10% or less. For each of the two kilns described above, how long should lumber be dried before it is used to build a house?

Investigation 4 Exponential Decay $\qquad$ **57**

Notes _____

_____

_____

_____

Mathematical Reflections 4

In this investigation, you explored situations that showed patterns of exponential decay.

Think about your answers to these questions. Discuss your ideas with other students and your teacher. Then, write a summary of your findings in your notebook.

1. How can you recognize an exponential decay pattern from a table of data?

2. How can you recognize an exponential decay pattern from a graph?

3. How can you tell that an equation represents exponential decay?

4. How are exponential growth relationships and exponential decay relationships similar? How are they different?

5. How are exponential decay relationships and decreasing linear relationships similar? How are they different?

STUDENT PAGE

Notes _____

_____

_____

_____

Investigation

ACE
Assignment Choices

Differentiated
Instruction
Solutions for All Learners

Problem 4.1

Core 1, 2, 8
Other Unassigned choices from previous problems

Problem 4.2

Core 3–5
Other *Connections* 9–11; *Extension* 13; unassigned choices from previous problems

Problem 4.3

Core 6, 7
Other *Connections* 12; unassigned choices from previous problems

Adapted For suggestions about adapting Exercise 1 and other ACE exercises, see the *CMP Special Needs Handbook*.
Connecting to Prior Units 9: *Moving Straight Ahead;* 10: *Bits and Pieces II;* 11: *Covering and Surrounding* and *Stretching and Shrinking;* 12: *Bits and Pieces I*

Applications

1. a.

Latisha's Licorice

Friend	Licorice Remaining (in.)
1	12
2	6
3	3
4	1.5
5	0.75
6	0.375
7	0.1875
8	0.09375

b.

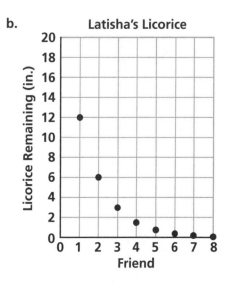

Latisha's Licorice

c.

Latisha's Licorice

Friend	Licorice Remaining (in.)
1	20
2	16
3	12
4	8
5	4
6	0

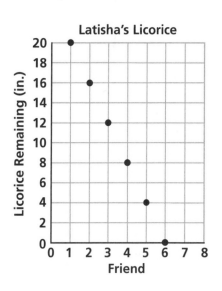

Latisha's Licorice

d. The first graph shows exponential decay; Latisha gave away less and less to each friend. The second graph is linear; each of the first six friends received the same amount. In the first graph, Latisha's licorice never runs out. In the second graph, the licorice runs out after 6 friends.

2.

Cuts	Area (in.²)
0	324
1	162
2	81
3	40.5
4	20.25
5	10.125
6	5.0625
7	2.53125
8	1.265625
9	0.6328125
10	0.31640625

a. $A = 324(\frac{1}{2})^n$

b. 9 cuts

c. If the paper were at least 4,096 in.², he would be able to make 12 cuts:
$1 \cdot 2^{12} = 4{,}096$.

3. **a.**

Days Since Dose	Penicillin in Blood (mg)
0	300
1	180
2	108
3	64.8
4	38.9
5	23.3
6	14.0
7	8.4

b. $d = 300(0.6^m)$

c. $d = 400(0.6^m)$, assuming the decay factor remains the same

4. Exponential growth because $2.1 > 1$

5. Exponential decay because $0.5 < 1$

6. a. The decay factor is $\frac{1}{3}$ and the y-intercept is 300.

b. $y = 300(\frac{1}{3})^x$

7. a.

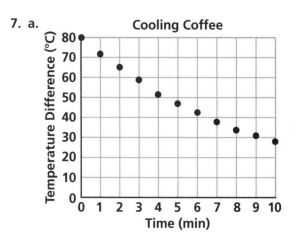

There is a slight curve in the graph, suggesting that the temperature dropped a bit more rapidly just after it was poured. The differences between the first several pairs of temperatures in the table reflect this pattern.

b. Averaging the ratios between successive temperature differences gives a decay factor of
$(0.90 + 0.90 + 0.89 + 0.90 + 0.90 + 0.91 + 0.88 + 0.89 + 0.91 + 0.90) \div 10 \approx 0.90$.

c. $d = 80(0.90^n)$, where d is temperature difference and n is time in min.

d. Theoretically, if the temperature decline followed an exponential pattern, the temperature would never exactly equal room temperature. However, the difference between coffee temperature and room temperature would have been less than 1°C after 42 min: $d = 80(0.90^{42}) = 0.96°C$.

Connections

8. a. Molecules : 3.34×10^{22}
  b. Red blood cells: 2.5×10^{13}
  c. Earth to sun: 9.3×10^7 mi; 1.5×10^8 km
  d. Age of universe: 1.8×10^{10} yr
     Big Bang temperature: 1.0×10^{11}°C

9. a.

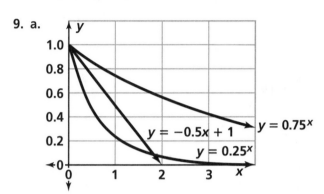

  b. The three graphs intersect at $(0, 1)$. The graphs of $y = -0.5x + 1$ and $y = (0.25)^x$ also intersect at about $(1.85, 0.075)$. In Quadrant II, there is a point of intersection for $y = -0.5x + 1$ and $y = (0.75)^x$.

  c. The graph of $y = (0.25)^x$ decreases faster than that of $y = -0.5x + 1$ until about $x = 0.7$. The graph of $y = -0.5x + 1$ decreases the fastest for x-values greater than 0.7.

  d. Because the graph of $y = -0.5x + 1$ is a straight line, it is not an example of exponential decay.

  e. The equation $y = -0.5x + 1$ does not include a variable exponent, so it is not an example of exponential decay.

10. a.

Hop	Location
1	$\frac{1}{2}$
2	$\frac{3}{4}$
3	$\frac{7}{8}$
4	$\frac{15}{16}$
5	$\frac{31}{32}$
6	$\frac{63}{64}$
7	$\frac{127}{128}$
8	$\frac{255}{256}$
9	$\frac{511}{512}$
10	$\frac{1{,}023}{1{,}024}$

  b. $1 - \left(\frac{1}{2}\right)^n$, or $\frac{2^n - 1}{2^n}$

  c. No; the numerator is always 1 less than the denominator. This means that the fraction approaches, but never reaches, 1.

11. a. circumference $= \pi d = 5\pi \approx 15.7$ in., area $= \pi r^2 = 6.25\pi \approx 19.6$ in.^{2}

  b. (Figure 2) **NOTE:** Students may round answers in different ways and at different stages. This is a good opportunity to have a discussion about rounding.

  c. diameter $= 5(0.9)^n$
     circumference $= 15.7(0.9)^n$
     area $= 19.6(0.81)^n$

  d. diameter $= 5(0.75)^n$
     circumference $= 15.7(0.75)^n$
     area $= 19.6(0.5625)^n$

  e. $0.75 = \frac{3}{4}$; $0.5625 = \frac{9}{16}$

Figure 2

Reduction Number	Diameter (in.)	Circumference (in.)	Area (in.²)
0	5.0	15.71	19.63
1	4.5	14.14	15.9
2	4.05	12.72	12.88
3	3.65	11.47	10.46
4	3.28	10.3	8.45
5	2.95	9.27	6.83

f. Possible answer: Yes; a 10% reduction can be represented by the expression $x - 0.10x$; 90% of original size can be represented by $0.9x$. These expressions are equivalent.
Note to the Teacher Common language is somewhat ambiguous about the meaning of "reduction in size." If we mean reduction in dimensions, the reasoning above applies. If we mean reduction in area, it does not apply.

12. a. 0.8. This is less than 0.9, so its product with any number will be less than the product of the same number and 0.9.

b. $\frac{2}{10}, \frac{2}{9}, (0.8)^4, (0.9)^4, (0.9)^2, 0.84, 90\%$

Extensions

13. (**Note:** A table is helpful for answering these questions. See Figure 3. Also, this would be a good time for students to learn how to display an answer in fractional form on their calculators. The decimal form of $(\frac{2}{3})^5$ is 0.1316872428, which is not very helpful when one is looking for patterns. See page 15 for a description of how to convert decimals to fractions with a calculator.)

a. $\frac{32}{243}$

b. $1 - \frac{32}{243} = \frac{211}{243}$

c. $m = (\frac{2}{3})^w$

d. $m = 1 - (\frac{2}{3})^w$

e. The graphs are mirror images of each other around the line $y = 0.5$. One approaches the x-axis, showing that the moisture remaining approaches 0; the other approaches the line $y = 1$, showing that the moisture removed approaches 100%.

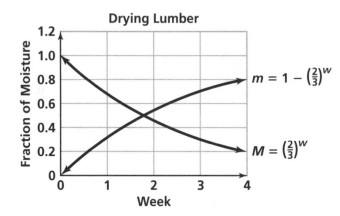

Drying Lumber

$m = 1 - (\frac{2}{3})^w$

$M = (\frac{2}{3})^w$

f. moisture remaining $= (\frac{3}{4})^w$

moisture removed $= 1 - (\frac{3}{4})^w$

Figure 3

Week	Fraction of Moisture Removed	Total Fraction of Moisture Removed	Fraction of Moisture Remaining
1	$\frac{1}{3}$	$\frac{1}{3}$	$\frac{2}{3}$
2	$\frac{1}{3} \times \frac{2}{3} = \frac{2}{9}$	$\frac{1}{3} + \frac{2}{9} = \frac{5}{9}$	$\frac{4}{9}$
3	$\frac{1}{3} \times \frac{4}{9} = \frac{4}{27}$	$\frac{5}{9} + \frac{4}{27} = \frac{19}{27}$	$\frac{8}{27}$
4	$\frac{1}{3} \times \frac{8}{27} = \frac{8}{81}$	$\frac{19}{27} + \frac{8}{81} = \frac{65}{81}$	$\frac{16}{81}$
5	$\frac{1}{3} \times \frac{16}{81} = \frac{16}{243}$	$\frac{65}{81} + \frac{16}{243} = \frac{211}{243}$	$\frac{32}{243}$

g. These graphs are also mirror images about the line $y = 0.5$. They are stretched out farther to the right, which indicates that the moisture removal proceeds more slowly. (Figure 4)

h. Possible answer: we need to go from a moisture content of 40% to one of 10%. For the first kiln, the equation is $0.1 = 0.4\left(\frac{2}{3}\right)^w$. Because $0.4\left(\frac{2}{3}\right)^3 \approx 11.9\%$ and $0.4\left(\frac{2}{3}\right)^4 = 7.9\%$, the first kiln would produce this loss in 3 to 4 wk. For the second kiln, the equation is $0.1 = 0.4\left(\frac{3}{4}\right)^w$. Because $0.4\left(\frac{3}{4}\right)^4 \approx 12.7\%$ and $0.4\left(\frac{2}{3}\right)^5 \approx 9.5\%$, the second kiln would produce this loss in 4 to 5 wk.

Possible Answers to Mathematical Reflections

1. If the x-values are equally spaced, and if there is a constant ratio between each y-value and the previous y-value and that ratio is between 0 and 1, then the data show an exponential decay pattern.

2. The pattern is a curve that drops downward from left to right, eventually becoming almost horizontal.

3. Exponential decay patterns have equations of the form $y = a \cdot b^x$, with $a > 0$ and b between 0 and 1.

4. Exponential growth and decay both have equations of the form $y = a \cdot b^x$, where $a > 0$. For exponential growth, b is greater than 1. For exponential decay, b is between 0 and 1. A graph of exponential decay is decreasing, and a graph of exponential growth is increasing. In a table, both exponential growth and decay are indicated by a constant ratio between each y-value and the previous y-value (assuming the x-values increase by a constant amount). However, in a growth situation, the ratio is greater than 1. In a decay situation, the ratio is between 0 and 1.

5. In both exponential decay situations and decreasing linear relationships, y decreases as x increases. In a table, we can see this difference easily. If the *difference* between consecutive y-values is constant and decreasing, the table exhibits a linear relationship. If the *ratio* of consecutive y-values is constant and between 0 and 1, the table exhibits an exponential decay pattern. A graph of a linear function looks like a straight line and has an x-intercept, and a graph of an exponential function is curved and does not have an x–intercept (if it is of the form $y = a \cdot b^x$, where $a > 1$), although it may sometimes appear linear depending on the scale.

Figure 4

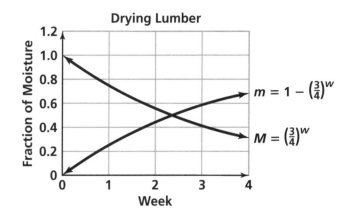

Drying Lumber

$m = 1 - \left(\frac{3}{4}\right)^w$

$M = \left(\frac{3}{4}\right)^w$

Investigation 5 Patterns With Exponents

Mathematical and Problem-Solving Goals

- Examine patterns in the exponential and standard forms of powers of whole numbers
- Use patterns in powers to estimate the ones digits for unknown powers
- Use patterns in powers to develop rules for operating with exponents
- Become skillful in operating with exponents in numeric and algebraic expressions
- Describe how varying the values of a and b in the equation $y = a(b^x)$ affects the graph of that equation

Summary of Problems

Problem 5.1 Predicting the Ones Digit

Students examine patterns in the ones digits of powers. They use these patterns to predict ones digits for powers that would be tedious to find directly.

Problem 5.2 Operating With Exponents

Students use their work in the previous problem to develop rules for operating with numerical expressions with exponents.

Problem 5.3 Exploring Exponential Equations

Students use graphing calculators to study how the values of a and b affect the graph of $y = a(b^x)$.

	Suggested Pacing	Materials for Students	Materials for Teachers	ACE Assignments
All	$4\frac{1}{2}$ days	Graphing calculators, student notebooks		
5.1	$1\frac{1}{2}$ days	Labsheet 5.1	Transparencies 5.1A and 5.1B, large sheet of poster paper (optional)	1–9, 44, 45, 52–55
5.2	$1\frac{1}{2}$ days	Completed Labsheet 5.1	Transparencies 5.2A and 5.2B	10–41, 46–48, 56–63
5.3	1 day		Overhead graphing calculator	42, 43, 49–51
MR	$\frac{1}{2}$ day			

Goals

- Examine patterns in the exponential and standard forms of powers of whole numbers

- Use patterns in powers to estimate the ones digits for unknown powers

In this problem, students start by looking at patterns in the ones digits of powers. For example, by examining the ones digits of the powers of 2 ($2^1 = 2, 2^2 = 4, 2^3 = 8, 2^4 = 16, 2^5 = 32, 2^6 = 64, 2^7 = 128, 2^8 = 256$, and so on) students see that the sequence 2, 4, 8, 6 repeats over and over. We say that the ones digits repeat in a cycle of four. The ones digits for powers of 9 are 9, 1, 9, 1, 9, 1, and so on. We say that the ones digits for the powers of 9 repeat in a cycle of 2. The ones digits for powers of 5 are all 5—that is, the ones digits repeat in a cycle of 1. The ones digits of the powers of any whole number repeat in a cycle of length 1, 2, or 4.

Students create a powers table for a^m for $a = 1$ to $a = 10$ and $m = 1$ to $m = 8$. They use the table to find patterns in order to predict the ones digits for powers such as $2^{100}, 6^{50}$, and 17^{20}, and to estimate the standard form of these powers.

Launch 5.1

Launch this problem by writing the values of $y = 2^x$, for whole-number x-values from 1 to 8. Write both the exponential and standard form for 2^x in the y-column.

x	y
1	2^1 or 2
2	2^2 or 4
3	2^3 or 8
4	2^4 or 16
5	2^5 or 32
6	2^6 or 64
7	2^7 or 128
8	2^8 or 256

Let students look for patterns in the table. Collect their discoveries on a large sheet of paper. If students can and are ready, let them give reasons for why the patterns occur. You may want to come back to these patterns later.

Use the Getting Ready to focus students on the patterns among the exponents and ones digits in the standard form of powers.

Suggested Questions Ask:

- *Look at the column of y-values in the table. What pattern do you see in how the ones digits of the standard form change?*

Students should notice that the ones digits repeat in cycles of four: 2, 4, 8, and 6. If necessary, extend the table to convince students that this pattern continues.

- *Can you predict the ones digit for 2^{15}?* (8) *What about 2^{50}?* (4)

Some students will continue the table or use their calculator to find 2^{15}. Hopefully, at least some students will use the pattern to reason as follows: The ones digits occur in cycles of four. The third complete cycle ends with 2^{12}, and the fourth cycle starts with 2^{13}. The number 2^{15} is the third number in this fourth cycle, so its ones digit is 8.

Students will not be able to find the ones digit of 2^{50} by using their calculators; the result will be displayed in scientific notation, and the ones digit will not be shown. Students will need to use the pattern previously described. Don't expect students to answer this quickly. You might postpone 2^{50} until later and give students more time to explore.

- *What other patterns do you see in the table?*

Here are some patterns students may notice. (Some of these have already been mentioned.)

- The ones digits are all even.

- To predict the ones digit, all you need to know is the cycle of repeating units digits and whether 2^x is the first, second, third, or fourth number in a cycle.

- If you divide the exponent by 4, the remainder tells you where the power is in a cycle.

- When you multiply two powers of 2, the exponent in the product is the sum of the exponents of the factors. For example, $2^3 \times 2^4 = 2^7$.

x	y
⋮	⋮
3	2^3 or 8
4	2^4 or 16
⋮	⋮
7	2^7 or 128

- *Find an x-value and values for the missing digits that will make this a true number sentence: $2^x = \underline{\ \ \ \ \ \ } 6$ ($x = 20$, which gives $2^{20} = 1{,}048{,}576$)*

Next, introduce Problem 5.1. Make sure students understand how the table is organized.

Students should fill out the powers table in Question A on their own and then work in groups of two or three for the rest of the problem.

(**Explore** 5.1)

Students should have no trouble filling in the table. Encourage them to take some care in completing the table because they will use it as a reference in the next problem.

Although the problem focuses on patterns in the ones digits, students may notice other interesting patterns as well. Here are some examples:

- Some numbers occur more than once in the powers chart. For example, 64 appears three times: $2^6 = 64$, $4^3 = 64$, and $8^2 = 64$.

- When you multiply powers of 2, the exponent of the product is the sum of the exponents of the factors. For example, $2^3 \times 2^4 = 2^{3+4} = 2^7$.

- The number of zeros in 10^n is n.

For Questions C and D, some students may try to continue the table or use their calculator to find the ones digits. But for very large exponents, continuing the table gets tedious, and the calculator rounds off after 10 digits. Students should begin to focus on the patterns in the ones digits.

Suggested Questions If students are having trouble with using the patterns of the ones digits, ask:

- *What are the lengths of the cycles of repeating ones digits?* (1, 2, or 4, depending on the base. For example, for the powers of 3, the ones digits 3, 9, 7, 1 repeat, so the cycle is of length 4.)

- *Which bases have cycles of length 4?* (2, 3, 7, and 8)

- *Which bases have a cycle of length 1?* (1, 5, 6, and 10)

- *Which bases have a cycle of length 2?* (4 and 9)

- *If you know the exponent, how can you use the pattern of the cycle to determine the ones digit of the power? For example, the ones digits for 2^n repeat in a cycle: 2, 4, 8, 6. How can we use this fact to find the ones digit of 2^{21}?* (For powers of 2, the exponents 1, 5, 9, 13, 17, 21, and so on correspond to a ones digit of 2. Students may recognize that each of these numbers is one more than a multiple of 4. In other words, when you divide these numbers by 4 you get a remainder of 1. The exponents 2, 6, 10, 14, 18, and so on, correspond to a ones digit of 4. Students may recognize that these numbers are 2 more than a multiple of 4. The exponents 3, 7, 11, 15, 19, and so on correspond to a ones digit of 8. These numbers are 3 more than a multiple of 4. Finally, the exponents 4, 8, 12, 16 and so on correspond to a ones digit of 6.)

Question D asks about powers of bases greater than those in the table. Students should reason that the ones digit of a power is determined by the ones digits of the base. For example, the ones digits for powers of 12 are the same as the ones digits for powers of 2, 22, and 92. The ones digits for powers of 17 are the same as the ones digits for powers of 7, 57, and 87. If students struggle with this idea, ask:

- *If you were to look at the ones digits for powers of 12, you would find that they follow the same pattern as the ones digits for the powers of 2. Why do you think this is true? What affects the ones digit?* (To get successive powers of 12, you multiply by 12, so the ones digit will be the same as the ones digit of 2 times the previous ones digit. For 12^1, the ones digit is 2; for 12^2, the ones digit is 4 because $2 \times 2 = 4$; for 12^3, the ones digit is 8 because $4 \times 2 = 8$; and for

12^4, the ones digit is 6 because $8 \times 2 = 16$. Then the ones digits start to repeat. A similar argument will work for all whole-number bases greater than 10.)

In Question E, remind students to use their knowledge about the patterns of the ones digit to narrow the choices. For example, for $a^{12} = 531{,}441$, a must be 1, 3, 7, or 9. Obviously, 1 is not a choice. And 9^{12} would be close to 10^{12}, which has 13 digits—much too large a number. The number 531,441 has only 6 digits. At this point, students should argue that 7^{12} is too large. They may use an argument similar to the following but with words, not symbols:

$7^2 \approx 50$, so $7^{12} = 7^2 \cdot 7^2 \cdot 7^2 \cdot 7^2 \cdot 7^2 \cdot 7^2 \approx$
$50 \cdot 50 \cdot 50 \cdot 50 \cdot 50 \cdot 50$, or
$5 \cdot 5 \cdot 5 \cdot 5 \cdot 5 \cdot 5 \cdot 10 \cdot 10 \cdot 10 \cdot 10 \cdot 10 \cdot 10$, which equals $5^6 \cdot 10^6$.

We know that 10^6 has 7 digits, which is too large, so the answer is $3^{12} = 531{,}441$.

Be sure to make note of interesting patterns, reasoning, and questions that arise during the Explore.

Summarize 5.1

It might be helpful to have a large poster of the completed powers table that students can refer to, both during this summary and for the next problem. You might also use the transparency provided for this problem.

Ask for general patterns students found. Post these on a sheet of chart paper. Ask students to give reasons for the patterns. Students may not be able to explain some of the patterns until the next problem, when the properties of exponents are developed.

Go over some of the powers in Questions C and D. Be sure to have students explain their strategies. After a student or group has explained a strategy, ask the rest of the class to verify the reasoning or to pose questions to the presenter so everyone is convinced of the validity of the reasoning. For further help with the patterns in the length of the cycle, the exponent, and the ones digit, you can use the table in Figure 1.

Save the completed powers table for the launch of Problem 5.2.

Be sure to assign ACE Exercise 54. It is needed for Problem 5.2.

Figure 1

x	2^x	Pattern	Ones Digit
1	$2^1 = 2$		2
2	$2^2 = 4$		4
3	$2^3 = 8$		8
4	$2^4 = 16$	**End of first cycle. The exponent 4 is a multiple of 4.**	6
5	$2^5 = 32$	The exponent 5 has a remainder of 1 when divided by 4.	2
6	$2^6 = 64$	The exponent 6 has a remainder of 2 when divided by 4.	4
7	$2^7 = 128$	The exponent 7 has a remainder of 3 when divided by 4.	8
8	$2^8 = 256$	**End of second cycle. The exponent 8 is a multiple of 4.**	6
9	$2^9 = \blacksquare$	The exponent 9 has a remainder of 1 when divided by 4.	2
10	$2^{10} = \blacksquare$	The exponent 10 has a remainder of 2 when divided by 4.	4
11	$2^{11} = \blacksquare$	The exponent 11 has a remainder of 3 when divided by 4.	8
12	$2^{12} = \blacksquare$	**End of third cycle. The exponent 12 is a multiple of 4.**	6
13	$2^{13} = \blacksquare$	The exponent 13 has a remainder of 1 when divided by 4.	2
14	$2^{14} = \blacksquare$	The exponent 14 has a remainder of 2 when divided by 4.	4
15	$2^{15} = \blacksquare$	The exponent 15 has a remainder of 3 when divided by 4.	8
16	$2^{16} = \blacksquare$	**End of fourth cycle. The exponent 16 is a multiple of 4.**	6
⋮	⋮	⋮	⋮
50	$2^{50} = \blacksquare$	The exponent 50 has a remainder of 2 when divided by 4. So the ones digit is 4.	4

Predicting the Ones Digit

PACING $1\frac{1}{2}$ days

Mathematical Goals

- Examine patterns in the exponential and standard forms of powers of whole numbers
- Use patterns in powers to estimate the ones digits for unknown powers

Launch

Launch this problem by writing the values of $y = 2^x$, for $x = 1$ to 8. Write both the exponential and standard form for 2^x in the y-column.

Let students look for patterns. Use the Getting Ready to focus students on the patterns.

- *Look at the column of y-values in the table. What pattern do you see in how the ones digits of the standard form change?*
- *Can you predict the ones digits for 2^{15}? What about 2^{50}?*
- *What other patterns do you see in the table?*

Students should fill out the powers table in Question A on their own and then work in groups of two or three for the rest of the problem.

Materials
- Transparencies 5.1A and 5.1B
- Labsheet 5.1

Vocabulary
- power

Explore

If students are having trouble using the patterns of the ones digits, ask:

- *What are the lengths of the cycles of repeating ones digits?*
- *Which bases have a cycle of length 4?*
- *Which bases have a cycle of length 1?*
- *Which bases have a cycle of length 2?*
- *If you know the exponent, how can you use the pattern of the cycle to determine the ones digit of the power?*
- *If you were to look at the ones digits for powers of 12, you would find that they follow the same pattern as the ones digits for the powers of 2. Why do you think this is true?*
- *What affects the ones digit?*

In Question E, remind students to use their knowledge about the patterns of the ones digit to narrow the choices down.

Make note of interesting patterns, reasoning, and questions that arise.

Summarize

Display a completed powers table on chart paper or a transparency for students to refer to, both during this summary and for the next problem.

Ask for general patterns. Ask students to give reasons for the patterns.

Go over some of the powers in Questions C and D. Be sure to have students explain their strategies.

Materials
- Student notebooks
- large sheet of poster paper (optional)

ACE Assignment Guide for Problem 5.1

Core 1–7, 54
Other *Applications* 8, 9; *Connections* 44, 45; *Extensions* 52, 53, 55; unassigned choices from previous problems

Adapted For suggestions about adapting ACE exercises, see the *CMP Special Needs Handbook.*
Connecting to Prior Units 44, 45: *Data Around Us*

Answers to Problem 5.1

A. Figure 2

B. See the Explore notes for patterns in the ones digits for each base. Here are some additional patterns students might notice.

- Square numbers a^2 have ones digits 1, 4, 9, 6, 5, 6, 9, 4, 1, 0. There is symmetry around the 5. This will repeat with each 10 square numbers.
- Fourth powers ($1^4, 2^4, 3^4$, etc.) have ones digits 0, 1, 5, and 6.
- The fifth powers ($1^5, 2^5, 3^5$, etc.) have ones digits 1, 2, 3, 4, 5, 6, 7, 8, 9, and 0, in that order.

C. **1.** 6. The even powers of 4 have 6 as a ones digit.
  2. 1. The even powers of 9 have 1 as a ones digit.
  3. 3. There is a cycle of length 4 in the ones digits of the powers of 3. 17 is the beginning of the fifth cycle.
  4. 5. Any power of 5 has a ones digit of 5.
  5. 0. Any power of 10 has a ones digit of 0.

D. **1.** 1. The ones digit of 31 is 1, so all powers of 31 will have a ones digit of 1.
  2. 4. The powers of 12 have the same ones digits as the corresponding powers of 2.
  3. 7. The powers of 17 have the same ones digits as the corresponding powers of 7.
  4. 1. The powers of 29 have the same ones digits as the corresponding powers of 9.

E. **1.** $3^{12} = 531,441$
  2. $9^9 = 387,420,489$
  3. $15^6 = 11,390,625$. The base must have a ones digit of 5. 5^6 can be ruled out without directly computing; we know it is too small because it is less than $10^6 = 1,000,000$.

F. **1.** $7^7 = \underline{823543}$
  2. $9^8 = \underline{43,046,721}$

Figure 2

Powers Table

x	1^x	2^x	3^x	4^x	5^x	6^x	7^x	8^x	9^x	10^x
1	1	2	3	4	5	6	7	8	9	10
2	1	4	9	16	25	36	49	64	81	100
3	1	8	27	64	125	216	343	512	729	1,000
4	1	16	81	256	625	1,296	2,401	4,096	6,561	10,000
5	1	32	243	1,024	3,125	7,776	16,807	32,768	59,049	100,000
6	1	64	729	4,096	15,625	46,656	117,649	262,144	531,441	1,000,000
7	1	128	2,187	16,384	78,125	279,936	823,543	2,097,152	4,782,969	10,000,000
8	1	256	6,561	65,536	390,625	1,679,616	5,764,801	16,777,216	43,046,721	100,000,000
Ones Digits of Powers	1	2, 4, 8, 6	3, 9, 7, 1	4, 6	5	6	7, 9, 3, 1	8, 4, 2, 6	9, 1	0

Operating With Exponents

Goals

- Examine patterns in the exponential and standard forms of powers of whole numbers

- Use patterns in powers to develop rules for operating with exponents

- Become skillful in operating with exponents in numeric and algebraic expressions

Students use the powers table from Problem 5.1 to find special relationships among numbers written in exponential form. For example, students may notice that $4^2 = 2^4$ or $(2^2)^2 = 2^{(2 \times 2)}$. This is an example of a general property of exponents: $(a^m)^n = a^{mn}$. In this problem, students use patterns among exponents to formulate several important properties:

$$(a^m)^n = a^{mn}$$

$$a^m \times a^n = a^{m+n}$$

$$a^m \times b^m = (a \times b)^m$$

$$a^m \div a^n = a^{m-n} \text{ (for } a \neq 0)$$

Launch 5.2

To launch this problem, refer to the completed powers table. Use the Getting Ready to encourage students to begin noticing patterns that will lead to the rules of exponents.

- *Federico noticed that 16 appears twice in the powers table. It is in the column for 2^x, for x = 4. It is also in the column for 4^x, for x = 2. He said this means that $2^4 = 4^2$. Write 2^4 as a product of 2s. Then, show that the product is equal to 4^2.*
  $[2 \cdot 2 \cdot 2 \cdot 2 = (2 \cdot 2) \cdot (2 \cdot 2) = 4 \cdot 4 = 4^2]$

- *Are there other numbers that appear more than once in the table? If so, write equations to show the equal exponential forms of the numbers. (Use different colors to circle these numbers. For example, 4 occurs as 2^2 and as 4^1, so $2^2 = 4^1$. Other examples are 8, 64, 9, 81, 256, and 729, 4,096, and 6,561.)*

Tell students that in this problem, they will look for a way to generalize these and other patterns for exponents.

Let students work in groups of three or four on this problem.

Explore 5.2

The questions are structured so that most students should be able to see the patterns. Students look at specific cases of each pattern first and are then asked to generalize the patterns.

If students have trouble explaining why a general rule works, have them connect the general rule to a specific case. For example, if students cannot explain why $a^m \times a^n = a^{m+n}$, ask them to first explain why $3^2 \times 3^4 = 3^6$. Students should be able to explain that the product of two 3s and four 3s is the product of two plus four, or six, 3s.

$$\underbrace{3 \times 3}_{\substack{\text{two 3s} \\ 3^2}} \times \underbrace{3 \times 3 \times 3 \times 3}_{\substack{\text{four 3s} \\ 3^4}} = \underbrace{3 \times 3 \times 3 \times 3 \times 3 \times 3}_{\substack{\text{six 3s} \\ 3^{2+4}}}$$

Help them generalize this to $a^m \times a^n$.

$$\underbrace{(a \times a \times \cdots \times a)}_{\substack{m \text{ as} \\ a^m}} \times \underbrace{(a \times a \times \cdots \times a)}_{\substack{n \text{ as} \\ a^n}} = \underbrace{(a \times a \times \cdots \times a)}_{\substack{(m+n) \text{ as} \\ a^{m+n}}}$$

The key to understanding why the rules of exponents work is for students to visualize the structure of a^m as the product of a used m times: $a \times a \times a \times \ldots \times a$.

Part (1) of Question D expresses $\frac{4^5}{4^6}$ as both 4^{-1} and $\frac{1}{4}$. Students may not be familiar with negative exponents. They are discussed in ACE Exercise 54, but students need not fully understand them to complete Question D. The example of $\frac{4^5}{4^6} = 4^{-1}$ illustrates that the general rule $\frac{a^m}{a^n} = a^{m-n}$ holds, even when the result has a negative exponent. Instead of using negative exponents, students can break the rule into two cases:

- If $m \geq n$, then $\frac{a^m}{a^n} = a^{m-n}$ for $a \neq 0$.

- If $m < n$, then $\frac{a^m}{a^n} = \frac{1}{a^{n-m}}$ for $a \neq 0$.

Be sure to check on how students are reasoning about a^0.

Summarize 5.2

Ask different groups to present their reasoning for each part of the problem. Use the completed powers table to illustrate the rules. For example, the rule $a^m \times a^n = a^{m+n}$ can be illustrated by looking at any column. The 3^x column is highlighted in Figure 3. Multiply two numbers in this column, for example, $9 \times 81 = 729$. The exponent for 729 is the sum of the exponents for the factors $(3^2 \times 3^4 = 3^{2+4} = 3^6)$. Ask students to give other examples. To understand the rules, it is essential that students see $3^2 \times 3^4$ as six 3s multiplied together: $3 \times 3 \times 3 \times 3 \times 3 \times 3$.

This would be a good time to ask students to explain the differences between 3^x, $3x$, and $3 + x$.

The rule $a^n \times b^n = (a \times b)^n$ is illustrated by looking at any row. The row corresponding to a^4 is highlighted in Figure 3. Multiply two numbers in this row, such as $16 \times 256 = 4,096$. In exponential form, this is $2^4 \times 4^4 = 8^4$. Students should think of a string of four 2s followed by four 4s.

The factors can be rearranged to form a string of four (2×4)s, or four 8s.
$(2 \times 2 \times 2 \times 2) \times (4 \times 4 \times 4 \times 4) =$
$(2 \times 4) \times (2 \times 4) \times (2 \times 4) \times (2 \times 4) =$
$8 \times 8 \times 8 \times 8 = 8^4$
Use the table to illustrate the other rules in a similar way.

Check for Understanding

Have students write numeric expressions, such as the following, in simpler exponential form:

$$\frac{2^5 \times 2^6}{2^9} \qquad \frac{3^4 \times 2^6}{6^9}$$

Depending on the goals for your course, you might also ask students to simplify algebraic expressions like these:

$$(x^2)^3 \qquad x^6 x^4 \qquad \frac{x^4 x^3}{x^7}$$

True or false:
$$2^3 \times 2^2 = 6^5 \qquad 4^2 + 4^3 = 4^5$$
$$5^3 \times 25 = 5^5 \qquad 18^4 = 3^4 \times 6^4$$

Figure 3

Powers Table

x	1^x	2^x	3^x	4^x	5^x	6^x	7^x	8^x	9^x	10^x
1	1	2	3	4	5	6	7	8	9	10
2	1	4	9	16	25	36	49	64	81	100
3	1	8	27	64	125	216	343	512	729	1,000
4	1	16	81	256	625	1,296	2,401	4,096	6,561	10,000
5	1	32	243	1,024	3,125	7,776	16,807	32,768	59,049	100,000
6	1	64	729	4,096	15,625	46,656	117,649	262,144	531,441	1,000,000
7	1	128	2,187	16,384	78,125	279,936	823,543	2,097,152	4,782,969	10,000,000
8	1	256	6,561	65,536	390,625	1,679,616	5,764,801	16,777,216	43,046,721	100,000,000
Ones Digits of Powers	1	2, 4, 8, 6	3, 9, 7, 1	4, 6	5	6	7, 9, 3, 1	8, 4, 2, 6	9, 1	0

5.2 Operating With Exponents

PACING $1\frac{1}{2}$ days

Mathematical Goals

- Examine patterns in the exponential and standard forms of powers of whole numbers
- Use patterns in powers to develop rules for operating with exponents
- Become skillful in operating with exponents in numeric and algebraic expressions

Launch

Refer to the completed powers table. Use the Getting Ready to encourage students to begin noticing patterns that will lead to the rules of exponents.

Tell students that in this problem, they will look for a way to generalize patterns for exponents.

Let the class work in groups of three or four.

Materials
- Transparencies 5.2A and 5.2B
- Students' completed tables from Problem 5.1

Explore

The questions are structured so that most students should be able to see the patterns. Students look at specific cases of each pattern first and are then asked to generalize the patterns.

The key to understanding why the rules of exponents work is for students to visualize the structure of a^m as the product of a used m times.

Be sure to check on how students are reasoning about a^0.

Summarize

Ask different groups to present their reasoning for each part of the problem. Use the completed powers table to illustrate the rules. For example, the rule $a^m \times a^n = a^{m+n}$ can be illustrated by looking at any column. Multiply two numbers in this column, such as $9 \times 81 = 729$. The exponent for 729 is the sum of the exponents of the factors ($3^2 \times 3^4 = 3^{2+4} = 3^6$). Ask students to give other examples.

This would be a good time to ask about the differences between $3x$, 3^x, and $3 + x$.

Materials
- Student notebooks

Check for Understanding

Have students write numeric expressions, such as the following, in simpler exponential form:

$$\frac{2^5 \times 2^6}{2^9} \qquad\qquad \frac{3^4 \times 2^6}{6^9}$$

Depending on the goals for your course, you might also ask students to simplify algebraic expressions like these:

$$(x)^3 \qquad x^6 x^4 \qquad \frac{x^4 x^3}{x^7}$$

ACE Assignment Guide for Problem 5.2

Differentiated Instruction
Solutions for All Learners

Core 10–27, 31

Other *Applications* 28–30, 32–41; *Connections* 46-48; *Extensions* 56–63; unassigned choices from previous problems

Adapted For suggestions about adapting Exercise 31 and other ACE exercises, see the *CMP Special Needs Handbook*.
Connecting to Prior Units 46, 47: *Filling and Wrapping* and *Stretching and Shrinking*; 48: *Prime Time*

Answers to Problem 5.2

A. 1. Students may calculate each product to verify the equality. For example, in part (a), $2^3 \times 2^2 = 2^5$ is true because $8 \times 4 = 32$. Others may reason that the left side has 2 used as a factor 5 times, which is equal to 32 or 2^5. They may also note that $2^3 \times 2^2 = (2 \times 2 \times 2) \times (2 \times 2) = 2^5$.

2. Examples will vary.

3. $a^m \times a^n = a^{m+n}$. This is true because the left side of the equality has a as a factor $m + n$ times. Or, some will write out:

$$a^m \times a^n = \underbrace{(a \times a \times \cdots \times a)}_{\substack{m \text{ times} \\ a^m}} \times \underbrace{(a \times a \times \cdots \times a)}_{\substack{n \text{ times} \\ a^n}}$$

$$= \underbrace{(a \times a \times \cdots \times a)}_{\substack{(m+n) \text{ times} \\ a^{m+n}}} = a^{m+n}$$

B. 1. Students may evaluate both sides or use the definition of exponents and the commutative property of multiplication:
$2 \cdot 2 \cdot 2 \cdot 3 \cdot 3 \cdot 3 = (2 \cdot 3)(2 \cdot 3)(2 \cdot 3) = (2 \cdot 3)^3 = 6^3$

2. Examples will vary.

3. $a^m \times b^m = (ab)^m$ Students can generalize the argument in part (1):

$$a^m \times b^m = \underbrace{(a \times a \times \cdots \times a)}_{\substack{m \text{ times} \\ a^m}} \times \underbrace{(b \times b \times \cdots \times b)}_{\substack{m \text{ times} \\ b^m}}$$

$$= \underbrace{(ab \times ab \times \cdots \times ab)}_{\substack{m \text{ times} \\ ab^m}} = ab^m$$

C. 1. Some students will just evaluate both sides. Here is a symbolic argument for part (a):
$4^2 = 4 \times 4 = 2^2 \times 2^2 = (2^2)^2 = 2 \times 2 \times 2 \times 2 = 2^4$

2. Examples will vary.

3. $(a^m)^n = a^{mn}$
Students can think of $(a^m)^n$ as a^m used as a factor n times. Each a^m is a string with a used as a factor m times. In all, there are n strings of m as or nm as. Symbolically,

$$(a^m)^n = \underbrace{a^m \times a^m \times \cdots \times a^m}_{n \text{ times}}$$

$$= \underbrace{\underbrace{(a\, a \cdots a)}_{m \text{ times}} \times \underbrace{(a\, a \cdots a)}_{m \text{ times}} \times \cdots \times \underbrace{(a\, a \cdots a)}_{m \text{ times}}}_{n \text{ times}}$$

$$= a^{mn}$$

D. 1. Students can evaluate both sides or write the numerators and denominators as factor strings, and then simplify so there are no common factors in the numerator and denominator.

$$\frac{3^5}{3^2} = \frac{3 \cdot 3 \cdot 3 \cdot 3 \cdot 3}{3 \cdot 3} = 3 \cdot 3 \cdot 3 = 3^3$$

$$\frac{4^6}{4^5} = \frac{4 \cdot 4 \cdot 4 \cdot 4 \cdot 4 \cdot 4}{4 \cdot 4 \cdot 4 \cdot 4 \cdot 4} = 4$$

$$\frac{4^5}{4^6} = \frac{4 \cdot 4 \cdot 4 \cdot 4 \cdot 4}{4 \cdot 4 \cdot 4 \cdot 4 \cdot 4 \cdot 4} = \frac{1}{4}$$

$$\frac{5^{10}}{5^{10}} = \frac{5 \cdot 5 \cdot 5 \cdot 5 \cdot 5 \cdot 5 \cdot 5 \cdot 5 \cdot 5 \cdot 5}{5 \cdot 5 \cdot 5 \cdot 5 \cdot 5 \cdot 5 \cdot 5 \cdot 5 \cdot 5 \cdot 5} = 1 = 5^0$$

2. Examples will vary.

3. $\frac{a^m}{a^n} = a^{m-n}$

Some students may claim that $\frac{a^m}{a^n} = a^{m-n}$ will lead to negative exponents if $m < n$. This is an opportunity to define a^{-n} as $\frac{1}{a^n}$.

E. $\frac{a^n}{a^n} = a^{n-n} = a^0$, but $\frac{a^n}{a^n} = 1$, so $a^0 = 1$. This is a subtle point. Some students might say that in the expression a^0, a is used as a factor 0 times, so the product should be 0. Some will use the same argument to say a^0 should be 1. Using the rules provides a logical argument that should help most students. Once a^{-n} is defined as $\frac{1}{a^n}$, the logic becomes a bit clearer.

5.3 Exploring Exponential Equations

Goal

- Describe how varying the values of a and b in the equation $y = a(b^x)$ affects the graph of that equation

This calculator-based activity will help students to generalize their understanding of how the parameters a and b in the exponential equation $y = a(b^x)$ affect the shape of the corresponding graphs. The calculator activities are similar to exponential situations involving change over time because the exponents can be non-whole numbers.

To graph four equations in the same window, students will enter them as y_1, y_2, y_3, and y_4. Ideally, each student will have his or her own calculator. If fewer calculators are available, let pairs of students work together. However, ask each student to make his or her own sketches of the graphs.

Launch 5.3

Remind students that the situations they have explored in this unit can be modeled by equations of the form $y = a(b^x)$, where a is the initial, or starting, value and b is the growth or decay factor. Remind them that in all the examples in this unit, a has been greater than 0. It might help to recall equations for some exponential growth and exponential decay situations the class has studied and ask students to identify the values of a and b in each equation. For example:

$b = 2^n$

$a = 4^t$

$A = 25(3^d)$

$b = 5(3^n)$

Check to see that students understand the meaning of the notation $0 \le x \le 5$.

Have students work in groups of three or four.

Explore 5.3

As you move about the class, check to see that students are discussing the effects of a and b on the graphs. In part (1) of Question A, groups should discuss the effect of increasing the value of b in the equation $y = b^x$ for values greater than 1. In part (2) of Question A, they should discuss the effect of increasing the value of b for values between 0 and 1. In Question B, the value of b in each part is fixed, allowing students to focus on the effects of varying the value of a.

The last parts of Questions A and B make excellent writing activities.

- Describe how you could predict the general shape of the graph of $y = b^x$ for a specific value of b.

- Describe how the value of a affects the graph of an equation of the form $y = a(b^x)$.

You might also ask groups to make posters illustrating their answers to these parts.

Summarize 5.3

You might ask a group of students to enter the equations and window settings for part (1) of Question A into the overhead graphing calculator if you have one. Alternatively, you could ask several groups to sketch their graphs on transparent grids or large sheets of paper.

With the graphs displayed, discuss how the graphs change when $a = 1$ and b is an increasing value greater than 1.

- *What similarities do you notice among the graphs? What differences do you notice?* (The graphs are all increasing curves. The greater b is, the faster the y-values increase.)

Similarly, display the graphs for part (2) of Question A, and discuss how they change when $a = 1$ and b is an increasingly greater number between 0 and 1.

- *What similarities do you notice among the graphs? What differences do you notice?* (The graphs are all decreasing curves. The greater b is, the more gradually the y-values decrease.)

Then ask:

- *How could you predict the shape of the graph for the equation* $y = b^x$ *when given a specific value of* b? (If $0 < b < 1$, the graph is a decreasing curve. If $b > 1$, the graph is an increasing curve.)

- *What would the graph look like if* b *were equal to 1?* (It would be a horizontal line.)

Follow a similar process to review Question B, displaying and discussing the graphs for each part.

- *How does the value of* a *affect the graph of* $y = a(b^x)$? [The value of a is the y-intercept. The greater the value of a, the higher the y-intercept of the graph is. And, as the value of a increases, there is a sharper increase (for a fixed value of b that is greater than 1) or decrease (for a fixed value of b that is less than 1) in the graph.]

You might want to use an equation from an earlier investigation to help students understand the role of a in a real-world context. In Problem 3.1, for example, the population of rabbits is given by the equation $P = 100(1.8)^t$. The value of a, which is 100, represents the initial population.

Check for Understanding

List a few exponential equations. Without sketching a graph or using a calculator, have students describe the shape of the graph, giving as much information as they can about the y-intercept and patterns of change.

$$y = 4^x \qquad y = 0.25^x \qquad y = 5(3^x)$$

Exploring Exponential Equations

Mathematical Goal

- Describe how varying the values of a and b in the equation $y = a(b^x)$ affects the graph of that equation

Launch

Remind students that the situations they have been studying can be modeled by $y = a(b^x)$, where a is the initial or starting value and b is the growth or decay factor. Remind them that in all the examples in this unit, a has been greater than 0. It might help to recall growth and decay equations the class has studied and ask students to identify a and b in each equation.

Check to see that students understand the notation $0 \le x \le 5$.

Have students work in groups of three or four.

Materials
- Graphing calculators
- Overhead graphing calculator (optional)

Explore

In part (1) of Question A, groups should discuss the effects on the graph of increasing the b value in $y = b^x$, where $b > 1$. In part (2) of Question A, they should discuss the effects on the graph of increasing b values for $0 < b < 1$. In Question B, the value of b in each part is fixed, allowing students to focus on the effects of varying the value of a.

The last parts in Questions A and B make good writing activities. You might also ask groups to make posters illustrating their answers to these parts.

Summarize

Have students display the graphs of part (1) of Question A on an overhead graphing calculator or transparency. Discuss how the graphs change for increasing values of b greater than one.

- *What similarities do you notice among the graphs? What differences do you notice?*

Repeat this process for the graphs in part (2) of Question A. Then ask:

- *How could you predict the shape of the graph for the equation $y = b^x$ when given a specific value of b?*

Display and discuss the graphs for each part of Question B.

- *How does the value of a affect the graph of $y = a(b^x)$?*

You might want to use an equation from an earlier investigation to help students understand the role of a in a real-world context.

Materials
- Student notebooks

Check for Understanding

List a few exponential equations. Without sketching a graph or using a calculator, have students describe the shape of the graph, giving as much information as they can about the y-intercept and patterns of change.

ACE Assignment Guide for Problem 5.3

Core 42, 43

Other *Connections* 49–51; unassigned choices from previous problems

Adapted For suggestions about adapting ACE exercises, see the *CMP Special Needs Handbook*.

Connecting to Prior Units 49: *Prime Time;* 51: *Bits and Pieces I*

Answers to Problem 5.3

A. 1. The greater b is, the faster the graph rises.

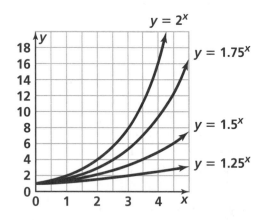

2. The smaller b is, the faster the graph falls.

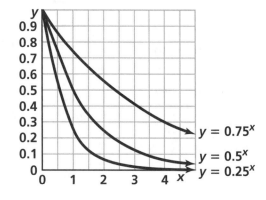

3. When b is greater than 1, the graph curves upward slowly at first and then very rapidly. When b is a positive number less than 1, the graph curves downward, rapidly at first and then more slowly until it is almost horizontal and very close to the x-axis. In both cases the y-intercept is 1, because $b^0 = 1$ for all nonzero values of b.

B. 1.

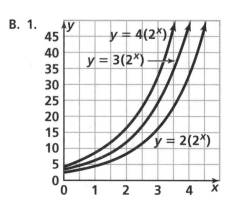

2.

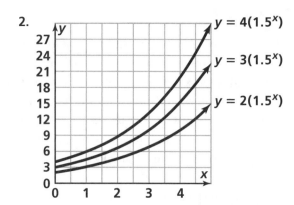

3.

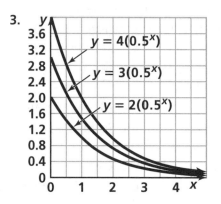

4. For an exponential function with the rule $y = a(b^x)$, the y-intercept is always equal to a. An increase in a makes the graph increase or decrease faster.

Patterns With Exponents

As you explored exponential relationships in previous investigations, you made tables of exponential growth. This table shows some values for $y = 2^x$. The y-values are given in both exponential and standard form.

x	y	
1	2^1 or	2
2	2^2 or	4
3	2^3 or	8
4	2^4 or	16
5	2^5 or	32
6	2^6 or	64
7	2^7 or	128
8	2^8 or	256

There are many interesting patterns in the table.

Getting Ready for Problem 5.1

- Look at the column of y-values in the table. What pattern do you see in how the ones digits of the standard forms change?
- Can you predict the ones digit for 2^{15}? What about 2^{50}?
- What other patterns do you see in the table?
- Find an x-value and values for the missing digits that will make this a true number sentence.

    $2^x = _____\,6$

Notes _____

_____

_____

_____

Predicting the Ones Digit

The values of a^x for a given number a are called *powers of a*. You just looked at powers of 2. In this problem, you will explore patterns in other powers.

Problem 5.1 **Predicting the Ones Digit**

A. Copy and complete this table.

Powers Table

x	1^x	2^x	3^x	4^x	5^x	6^x	7^x	8^x	9^x	10^x
1	1	2								
2	1	4								
3	1	8								
4	1	16								
5	1	32								
6	1	64								
7	1	128								
8	1	256								
Ones Digits of the Powers	1	2, 4, 8, 6								

B. Describe patterns you see in the ones digits of the powers.

C. Predict the ones digit in the standard form of each number.
   1. 4^{12} **2.** 9^{20} **3.** 3^{17} **4.** 5^{100} **5.** 10^{500}

D. Predict the ones digit in the standard form of each number.
   1. 31^{10} **2.** 12^{10} **3.** 17^{21} **4.** 29^{10}

STUDENT PAGE

Notes _____

_____

_____

_____

E. Find the value of a that makes each number sentence true.

   1. $a^{12} = 531,441$ **2.** $a^9 = 387,420,489$ **3.** $a^6 = 11,390,625$

F. Find a value for a and values for the missing digits to make each number sentence true. Explain your reasoning.

   1. $a^7 = \_\_\ \_\_\ \_\_\ \_\_\ \_\_\ 3$ **2.** $a^8 = \_\_\ \_\_\ \_\_\ \_\_\ \_\_\ \_\_\ 1$

ACE Homework starts on page 64.

5.2 Operating With Exponents

In the last problem, you explored patterns in the values of a^x for different values of a. You used the patterns you discovered to make predictions. For example, you predicted the ones digit in the standard form of 4^{12}. In this problem, you will look at other interesting patterns that lead to some important properties of exponents.

Getting Ready for Problem

- Federico noticed that 16 appears twice in the powers table. It is in the column for 2^x, for $x = 4$. It is also in the column for 4^x, for $x = 2$. He said this means that $2^4 = 4^2$. Write 2^4 as a product of 2's. Then, show that the product is equal to 4^2.

- Are there other numbers that appear more than once in the table? If so, write equations to show the equivalent exponential forms of the numbers.

Notes _____

_____

_____

_____

Use properties of real numbers and your table from Problem 5.1 to help you answer these questions.

A. 1. Explain why each of the following statements is true.

    a. $2^3 \times 2^2 = 2^5$ **b.** $3^4 \times 3^3 = 3^7$ **c.** $6^3 \times 6^5 = 6^8$

    2. Give another example that fits the pattern in part (1).

    3. Complete the following equation to show how you can find the exponent of the product when you multiply two powers with the same base. Explain your reasoning.

$$a^m \times a^n = a^{\blacksquare}$$

B. 1. Explain why each of the following statements is true.

    a. $2^3 \times 3^3 = 6^3$ **b.** $5^3 \times 6^3 = 30^3$ **c.** $10^4 \times 4^4 = 40^4$

    2. Give another example that fits the pattern in part (1).

    3. Complete the following equation to show how you can find the base and exponent of the product when you multiply two powers with the same exponent. Explain your reasoning.

$$a^m \times b^m = \underline{\ ?\ }$$

C. 1. Explain why each of the following statements is true.

    a. $4^2 = (2^2)^2 = 2^4$

    b. $9^2 = (3^2)^2 = 3^4$

    c. $125^2 = (5^3)^2 = 5^6$

    2. Give another example that fits the pattern in part (1).

    3. Complete the following equation to show how you can find the base and exponent when a power is raised to a power. Explain.

$$(a^m)^n = \underline{\ ?\ }$$

D. 1. Explain why each of the following statements is true.

    a. $\dfrac{3^5}{3^2} = 3^3$ **b.** $\dfrac{4^6}{4^5} = 4^1$ **c.** $\dfrac{5^{10}}{5^{10}} = 5^0$

    2. Tom says $\dfrac{4^5}{4^6} = 4^{-1}$. Mary says $\dfrac{4^5}{4^6} = \dfrac{1}{4^1}$. Who is correct and why?

    3. Complete the following equation to show how you can find the base and exponent of the quotient when you divide two powers with the same base. (Assume a is not 0.) Explain your reasoning.

$$\frac{a^m}{a^n} = \underline{\ ?\ }$$

E. Use the pattern from Question D to explain why $a^0 = 1$ for any nonzero number a.

ACE Homework starts on page 64.

Notes _____

_____

_____

_____

5.3 Exploring Exponential Equations

In this unit, you have studied situations that show patterns of exponential growth or exponential decay. All of these situations are modeled by equations of the form $y = a(b^x)$, where a is the starting value and b is the growth or decay factor.

Problem 5.3 Exploring Exponential Equations

You can use your graphing calculator to explore how the values of a and b affect the graph of $y = a(b^x)$.

A. First, let $a = 1$ and explore how the value of b affects the graph of $y = b^x$.

1. Graph these four equations in the same window. Use window settings that show x-values from -5 to 5 and y-values from -5 to 20. Record your observations.

$y = 1.25^x$ $\qquad$ $y = 1.5^x$ $\qquad$ $y = 1.75^x$ $\qquad$ $y = 2^x$

2. Next, graph these three equations in the same window. Use window settings that show $-5 \le x \le 5$ and $-1 \le y \le 2$. Record your observations.

$y = 0.25^x$ $\qquad$ $y = 0.5^x$ $\qquad$ $y = 0.75^x$

3. Describe how you could predict the general shape of the graph of $y = b^x$ for a specific value of b.

B. Next, you will look at how the value of a affects the graph of $y = a(b^x)$. You will need to adjust the window settings as you work. Graph each set of equations in the same window. Record your observations for each set.

1. $y = 2(2^x)$ $\qquad$ $y = 3(2^x)$ $\qquad$ $y = 4(2^x)$
2. $y = 2(1.5^x)$ $\qquad$ $y = 3(1.5^x)$ $\qquad$ $y = 4(1.5^x)$
3. $y = 2(0.5^x)$ $\qquad$ $y = 3(0.5^x)$ $\qquad$ $y = 4(0.5^x)$
4. Describe how the value of a affects the graph of an equation of the form $y = a(b^x)$.

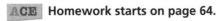 **ACE** Homework starts on page 64.

Notes _____

_____

_____

_____

Applications

Predict the ones digit for the standard form of the number.

1. 7^{100} **2.** 6^{200} **3.** 17^{100} **4.** 31^{10} **5.** 12^{100}

active math
online

For: Pattern Iterator
Visit: PHSchool.com
Web Code: apd-3500

For Exercises 6 and 7, find the value of a that makes the number sentence true.

6. $a^7 = 823{,}543$ **7.** $a^6 = 1{,}771{,}561$

8. Explain how you can use your calculator to find the ones digit of the standard form of 3^{30}.

9. Multiple Choice In the powers table you completed in Problem 5.1, look for patterns in the ones digit of square numbers. Which number is *not* a square number? Explain.

    A. 289   **B.** 784   **C.** 1,392   **D.** 10,000

Tell how many zeros are in the standard form of the number.

10. 10^{10} **11.** 10^{50} **12.** 10^{100}

Find the least value of x that will make the statement true.

13. $9^6 < 10^x$ **14.** $3^{14} < 10^x$

For Exercises 15–17, identify the greater number in each pair.

15. 6^{10} or 7^{10} **16.** 8^{10} or 10^8 **17.** 6^9 or 9^6

18. Multiple Choice Which expression is equivalent to $2^9 \times 2^{10}$?

    F. 2^{90} **G.** 2^{19} **H.** 4^{19} **J.** 2^{18}

Use the properties of exponents to write each expression as a single power. Check your answers.

19. $5^6 \times 8^6$ **20.** $(7^5)^3$ **21.** $\dfrac{8^{15}}{8^{10}}$

STUDENT PAGE

Notes _____

_____

_____

_____

For Exercises 22–27, tell whether the statement is *true* or *false*. Explain.

Go Online
PHSchool.com
For: Multiple-Choice Skills
Practice
Web Code: apa-3554

22. $6^3 \times 6^5 = 6^8$

23. $2^3 \times 3^2 = 6^5$

24. $3^8 = 9^4$

25. $4^3 + 5^3 = 9^3$

26. $2^3 + 2^5 = 2^3(1 + 2^2)$

27. $\dfrac{5^{12}}{5^4} = 5^3$

28. Multiple Choice Which number is the ones digit of $2^{10} \times 3^{10}$?

A. 2   **B.** 4   **C.** 6   **D.** 8

For Exercises 29 and 30, find the ones digit of the product.

29. $4^{15} \times 3^{15}$

30. $7^{15} \times 4^{20}$

31. Manuela said it must be true that $2^{10} = 2^4 \cdot 2^6$ because she can group $2 \cdot 2 \cdot 2 \cdot 2 \cdot 2 \cdot 2 \cdot 2 \cdot 2 \cdot 2 \cdot 2$ as $(2 \cdot 2 \cdot 2 \cdot 2) \cdot (2 \cdot 2 \cdot 2 \cdot 2 \cdot 2 \cdot 2)$.

$2 \cdot 2 \cdot 2 \cdot 2 = 2^4$

  a. Verify that Manuela is correct by evaluating both sides of the equation $2^{10} = 2^4 \cdot 2^6$.

  b. Use Manuela's idea of grouping factors to write three other expressions that are equivalent to 2^{10}. Evaluate each expression you find to verify that it is equivalent to 2^{10}.

  c. The standard form for 2^7 is 128, and the standard form for 2^5 is 32. Use these facts to evaluate 2^{12}. Explain your work.

  d. Test Manuela's idea to see if it works for exponential expressions with other bases, such as 3^8 or $(1.5)^{11}$. Test several cases. Give an argument supporting your conclusion.

Investigation 5 Patterns With Exponents   **65**

Notes _____

_____

_____

_____

Tell whether the expression is equivalent to 1.25^{10}. Explain your reasoning.

32. $(1.25)^5 \cdot (1.25)^5$

33. $(1.25)^3 \times (1.25)^7$

34. $(1.25) \times 10$

35. $(1.25) + 10$

36. $(1.25^5)^2$

37. $(1.25)^5 \cdot (1.25)^2$

For Exercises 38–41, tell whether the expression is equivalent to $(1.5)^7$. Explain your reasoning.

38. $1.5^5 \times 1.5^2$

39. $1.5^3 \times 1.5^4$

40. 1.5×7

41. $(1.5) + 7$

42. Without actually graphing these equations, describe and compare their graphs. Be as specific as you can.

$$y = 4^x \qquad y = 0.25^x \qquad y = 10(4^x) \qquad y = 10(0.25^x)$$

Homework Help Online
PHSchool.com
For: Help with Exercise 42
Web Code: ape-3542

43. Each graph below represents an exponential equation of the form $y = ab^x$.

a. For which of the three functions is the value of a greatest?

b. For which of the three functions is the value of b greatest?

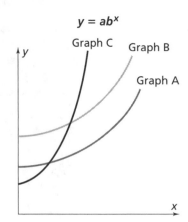

$y = ab^x$

Graph C Graph B

Graph A

Connections

For Exercises 44 and 45, tell whether the statement is *true* or *false*. Do not do an exact calculation. Explain your reasoning.

44. $(1.56892 \times 10^5) - (2.3456 \times 10^4) < 0$

45. $\dfrac{3.96395 \times 10^5}{2.888211 \times 10^7} > 1$

Notes _____

_____

_____

_____

46. Suppose you start with a unit cube (a cube with edges of length 1 unit). In parts (a)–(c), give the volume and surface area of the cube that results from the given transformation.

  a. Each edge length is doubled.

  b. Each edge length is tripled.

  c. Each edge is enlarged by a scale factor of 100.

47. Suppose you start with a cylinder with a radius of 1 unit and a height of 1 unit. In parts (a)–(c), give the volume of the cylinder that results from the given transformation.

  a. The radius and height are doubled.

  b. The radius and height are tripled.

  c. The radius and height are enlarged by a scale factor of 100.

48. a. Tell which of the following numbers are prime. (There may be more than one.)

  $2^2 - 1$ $2^3 - 1$ $2^4 - 1$ $2^5 - 1$ $2^6 - 1$

  b. Find another prime number that can be written in the form $2^n - 1$.

49. In parts (a)–(d), find the sum of the proper factors for the number.

  a. 2^2 **b.** 2^3 **c.** 2^4 **d.** 2^5

  e. What do you notice about the sums in parts (a)–(d)?

50. Grandville has a population of 1,000. Its population is expected to decrease by 4% a year for the next several years. Tinytown has a population of 100. Its population is expected to increase by 4% a year for the next several years. Will the populations of the two towns ever be the same? Explain.

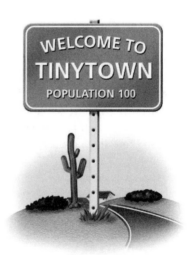

STUDENT PAGE

Notes _____

_____

_____

_____

51. The expression $\frac{20}{10^2}$ can be written in equivalent forms, including $\frac{2}{10}$, $\frac{1}{5}$, 0.2, and $\frac{2(10^2)}{10^3}$. In parts (a) and (b), write two equivalent forms for the expression.

a. $\frac{3(10)^5}{10^7}$

b. $\frac{5(10)^5}{2.5(10)^7}$

Extensions

52. a. Find the sum for each row.

Row 1: $\frac{1}{2}$

Row 2: $\frac{1}{2} + \left(\frac{1}{2}\right)^2$

Row 3: $\frac{1}{2} + \left(\frac{1}{2}\right)^2 + \left(\frac{1}{2}\right)^3$

Row 4: $\frac{1}{2} + \left(\frac{1}{2}\right)^2 + \left(\frac{1}{2}\right)^3 + \left(\frac{1}{2}\right)^4$

b. Study the pattern. Suppose the pattern continues. Write the expression that would be in row 5, and find its sum.

c. What would be the sum of the expression in row 10? What would be the sum for row 20?

d. Describe the pattern of sums in words and with a symbolic expression.

e. For which row does the sum first exceed 0.9?

f. As the row number increases, the sum gets closer and closer to what number?

g. Celeste claims the pattern is related to the pattern of the areas of the ballots cut in Problem 4.1. She drew this picture to explain her thinking. What relationship do you think she has observed?

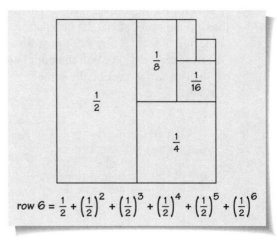

$$\text{row } 6 = \frac{1}{2} + \left(\frac{1}{2}\right)^2 + \left(\frac{1}{2}\right)^3 + \left(\frac{1}{2}\right)^4 + \left(\frac{1}{2}\right)^5 + \left(\frac{1}{2}\right)^6$$

Notes _____

_____

_____

_____

53. a. Find the sum for each row.

Row 1: $\frac{1}{3}$

Row 2: $\frac{1}{3} + \left(\frac{1}{3}\right)^2$

Row 3: $\frac{1}{3} + \left(\frac{1}{3}\right)^2 + \left(\frac{1}{3}\right)^3$

Row 4: $\frac{1}{3} + \left(\frac{1}{3}\right)^2 + \left(\frac{1}{3}\right)^3 + \left(\frac{1}{3}\right)^4$

b. Study the pattern. Suppose the pattern continues. Write the expression that would be in row 5, and find its sum.

c. What would be the sum of the expression in row 10? What would be the sum for row 20?

d. Describe the pattern of sums in words and with an equation.

e. As the row number increases, the sum gets closer and closer to what number?

54. Negative numbers can be used as exponents. Parts (a) and (b) will help you understand negative exponents.

a. Use your calculator to find the value of 2^x for x-values -1, -2, and -3.

b. Use your calculator to find the value of $\left(\frac{1}{2}\right)^x$ for x-values 1, 2, and 3.

c. What observation can you make from your computations in parts (a) and (b)?

d. Write each number as a power with a positive exponent.

3^{-1} 4^{-2} 5^{-3}

Notes _____

_____

_____

_____

55. a. Copy and complete this table.

Standard Form	Exponential Form
10,000	10^4
1,000	10^3
100	10^2
10	10^1
1	10^0
$\frac{1}{10} = 0.1$	10^{-1}
$\frac{1}{100} = 0.01$	10^{-2}
$\frac{1}{1,000} = 0.001$	■
$\frac{1}{10,000} = 0.0001$	■
■	10^{-5}
■	10^{-6}

b. Write each number in standard form as a decimal.

3×10^{-1} $\qquad$ 1.5×10^{-2} $\qquad$ 1.5×10^{-3}

56. If you use your calculator to compute $2 \div 2^{12}$, the display will probably show one of the following:

4.8828125ᴇ ⁻4 $\qquad$ or $\qquad$ 4.8828125 ⁻4

Both displays mean 4.8828125×10^{-4}. This number is in scientific notation because it is a number greater than or equal to 1, but less than 10 (in this case, 4.8828125), times a power of 10 (in this case, 10^{-4}). You can convert 4.8828125×10^{-4} to standard form as shown:

$4.8828125 \times 10^{-4} = 4.8828125 \times \frac{1}{10,000} = 0.00048828125$

a. Write each number in standard notation.

1.2×10^{-1} $\qquad$ 1.2×10^{-2} $\qquad$ 1.2×10^{-3} $\qquad$ 1.2×10^{-8}

b. Using what you discovered in part (a), explain how you would write 1.2×10^{-n} in standard notation where n is any whole number greater than or equal to 1.

c. Write each number in scientific notation.

2,000,000	28,000,000	19,900,000,000
0.12489	0.0058421998	0.0010201

Notes

57. When Tia found $0.0000015 \div 1{,}000{,}000$ on her calculator, she got $1.5\text{E} ^-12$, which means 1.5×10^{-12}.

   a. Write a different division problem that will give the result $1.5\text{E} ^-12$ on your calculator.

   b. Write a multiplication problem that will give the result $1.5\text{E} ^-12$ on your calculator.

58. The average radius of the moon is 1.74×10^6 meters.

   a. Express the average radius of the moon in standard notation.

   b. The largest circle that will fit on this page has a radius of 10.795 cm. Express this radius in meters, using scientific notation.

   c. Suppose a circle has the same radius as the moon. By what scale factor would the circle have to be reduced to fit on this page?

59. The number 2^7 is written in standard form as 128 and in scientific notation as 1.28×10^2. The number $\left(\frac{1}{2}\right)^7$ is written in standard form as 0.0078125 and in scientific notation as 7.812×10^{-3}. Write each number in scientific notation.

   a. 2^8 **b.** $\left(\frac{1}{2}\right)^8$ **c.** 20^8 **d.** $\left(\frac{1}{20}\right)^8$

60. a. The y-values in the table below are decreasing by a factor of $\frac{1}{3}$. Copy and complete the table.

x	0	1	2	3	4	5	6	7	8
y	30	10	▪	▪	▪	▪	▪	▪	▪

   b. Using a calculator to find the y-value when x is 12 gives the result $5.645029269\text{E} ^-5$. What does this mean?

   c. Write the y-values for $x = 8, 9, 10,$ and 11 in scientific notation.

Notes _____

_____

_____

_____

61. Chen, from Problem 4.1, decides to make his ballots starting with a sheet of paper with an area of 1 square foot.

Number of Cuts	Area (ft²)
0	1
1	$\frac{1}{2}$
2	$\frac{1}{4}$
3	▧
4	▧
5	▧
6	▧
7	▧
8	▧

a. Copy and complete this table to show the area of each ballot after each of the first 8 cuts.

b. Write an equation for the area A of a ballot after any cut n.

c. Use your equation to find the area of a ballot after 20 cuts. Write your answer in scientific notation.

62. In 1803, the U.S. bought the 828,000-square-mile Louisiana Purchase for $15,000,000. Suppose one of your ancestors was given 1 acre of the Louisiana Purchase. Assuming an annual inflation rate of 4%, what is the value of this acre in 2006? (640 acres = 1 square mile)

63. Use the properties of exponents to show that each statement is true.

a. $\frac{1}{2}(2^n) = 2^{n-1}$ b. $4^{n-1} = \frac{1}{4}(4)^n$ c. $25(5^{n-2}) = 5^n$

Notes _____

_____

_____

_____

Mathematical Reflections 5

In this investigation, you explored properties of exponents and you looked at how the values of *a* and *b* affect the graph of $y = a(b^x)$.

Think about your answers to these questions. Discuss your ideas with other students and your teacher. Then, write a summary of your findings in your notebook.

1. Describe some of the rules for operating with exponents.

2. Assume *a* is a fixed positive number. Describe the graph of $y = a(b^x)$ if

   a. *b* is greater than 1.

   b. *b* is equal to 1.

   c. *b* is between 0 and 1.

3. Assume *b* is a fixed number greater than 1. Describe the graph of $y = a(b^x)$ if

   a. *a* is greater than 1.

   b. *a* is equal to 1.

   c. *a* is between 0 and 1.

STUDENT PAGE

Notes _____

_____

_____

_____

STUDENT PAGE

Answers Applications

Investigation 5

ACE Assignment Choices

Differentiated Instruction
Solutions for All Learners

Problem 5.1
Core 1–7, 54
Other *Applications* 8, 9; *Connections* 44, 45; *Extensions* 52, 53, 55; unassigned choices from previous problems

Problem 5.2
Core 10–27, 31
Other *Applications* 28–30, 32–41; *Connections* 46–48; *Extensions* 56–63; unassigned choices from previous problems

Problem 5.3
Core 42, 43
Other *Connections* 49–51; unassigned choices from previous problems

Adapted For suggestions about adapting Exercise 31 and other ACE exercises, see the *CMP Special Needs Handbook*.
Connecting to Prior Units 51: *Bits and Pieces I*; 46, 47: *Filling and Wrapping* and *Stretching and Shrinking*; 48, 49: *Prime Time*

Applications

1. 9. The ones digits for powers of 7 cycle through 7, 9, 3, and 1. Because the exponent, 100, is a multiple of 4, the ones digit will match the fourth number in the cycle, which is 1.

2. 6. The only possibility for the ones digit for a power of 6 is 6.

3. 9. The same reasoning from ACE Exercise 1 holds because the ones digit of 17 is 7. 7^{100} and 17^{100} have the same ones digit.

4. 1. To get successive powers of 31, you repeatedly multiply by 31, and the ones digit is always 1 times the previous ones digit. So the ones digit is always a power of 1, or 1.

5. 6. The possibilities for the ones digit when the base is 12 are the same as when the base is 2. So, the ones digits cycle through 2, 4, 8, and 6.

Because the exponent, 100, is a multiple of 4, the ones digit will be the fourth number in the cycle, which is 6.

6. 7. The possibilities for *a* include 3 and 7 because the ones digit in 823,543 is 3. Because 823,543 has 6 digits and the power is 7, 3 is too small, so *a* must equal 7.

7. 11. *a* could be any number with a ones digit of 1, 3, 7, or 9. Because 1,771,561 has 7 digits and $10^6 = 1,000,000$ has 7 digits, *a* must be greater than 10 but close to 10, so *a* is 11.

8. Possible answer: The ones digit is 9. You can find 3^{15}, which is 14,348,907. The expression 3^{30} is equivalent to a product string of thirty 3s, which is the same as the product of two strings of fifteen 3s. So, $3^{30} = 3^{15} \times 3^{15}$. Therefore, the ones digit of 3^{30} is the same as the ones digit of 7×7 (the ones digit of 3^{15} times itself).

9. C. Square numbers have a ones digit of 1, 4, 9, 6, 5, or 0, so 1,392 is not a square number. However, 289 and 10,000 could be square numbers because they end in 0 and 9. In fact, $17^2 = 289$ and $100^2 = 10,000$.

10. 10 zeros
11. 50 zeros
12. 100 zeros
13. 6
14. 7
15. 7^{10}
16. 8^{10}
17. 6^9

Note to the Teacher Students may use their calculators for Exercises 15–17, but they should be able to use the rules of exponents and some estimation or mental arithmetic. The reasoning for $6^9 > 9^6$, for example, might look like this:
$6^9 = (2 \times 3)^9 = 2^9 \times 3^9 = 2^9 \times 3^3 \times 3^6$
and
$9^6 = (3 \times 3)^6 = 3^6 \times 3^6 = 3^3 \times 3^3 \times 3^6$
Comparing these comes down to comparing 2^9 and 3^3. Because $2^9 > 3^3$, $6^9 > 9^6$.

18. G **19.** 40^6

20. 7^{15} **21.** 8^5

22. True; this is an example of $a^m \times a^n = a^{m+n}$

23. False; $2^3 \cdot 3^2 = 8 \cdot 9 = 72$ and $72 \neq 6^5$

24. True;
$3^8 = (3 \cdot 3)(3 \cdot 3)(3 \cdot 3)(3 \cdot 3) = (3^2)^4 = 9^4$

25. False; $4^3 + 5^3 = 64 + 125 = 189$ and $189 \neq 9^3$

26. True; by the distributive property,
$2^3(1 + 2^2) = (2^3 \cdot 1) + (2^3 \cdot 2^2) = 2^3 + 2^5$.
Or, students may evaluate both sides and find that both sides are equal to 40.

27. False. $\dfrac{5^{12}}{5^4} = 5^8 \neq 5^3$

28. C

29. 8. Because $4^{15} \times 3^{15} = (4 \times 3)^{15} = 12^{15}$, the ones digit is the same as the ones digit for $2^{15} = 32{,}768$.

30. 8. The ones digits for powers of 7 occur in cycles of 7, 9, 3, 1. Because 15 divided by 4 leaves a remainder of 3, the ones digit of 7^{15} is the third digit in the cycle, which is 3. The ones digits for powers of 4 occur in cycles of 4, 6. Because 20 is evenly divisible by 2, the ones digit of 4^{20} is the second digit in the cycle, which is 6. So, the ones digit of $7^{15} \times 4^{20}$ is the ones digit of $3 \times 6 = 18$.

31. a. Manuela is correct because $2^{10} = 1{,}024$ and $2^4 \times 2^6 = 16 \times 64 = 1{,}024$.

  b. Possible answers:
  $2^2 \times 2^8 = 4 \times 256 = 1{,}024$
  $2^3 \times 2^7 = 8 \times 128 = 1{,}024$
  $2^2 \times 2^2 \times 2^6 = 4 \times 4 \times 64 = 1{,}024$

  c. 4,096. Because $2^7 = 128$ and $2^5 = 32$, 2^{12} is $2^7 \times 2^5 = 128 \times 32 = 4{,}096$.

  d. It works for other cases because you are just using the associative property of multiplication. She is grouping strings of the same factor into two groups.

32. Yes; it has exactly 10 factors of 1.25.

33. Yes; it has exactly 10 factors of 1.25.

34. No; $(1.25)^{10}$ is about 9.3 and $(1.25) \times 10$ is 12.5.

35. No; $(1.25)^{10}$ is about 9.3 and $(1.25) + 10 = 11.25$.

36. Yes; $(1.25^5)^2 = 1.25^5 \times 1.25^5$, which has exactly 10 factors of 1.25.

37. No; $1.25^5 \times 1.25^2$ has exactly seven factors of 1.25, so it is equal to $(1.25)^7$, not $(1.25)^{10}$.

38. Yes; it has exactly 7 factors of 1.5.

39. Yes; it has exactly 7 factors of 1.5.

40. No; $(1.5)^7$ is about 17 and $1.5 \times 7 = 10.5$.

41. No; $(1.5)^7$ is about 17 and $1.5 + 7 = 8.5$.

42. The graphs of $y = 4^x$ and $y = 10(4^x)$ have the same growth factor of 4, so they are both exponential growth patterns. The graphs $y = 0.25^x$ and $y = 10(0.25)^x$ are exponential decay patterns and have the same decay factor of 0.25. The graphs of $y = 4^x$ and $y = 0.25^x$ have a y-intercept of $(0, 1)$. The graphs of $y = 10(4^x)$ and $y = 10(0.25)^x$ have y-intercepts $(0, 10)$.

43. a. Graph B
  b. Graph C

Connections

44. False; because $1.56892 \times 10^5 = 156{,}892$ is greater than $2.3456 \times 10^4 = 23{,}456$, the difference is greater than zero.

45. False; because $3.96395 \times 10^5 = 396{,}395$ is less than $2.888211 \times 10^7 = 28{,}882{,}110$, the quotient is less than 1.

46. a. Volume: 8 units^3; surface area: 24 units^2. The side lengths increase to 2 units. The new volume is $2^3 = 2 \cdot 2 \cdot 2 = 8$ units^3. Because there are six square faces, each with area $2^2 = 4$, the total surface area is $6 \cdot 2^2 = 24$ units^3.

  b. Volume: 27 units^3; surface area: 54 units^2. The side lengths increase to 3 units. The new volume is $3^3 = 3 \cdot 3 \cdot 3 = 27$ units^3, and the new surface area is $6 \cdot 3^2 = 54$ units^2.

  c. Volume: 1,000,000 units^3; surface area: 54 units^2. The side lengths increase to 100 units each. The new volume is $100^3 = 100 \cdot 100 \cdot 100 = 1{,}000{,}000$ units^3, and the new surface area is $6 \cdot 100^2 = 60{,}000$ units^2.

47. a. 8π units^3. The resulting cylinder has a radius of 2 units and a height of 2 units, so the volume is $\pi(2)^2 \times 2 = 8\pi$ units^3.

  b. 27π units^3. The resulting cylinder has a radius of 3 units and a height of 3 units, so the volume is $\pi(3)^2 \times 3 = 27\pi$ units^3.

c. 1,000,000π units^3. The resulting cylinder has a radius of 100 units and a height of 100 units, so the volume is $\pi(100)^2 \times 100 = 1{,}000{,}000\pi$ units^3.

48. a. The following are prime: $2^2 - 1 = 3$; $2^3 - 1 = 7; 2^5 - 1 = 31$

b. Other primes that fit this pattern include $2^7 - 1 = 127$ and $2^{13} - 1 = 8{,}191$.

49. a. The sum of the proper factors of 2^2 is 3.

b. The sum of the proper factors for 2^3, or 8, is $1 + 2 + 4 = 7$.

c. The sum of the proper factors for 2^4, or 16, is $1 + 2 + 4 + 8 = 15$.

d. The sum of the proper factors for 2^5, or 32, is $1 + 2 + 4 + 8 + 16 = 31$.

e. The sum of the proper factors of a power of 2 is always 1 less than the number.

50. Yes; the two towns will have the same populations if they continue to change at the same rates. Even though Grandville has a greater starting population, its population is decreasing, and in Tinytown, the population is increasing. So, eventually, the graphs will cross. However, it will take over 28 years for this to happen.

51. a. Possible answers: $\dfrac{3(10)^5}{10^7}, 3 \times 10^{-2}, 0.03, \dfrac{3}{100}$.

b. Possible answers: $\dfrac{5(10)^5}{2.5(10)^7}, 2 \times 10^{-2}, 0.02,$ $\dfrac{2}{100}, \dfrac{1}{50}$

Extensions

52. a. Row 1: $\frac{1}{2}$, row 2: $\frac{3}{4}$, row 3: $\frac{7}{8}$, row 4: $\frac{15}{16}$

b. $\frac{1}{2} + \left(\frac{1}{2}\right)^2 + \left(\frac{1}{2}\right)^3 + \left(\frac{1}{2}\right)^4 + \left(\frac{1}{2}\right)^5 = \frac{31}{32}$

c. $\dfrac{1{,}023}{1{,}024}, \dfrac{1{,}048{,}575}{1{,}048{,}576}$

d. The sum of each row is a fraction with a denominator equal to 2 raised to the power of that row number, and a numerator that is 1 less than the denominator. In the nth row, the sum will be $\dfrac{2^n - 1}{2^n}$.

e. Row 4

f. 1

g. The pattern is similar to adding the areas of one of the ballots produced by each cut. It may appear that this total area will eventually equal the area of the original

sheet, but the pattern demonstrates that the total of the areas of the ballots will never actually equal the area of the whole piece.

53. a. Row 1: $\frac{1}{3}$, row 2: $\frac{4}{9}$, row 3: $\frac{13}{27}$, row 4: $\frac{40}{81}$

b. $\frac{1}{3} + \left(\frac{1}{3}\right)^2 + \left(\frac{1}{3}\right)^3 + \left(\frac{1}{3}\right)^4 + \left(\frac{1}{3}\right)^5 = \frac{121}{243}$

c. Row 10: $\dfrac{29{,}524}{59{,}049}$; row 20: $\dfrac{1{,}743{,}392{,}200}{3{,}486{,}784{,}401}$

d. The sum of each row is a fraction with a denominator equal to 3 raised to the power of that row number, and a numerator that is half of the number that is 1 less than the denominator. Each row is a sum of powers of $\frac{1}{3}$. In the nth row, the sum will be $\dfrac{\frac{3^n - 1}{2}}{3^n}$.

e. The sum seems to be approaching 0.5.

54. a. $2^{-1} = \frac{1}{2}, 2^{-2} = \frac{1}{4}, 2^{-3} = \frac{1}{8}$

b. $\left(\frac{1}{2}\right)^1 = \frac{1}{2}, \left(\frac{1}{2}\right)^2 = \frac{1}{4}, \left(\frac{1}{2}\right)^3 = \frac{1}{8}$

c. Students should notice that 2^x and $\left(\frac{1}{2}\right)^x$ have the same value when numbers of the opposite sign with the same absolute value are substituted. In other words, $2^{-x} = \left(\frac{1}{2}\right)^x$.

d. $3^{-1} = \left(\frac{1}{3}\right)^1, 4^{-2} = \left(\frac{1}{4}\right)^2$, and $5^{-3} = \left(\frac{1}{5}\right)^3$

55. a.

Standard Form	Exponential Form
10,000	10^4
1,000	10^3
100	10^2
10	10^1
1	10^0
$\frac{1}{10} = 0.1$	10^{-1}
$\frac{1}{100} = 0.01$	10^{-2}
$\frac{1}{1{,}000} = 0.001$	10^{-3}
$\frac{1}{10{,}000} = 0.0001$	10^{-4}
$\frac{1}{100{,}000} = 0.00001$	10^{-5}
$\frac{1}{1{,}000{,}000} = 0.000001$	10^{-6}

b. 0.3, 0.015, 0.0015

56. a. $0.12, 0.012, 0.0012, 0.000000012$

  b. Because $1.2 \times 10^{-n} = 1.2 \times \frac{1}{10^n}$, the standard form is 1.2 divided by the nth power of 10. When dividing by a power of 10, the decimal point in the number moves to the left. Because 1.2 is divided by the nth power of 10, the decimal place is moved to the left n places; thus, $1.2 \times \frac{1}{10^n} = \underbrace{0.0000\cdots0000012}_{n-1 \text{ zeros}}$.

  c. 2.0×10^6,
  2.8×10^7,
  1.99×10^{10},
  1.2489×10^{-1},
  5.8421998×10^{-3},
  1.0201×10^{-3}

57. a. Possible answer: $\frac{1.5 \times 10^{-4}}{10^8}$

  b. Possible answer: $1.5 \times 10^{-4} \times 10^{-8}$

58. a. 1,740,000 meters

  b. 1.0795×10^1

  c. The scale that would make the image fit exactly is 6.204×10^{-6}. Any scale factor smaller than this will make the image small enough to fit.

59. a. $2^8 = 256$, or 2.56×10^2.

  b. $\left(\frac{1}{2}\right)^8 = \frac{1}{256} = 2^{-8}$, or
  $0.00390625 = 3.90625 \times 10^{-3}$.

  c. $20^8 = 25,600,000,000$, or 2.56×10^{10}

  d. $\left(\frac{1}{20}\right)^8 = \frac{1}{25,600,000,000} = 20^{-8}$ or
  $0.0000000000390625 = 3.90625 \times 10^{-11}$

60. a. $3\frac{1}{3}, 1\frac{1}{9}, \frac{10}{27}, \frac{10}{81}, \frac{10}{243}, \frac{10}{729}, \frac{10}{2,187}$

  b. This means $5.645029269 \times 10^{-5}$. In standard notation, this is 0.00005645029269.

  c. $4.57 \times 10^{-3}, 1.52 \times 10^{-3}, 5.08 \times 10^{-4}$,
  1.69×10^{-4}

61. a.

Number of Cuts	Area (sq. ft)
0	1
1	$\frac{1}{2}$
2	$\frac{1}{4}$
3	$\frac{1}{8}$
4	$\frac{1}{16}$
5	$\frac{1}{32}$
6	$\frac{1}{64}$
7	$\frac{1}{128}$
8	$\frac{1}{256}$

  b. $A = \left(\frac{1}{2}\right)^n$

  c. About 9.54×10^{-7} ft^2. This doesn't make sense because a piece of paper could not be cut this small.

62. About $86.08 per acre. The growth factor is 1.04. The cost has been inflating for 203 years ($2006 - 1803 = 203$). Find the initial price per sq. mi: $\$15,000,000 \div 828,000$ sq. mi $\approx \$18.13$ per sq. mile. To get the initial price per acre, divide this value by 640: $\$18.13$ per mile $\div 640$ acres per mile $\approx \$0.03$ per acre. Thus, the value of 1 acre of land in 2006 is $(\$0.03)(1.04)^{20} \approx \$86.08$.

63. a. $\frac{1}{2}(2)^n = 2^{-1} \cdot 2^n = 2^{n-1}$

  b. $4^{n-1} = 4^n \cdot 4^{-1} = 4^{-1} \cdot 4^n = \frac{1}{4}(4)^n$

  c. $25(5^{n-2}) = 5^2 \cdot 5^{n-2} = 5^{n-2+2} = 5^n$

Possible Answers to Mathematical Reflections

1. To multiply powers with the same base, keep the same base and add the exponents:
$a^m \times a^n = a^{m+n}$

To multiply powers with the same exponent, multiply the bases and keep the exponent:
$a^m \times b^m = (ab)^m$

To raise a power to a power, keep the base and multiply the exponents:
$(a^m)^n = a^{mn}$

To divide powers of the same base, keep the base and use the numerator exponent minus the denominator exponent as the exponent: $\frac{a^m}{a^n} = a^{m-n}$, for $a \neq 0$

If the exponent in the denominator is greater than the exponent in the numerator, this division rule results in a negative exponent. There is a different form of the rule that always gives a positive exponent: If the exponent of the numerator is greater than the exponent of the denominator, then use the rule above. If the exponent of the denominator is greater than the exponent of the numerator, then the result is a fraction with a numerator of 1 and a base equal to the base raised to the denominator exponent minus the numerator exponent:

$\frac{a^m}{a^n} = a^{m-n}$ if $m \geq n$

$\quad = \frac{1}{a^{n-m}}$ if $m < n$

(**Note:** Students should know why these rules work.)

2. **a.** When b is greater than 1, the graph curves upward slowly at first and then very rapidly.

   b. When b is equal to 1, the graph is a horizontal line.

   c. When b is between 0 and 1, the graph curves downward rapidly at first, then more slowly, until it is almost horizontal and very close to the x-axis.

3. **a.** When a is greater than 1, the y-intercept is greater than 1.

   b. When a is equal to 1, the intercept is 1.

   c. When a is between 0 and 1, the y-intercept is less than 1.

Answers to Looking Back and Looking Ahead

1. **a.** $p = 10(n - 1) + 5$ or $p = 10n - 5$, for $n \geq 1$.

   b. 6 correct answers will give a prize of $55. 8 correct answers will give a prize of $75. 11 correct answers will give a prize of $105. It is not possible to win exactly $50 or exactly $100.

c.

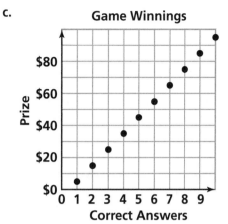

Game Winnings

2. **a.** $p = 5(2^{n-1})$, for $n > 1$

   b. Four correct answers will give a prize of only $40. Five correct answers will give a prize of $80. Six correct answers will give a prize of $160. It is not possible to win exactly $50, $75, or $100.

c.

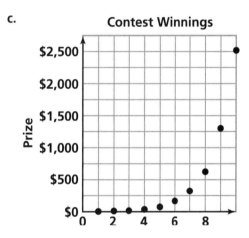

Contest Winnings

   d. Possible answer: Lucy's proposal gives a linear relationship while Pedro's proposal is exponential. Contestants would probably prefer Pedro's proposal because they would get more money after three correct answers.

3. **a.** 2^n

   b. $3{,}600(0.5)^n$

4. False; $3^5 \times 6^5 = 18^5$, which is not equal to 9^5.

5. True; $8^5 = 2^{15}$ and $4^6 = 2^{12}$, so $8^5 \times 4^6 = 2^{15} \times 2^{12} = 2^{27}$.

6. True; $2^0 = 1$

7. If you look at the y-values for consecutive x-values, each y-value will be a constant factor times the previous y-value. The value of a is the initial y-value, or the y-value for $x = 0$. The value of b is the growth factor, or the constant each y-value is multiplied by to get the next y-value.

8. Exponential growth or decay is suggested when the pattern is a curve like the following graphs. In the equation, a represents the initial y-value, or the y-intercept, and b represents the growth factor. When the value of b is between 0 and 1, the graph shows exponential decay. Smaller values of b correspond to sharper rates of decay. When the value of b is greater than 1, the pattern is exponential growth, and larger values of b correspond to greater growth rates.

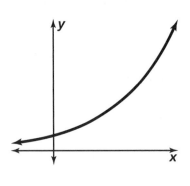

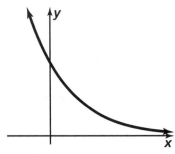

9. In linear relationships, y changes at a constant rate. That is, each time x increases by a fixed amount, y changes by a fixed amount. In exponential relationships, the rate of change is not constant; as x increases by a fixed amount,

y is multiplied by a constant factor. A graph of a linear relationship is a straight line, while the graph of an exponential relationship is a curve. An equation for a linear relationship can be written in the form $y = mx + b$, where b is the y-intercept and m is the rate of change. The equation for an exponential relationship can be written in the form $y = a(b^x)$, where a is the y-intercept and b is the growth factor.

10. $(a^m)^n = a^{mn}$

$a^m \times a^n = a^{m+n}$

$a^m \times b^m = (a \times b)^m$

$a^m \div a^n = a^{m-n}$ for $(a \neq 0)$

To show why $a^m \times a^n = a^{m+n}$, write a^m and a^n as strings of factors:

$$a^m \times a^n = \underbrace{(a \times a \times \cdots \times a)}_{\substack{m \text{ times} \\ a^m}} \times \underbrace{(a \times a \times \cdots \times a)}_{\substack{n \text{ times} \\ a^n}}$$

$$= \underbrace{(a \times a \times \cdots \times a)}_{\substack{(m+n) \text{ times} \\ a^{m+n}}}$$

$$= a^{m+n}$$

Here is why $a^m \times b^m = (a \times b)^m$, works:

$$a^m \times b^m = \underbrace{(a \times a \times \cdots \times a)}_{\substack{m \text{ times} \\ a^m}} \times \underbrace{(b \times b \times \cdots \times b)}_{\substack{m \text{ times} \\ b^m}}$$

$$= \underbrace{(ab \times ab \times \cdots \times ab)}_{\substack{m \text{ times} \\ ab^m}}$$

$$= ab^m$$

And, here is why $(a^m)^n = a^{mn}$ works: $(a^m)^n$

$$= \underbrace{a^m \times a^m \times \cdots \times a^m}_{n \text{ times}}$$

$$= \underbrace{\underbrace{(a \times a \times \cdots \times a)}_{m \text{ times}} \times \underbrace{(a \times a \times \cdots \times a)}_{m \text{ times}} \times \cdots \times \underbrace{(a \times a)}_{m}}_{n \text{ times}}$$

$$= a^{mn}$$

Guide to the Unit Project

Assigning the Unit Project

The optional unit project, the Half-Life project, gives students an opportunity to apply what they have learned about exponential relationships to a real-world situation, radioactive decay.

We recommend that students work on the project with a partner. Each pair will need 100 cubes (wooden, plastic, or sugar) to conduct the simulation. If it is not possible to have students mark on the cubes, supply them with stickers that can be removed later. Students can also use number cubes and choose one number to represent the marked side. The cubes can be shared.

Some teachers launch the project at the start of Investigation 4 and use the last several minutes of class each day for a few groups to experiment and collect data. By the end of Investigation 4, all groups have their data. A class period is then used for groups to finish the project.

Sample results and answers to the questions are presented here.

Sample Results and Answers

Following are the data collected by a group of students who conducted this experiment.

Roll	Cubes Left	Roll	Cubes Left
0	100	13	11
1	80	14	8
2	64	15	5
3	53	16	4
4	46	17	4
5	37	18	4
6	33	19	4
7	28	20	4
8	26	21	4
9	19	22	4
10	15	23	2
11	13	24	2
12	12	25	1

The students made a graph similar to the following one.

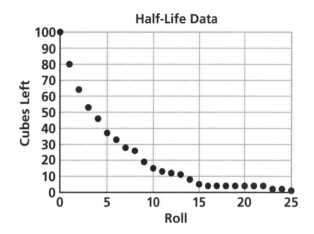

The answers below are based on the sample data.

1. **a.** It took 4 days to reduce the 100 atoms to 46 atoms.

   b. It took 5 days to reduce the 46 atoms to 19 atoms.

   c. Averaging these two results gives a half-life of about 4.5 days.

2. **a.** After 1 day, $\frac{5}{6}$ of the atoms remain.

   b. The decay rate is $\frac{5}{6}$, so an equation is
   $$n = 100\left(\tfrac{5}{6}\right)^d.$$

c. A table can be made from the equation. The table indicates that iodine-124 has a half-life of about 4 days (when 48 atoms remain).

Roll	Cubes Left	Roll	Cubes Left
0	100	13	9
1	83	14	8
2	69	15	6
3	58	16	5
4	48	17	5
5	40	18	4
6	33	19	3
7	28	20	3
8	23	21	2
9	19	22	2
10	16	23	2
11	13	24	1
12	11		

d. The half-life of 4 days is fairly close to our experimental half-life of 4.5 days.

3. Answers will vary. Cubes can easily be used to model decay rates of $\frac{4}{6}$ or $\frac{2}{3}$ [with an equation of $n = 100\left(\frac{2}{3}\right)^d$ and a half-life of about 2 days], $\frac{3}{6}$ or $\frac{1}{2}$ [with an equation of $n = 100\left(\frac{1}{2}\right)^d$ and a half-life of about 1 day], or $\frac{1}{3}$ (with an equation of $n = 100\left(\frac{1}{3}\right)^d$ and a half-life of less than 1 day) and $\frac{1}{6}$ [with an equation of $n = 100\left(\frac{1}{6}\right)^d$ and a half-life of significantly less than 1 day].

The student edition pages for this investigation begin on the next page.

Notes _____

_____

_____

_____

Unit Project

Half-Life

Most things around you are composed of atoms that are stable. However, the atoms that make up *radioactive* substances are unstable—they break down in a process known as *radioactive decay*. As these substances decay, they emit radiation. At high levels, radiation can be dangerous.

The rate of decay varies from substance to substance. The term *half-life* describes the time it takes for half of the atoms in a radioactive sample to decay. For example, the half-life of carbon-11 is 20 minutes. This means that 2,000 carbon-11 atoms will be reduced to 1,000 carbon-11 atoms in 20 minutes, and to 500 carbon-11 atoms in 40 minutes.

Half-lives vary from a fraction of a second to billions of years. For example, the half-life of polonium-214 is 0.00016 seconds. The half-life of rubidium-87 is 49 billion years.

In this experiment, you will model the decay of a radioactive substance known as iodine-124. About $\frac{1}{6}$ of the atoms in a sample of iodine-124 decay each day. This experiment will help you determine the half-life of this substance.

Follow these steps to conduct your experiment:

- Use 100 cubes to represent 100 iodine-124 atoms. Mark one face of each cube.

- Place all 100 cubes in a container, shake the container, and pour the cubes onto the table.

- The cubes for which the mark is facing up represent atoms that have decayed on the first day. Remove these cubes, and record the number of cubes that remain. Place the remaining cubes in the container.

- Repeat this process to find the number of atoms that remain after the second day.

- Repeat this process until one cube or no cubes remain.

When you complete your experiment, answer the questions on the next page.

Notes

1. a. In your experiment, how many days did it take to reduce the 100 iodine-124 atoms to 50 atoms? In other words, how many times did you have to roll the cubes until about 50 cubes remained?

b. How many days did it take to reduce 50 iodine-124 atoms to 25 atoms?

c. Based on your answers to parts (a) and (b), what do you think the half-life of iodine-124 is?

2. a. In a sample of real iodine-124, $\frac{1}{6}$ of the atoms decay after 1 day. What fraction of the atoms remain after 1 day?

b. Suppose a sample contains 100 iodine-124 atoms. Use your answer from part (a) to write an equation for the number of atoms n remaining in the sample after d days.

c. Use your equation to find the half-life of iodine-124.

d. How does the half-life you found based on your equation compare to the half-life you found from your experiment?

3. a. Make up a problem involving a radioactive substance with a different rate of decay that can be modeled by an experiment involving cubes or other common objects. Describe the situation and your experiment.

b. Conduct your experiment and record your results.

c. Use the results of your experiment to predict the half-life of your substance.

d. Use what you know about the rate of decay to write an equation that models the decay of your substance.

e. Use your equation to find the half-life of your substance.

Write a report summarizing your findings about decay rates and half-lives. Your report should include tables and graphs justifying your answers to the questions above.

Notes _____

_____

_____

_____

Looking Back and Looking Ahead

Working on the problems in this unit developed your skills in recognizing and applying *exponential relationships* between variables.

Go Online
PHSchool.com
For: Vocabulary Review Puzzle
Web Code: apj-3051

You wrote equations of the form $y = a(b^x)$ to describe *exponential growth* of populations and investments and *exponential decay* of medicines and radioactive materials. You used equations to produce tables and graphs of the relationships. You used those tables and graphs to make predictions and solve equations.

Use Your Understanding: Algebraic Reasoning

To test your understanding and skill in finding and applying exponential models, solve these problems that arise as the student council at Lincoln Middle School plans a fundraising event.

The students want to have a quiz show called *Who Wants to Be Rich?* Contestants will be asked a series of questions. A contestant will play until he or she misses a question. The total prize money will grow with each question answered correctly.

1. Lucy proposes that a contestant receive $5 for answering the first question correctly. For each additional correct answer, the total prize would increase by $10.

   a. For Lucy's proposal, what equation gives the total prize *p* for correctly answering *n* questions?

   b. How many questions would a contestant need to answer correctly to win at least $50? To win at least $75? To win at least $100?

   c. Sketch a graph of the (n, p) data for $n = 1$ to 10.

Notes _____

_____

_____

_____

2. Pedro also thinks the first question should be worth $5. However, he thinks a contestant's winnings should double with each subsequent correct answer.

   a. For Pedro's proposal, what equation gives the total prize p for correctly answering n questions?

   b. How many questions will a contestant need to answer correctly to win at least $50? To win at least $75? To win at least $100?

   c. Sketch a graph of the (n, p) data for $n = 1$ to 10.

   d. Compare Pedro's proposal with Lucy's proposal in Exercise 1.

3. The council decides that contestants for *Who Wants to Be Rich?* will be chosen by a random drawing. Students and guests at the fundraiser will buy tickets like the one at right. The purchaser will keep half of the ticket and add the other half to the entries for the drawing.

   a. To make the tickets, council members will take a large piece of paper and fold it in half many times to make a grid of small rectangles. How many rectangles will there be after n folds?

   b. The initial piece of paper will be a square with sides measuring 60 centimeters. What will be the area of each rectangle after n folds?

Decide whether each statement is *true* or *false*. Explain.

   4. $3^5 \times 6^5 = 9^5$ **5.** $8^5 \times 4^6 = 2^{27}$ **6.** $\dfrac{2^0 \times 6^7}{3^7} = 2^7$

Notes _____

_____

_____

_____

Explain Your Reasoning

To answer Questions 1–3, you had to use algebraic knowledge about number patterns, graphs, and equations. You had to recognize linear and exponential patterns from verbal descriptions and represent those patterns with equations and graphs.

7. How can you decide whether a data pattern can be modeled by an exponential equation of the form $y = a(b^x)$? How will the values of a and b relate to the data pattern?

8. Describe the possible shapes for graphs of exponential relationships. How can the shape of an exponential graph be predicted from the values of a and b in the equation?

9. How are the data patterns, graphs, and equations for exponential relationships similar to and different from those for linear relationships?

10. Describe the rules for exponents that you used in Questions 4–6. Choose one of the rules and explain why it works.

Look Ahead

The algebraic ideas and techniques you developed and used in this unit will be applied and extended in future units of *Connected Mathematics* and in problems of science and business. In upcoming units, you will study other important families of algebraic models and you will learn strategies for finding and using those models to solve problems.

Notes _____

_____

_____

_____

B

base The number that is raised to a power in an exponential expression. In the expression 3^5, read "3 to the fifth power", 5 is the exponent and 3 is the base.

base El número que se eleva a una potencia en una expresión exponencial. En la expresión 3^5, que se lee "3 elevado a la quinta potencia", 3 es la base y 5 es el exponente.

C

compound growth Another term for exponential growth, usually used when talking about the monetary value of an investment. The change in the balance of a savings account shows compound growth because the bank pays interest not only on the original investment, but on the interest earned.

crecimiento compuesto Otro término para crecimiento exponencial, normalmente usado para referirse al valor monetario de una inversión. El cambio en el saldo de una cuenta de ahorros muestra un crecimiento compuesto, ya que el banco paga intereses no sólo sobre la inversión original, sino sobre los intereses ganados.

D

decay factor The constant factor that each value in an exponential decay pattern is multiplied by to get the next value. The decay factor is the base in an exponential decay equation. For example, in the equation $A = 64(0.5)n$, where A is the area of a ballot and n is the number of cuts, the decay factor is 0.5. It indicates that the area of a ballot after any number of cuts is 0.5 times the area after the previous number of cuts. In a table of (x, y) values for an exponential decay relationship (with x-values increasing by 1), the decay factor is the ratio of any y-value to the previous y-value.

factor de disminución El factor constante por el cual se multiplica cada valor en un patrón de disminución exponencial para obtener el valor siguiente. El factor de disminución es la base en una ecuación de disminución exponencial. Por ejemplo, en la ecuación $A = 64(0.5)n$, donde A es el área de una papeleta y n es el número de cortes, el factor de disminución es 0.5. Esto indica que el área de una papeleta después de un número cualquiera de cortes es 0.5 veces el área después del número anterior de cortes. En una tabla de valores (x, y) para una relación de disminución exponencial (donde el valor x crece de a 1), el factor de disminución es la razón entre cualquier valor de y y su valor anterior.

decay rate The percent decrease in an exponential decay pattern. A discount, expressed as a percent, is a decay rate. In general, for an exponential pattern with decay factor b, the decay rate is $1 - b$.

tasa de disminución El porcentaje de reducción en un patrón de disminución exponencial. Un descuento, expresado como porcentaje, es una tasa de disminución. En general, para un patrón exponencial con factor de disminución b, la tasa de disminución es $1 - b$.

English/Spanish Glossary **79**

Notes _____

_____

_____

_____

exponent A number that indicates how many times another number (the base) is to be used as a factor. Exponents are written as raised numbers to the right of the base. In the expression 3^5, read "3 to the fifth power", 5 is the exponent and 3 is the base, so 3^5 means $3 \cdot 3 \cdot 3 \cdot 3 \cdot 3$. In the formula for the area of a square, $A = s^2$, the 2 is an exponent. This formula can also be written as $A = s \cdot s$.

exponente Es un número que indica la cantidad de veces que otro número (la base) se va a usar como factor. Los exponentes se escriben como números elevados a la derecha de la base. En la expresión 3^5, que se lee como "3 elevado a la quinta potencia", 5 es el exponente y 3 es la base. Así, 3^5 significa $3 \cdot 3 \cdot 3 \cdot 3 \cdot 3$. En la fórmula para calcular el área de un cuadrado, $A = s^2$, el 2 es un exponente. Esta fórmula también se puede escribir como $A = s \cdot s$.

exponential decay A pattern of decrease in which each value is found by multiplying the previous value by a constant factor greater than 0 and less than 1. For example, the pattern $27, 9, 3, 1, \frac{1}{3}, \frac{1}{9}, \ldots$ shows exponential decay in which each value is $\frac{1}{3}$ times the previous value.

disminución exponencial Un patrón de disminución en el cual cada valor se calcula multiplicando el valor anterior por un factor constante mayor que 0 y menor que 1. Por ejemplo, el patrón $27, 9, 3, 1, \frac{1}{3}, \frac{1}{9}, \ldots$ muestra una disminución exponencial en la que cada valor es $\frac{1}{3}$ del valor anterior.

exponential form A quantity expressed as a number raised to a power. In exponential form, 32 can be written as 2^5.

forma exponencial Una cantidad que se expresa como un número elevado a una potencia. En forma exponencial, 32 puede escribirse como 2^5.

exponential growth A pattern of increase in which each value is found by multiplying the previous value by a constant factor greater than 1. For example, the doubling pattern $1, 2, 4, 8, 16, 32, \ldots$ shows exponential growth in which each value is 2 times the previous value.

crecimiento exponencial Un patrón de crecimiento en el cual cada valor se calcula multiplicando el valor anterior por un factor constante mayor que 1. Por ejemplo, el patrón $1, 2, 4, 8, 16, 32, \ldots$ muestra un crecimiento exponencial en el que cada valor es el doble del valor anterior.

exponential relationship A relationship that shows exponential growth or decay.

relación exponencial Una relación que muestra crecimiento o disminución exponencial.

Notes

growth factor The constant factor that each value in an exponential growth pattern is multiplied by to get the next value. The growth factor is the base in an exponential growth equation. For example, in the equation $A = 25(3)^d$, where A is the area of a patch of mold and d is the number of days, the growth factor is 3. It indicates that the area of the mold for any day is 3 times the area for the previous day. In a table of (x, y) values for an exponential growth relationship (with x-values increasing by 1), the growth factor is the ratio of any y-value to the previous y-value.

factor de crecimiento El factor constante por el cual se multiplica cada valor en un patrón de crecimiento exponencial para obtener el valor siguiente. El factor de crecimiento es la base en una ecuación de crecimiento exponencial. Por ejemplo, en la ecuación $A = 25(3)^d$, donde A es el área enmohecida y d es el número de días, el factor de crecimiento es 3. Esto indica que el área enmohecida en un día cualquiera es 3 veces el área del día anterior. En una tabla de valores (x, y) para una relación de crecimiento exponencial (donde el valor de x aumenta de a 1), el factor exponencial es la razón entre cualquier valor de y y su valor anterior.

growth rate The percent increase in an exponential growth pattern. For example, in Problem 3.1, the number of rabbits increased from 100 to 180 from year 0 to year 1, an 80% increase. From year 1 to year 2, the number of rabbits increased from 180 to 324, an 80% increase. The growth rate for this rabbit population is 80%. Interest, expressed as a percent, is a growth rate. For an exponential growth pattern with a growth factor of b, the growth rate is $b - 1$.

tasa de crecimiento El porcentaje de crecimiento en un patrón de crecimiento exponencial. Por ejemplo, en el Problema 3.1, el número de conejos aumentó de 100 a 180 del año 0 al año 1, un aumento del 80%. Del año 1 al año 2, el número de conejos aumentó de 180 a 324, un aumento del 80%. La tasa de crecimiento para esta población de conejos es del 80%. El interés, expresado como porcentaje, es una tasa de crecimiento. Para un patrón de crecimiento exponencial con un factor de crecimiento b, la tasa de crecimiento es $b - 1$.

scientific notation A short way to write very large or very small numbers. A number is in scientific notation if it is of the form $a \times 10^n$, where n is an integer and $1 \leq a < 10$.

notación científica Una manera corta de escribir números muy grandes o muy pequeños. Un número está e notación científica si está en la forma $a \times 10^n$, donde n es un entero y $1 \leq a < 10$.

standard form The most common way we express quantities. For example, 27 is the standard form of 3^3.

forma normal La manera más común de expresar una cantidad. Por ejemplo, 27 es la forma normal de 3^3.

English/Spanish Glossary

English/Spanish Glossary   **81**

STUDENT PAGE

STUDENT PAGE

Notes

Academic vocabulary words are words that you see in textbooks and on tests. These are not math vocabulary terms, but knowing them will help you succeed in mathematics.

Las palabras de vocabulario académico son palabras que ves en los libros de texto y en las pruebas. Éstos no son términos de vocabulario de matemáticas, pero conocerlos te ayudará a tener éxito en matemáticas.

D

decide To use the given information and any related facts to find a value or make a determination.
related terms: determine, find, conclude

Sample: **Study the pattern in the table. Decide whether the relationship is linear or exponential.**

x	−1	0	1	2	3
y	−9	−7	−5	−3	−1

Each y-value increases by 2 when each x-value increases by 1. The relationship is linear.

decidir Usar la información dada y cualesquiera datos relacionados para hallar un valor o tomar una determinación.
términos relacionados: determinar, hallar, concluir

Ejemplo: **Estudia el patrón en la tabla. Decide si la relación es lineal o exponencial.**

x	−1	0	1	2	3
y	−9	−7	−5	−3	−1

Cada valor de y aumenta en 2 cuando cada valor de x aumenta en 1. La relación es lineal.

---

describe To explain using details. You can describe a situation using words, numbers, graphs, tables, or any combination of these.
related terms: explain, tell, present, detail

Sample: **Consider the following equations.**

Equation 1: $y = 3x + 5$ Equation 2: $y = 5(3^x)$

Use a table to describe the change in y-values as the x-values increase in both equations.

x	0	1	2	3	4
$y = 3x + 5$	5	8	11	14	17
$y = 5(3^x)$	5	15	45	135	675

In $y = 3x + 5$, the value of y increases by 3 when x increases by 1. In $y = 5(3^x)$, the value of y increases by a factor of 3 when x increases by 1.

describir Explicar usando detalles. Puedes describir una situación usando palabras, números, gráficas, tablas o cualquier combinación de éstos.
términos relacionados: explicar, decir, presentar, dar detalles

Ejemplo: **Considera las siguientes ecuaciones.**

Ecuación 1: $y = 3x + 5$ Ecuación 2: $y = 5(3^x)$

Usa una tabla para describir el cambio en los valores de y a medida que los valores de x se incrementan en ambas ecuaciones.

x	0	1	2	3	4
$y = 3x + 5$	5	8	11	14	17
$y = 5(3^x)$	5	15	45	135	675

In $y = 3x + 5$, el valor de y aumenta en 3 cuando x aumenta en 1. En $y = 5(3^x)$, el valor de y aumenta por un factor de 3 cuando x aumenta en 1.

Notes _____

_____

_____

_____

explain To give facts and details that make an idea easier to understand. Explaining something can involve a written summary supported by factual information, a diagram, chart, table, or any combination of these.

related terms: describe, justify, tell

Sample: Etymologists are working with a population of mosquitoes that have a growth factor of 8. After 1 month there are 6,000 mosquitoes. In two months, there are 48,000 mosquitoes.

Write an equation for the population after any number of months. Explain each part of your equation.

I first find the initial population of mosquitoes by dividing 6,000 by 8 to get 750. I can then model the population growth with the equation $y = 750(8^m)$, where 750 represents the initial population, 8 is the growth factor, m is the number of months, and y is the population of mosquitoes after m months.

explicar Dar hechos y detalles que hacen que una idea sea más fácil de comprender. Explicar puede implicar un resumen escrito apoyado por un diagrama, un gráfica, una tabla o cualquier combinación de éstos.

términos relacionados: describir, justificar, decir

Ejemplo: Los entomólogos trabajan con una población de mosquitos que tiene un factor de crecimiento de 8. Después de 1 mes hay 6,000 mosquitos. En dos meses, hay 48,000 mosquitos.

Escribe una ecuación para la población después de cualquier número de meses. Explica cada parte de tu ecuación.

Primero hallo la población inicial de mosquitos dividiendo 6,000 entre 8 para obtener 750. Luego puedo modelar el crecimiento de la población con la ecuación $y = 750(8^m)$, donde 750 representa la población inicial, 8 es el factor de crecimiento, m es el número de meses y y es la población de mosquitos luego de m meses.

predict To make an educated guess based on the analysis of real data.

related terms: estimate, guess, expect

Sample: Predict the ones digit for the expression 3^{11}.

3^1	3
3^2	9
3^3	27
3^4	81
3^5	243
3^6	729
3^7	2187
3^8	6561

The pattern for the ones digit of the powers of 3 is 3, 9, 7, 1, as the exponent increases by 1. If I continue the pattern, 3^9 will end with a 3, 3^{10} will end with a 7, and 3^{11} will end with a 1.

predecir Hacer una conjetura informada basada en el análisis de datos reales.

términos relacionados: estimar, conjeturar, esperar

Ejemplo: Predice el dígito de las unidades para la expresión 3^{11}.

3^1	3
3^2	9
3^3	27
3^4	81
3^5	243
3^6	729
3^7	2187
3^8	6561

El patrón para el dígito de las unidades de las potencias de 3 es 3, 9, 7, 1, a medida que el exponente aumenta en 1. Si continúo el patrón, 3^9 terminará con un 3, 3^{10} terminará con un 7, y 3^{11} terminará con un 1.

Academic Vocabulary **83**

STUDENT PAGE

STUDENT PAGE

Academic Vocabulary

Notes _____

_____

_____

_____

84   Growing, Growing, Growing

Notes _____

_____

_____

_____

STUDENT PAGE

Index

Notes _____

_____

_____

_____

Team Credits

The people who made up the **Connected Mathematics 2** team—representing editorial, editorial services, design services, and production services—are listed below. Bold type denotes core team members.

Leora Adler, Judith Buice, Kerry Cashman, Patrick Culleton, Sheila DeFazio, Katie Hallahan, Richard Heater, **Barbara Hollingdale, Jayne Holman,** Karen Holtzman, **Etta Jacobs,** Christine Lee, Carolyn Lock, Catherine Maglio, **Dotti Marshall,** Rich McMahon, Eve Melnechuk, Kristin Mingrone, Terri Mitchell, **Marsha Novak,** Irene Rubin, Donna Russo, Robin Samper, Siri Schwartzman, **Nancy Smith,** Emily Soltanoff, **Mark Tricca,** Paula Vergith, Roberta Warshaw, Helen Young

Additional Credits

Diana Bonfilio, Mairead Reddin, Michael Torocsik, nSight, Inc.

Technical Illustration

WestWords, Inc.

Cover Design

tom white.images

Photos

2 t, Jacques Jangoux/Alamy; **2 b,** (ZF) Virgo/Corbis; **3 t,** Inga Spence/Visuals Unlimited; **3 b,** AP Photo/Chuck Burton; **13,** Dr. Stanley Flegler/Visuals Unlimited; **14,** Tim Pannell/Masterfile; **21,** Nicolas Granier/Peter Arnold, Inc.; **21 inset,** Jacques Jangoux/Alamy; **22,** Photodisc/Getty Images, Inc.; **23,** Sheldon, Allen Blake/Animals Animals-Earth Scenes; **25,** Wolfgang Kaehler/Corbis; **26,** David Young-Wolff/PhotoEdit; **33,** Steve Maslowski/Visuals Unlimited; **34,** Geoff Dann/Dorling Kindersley; **35,** Topham/The Image Works; **36 t,** (ZF) Virgo/Corbis; **36 b,** Steve Allen/AGE Fotostock; **38,** Michael Wickes/The Image Works; **40,** Creatas/AGE Fotostock; **41,** DK Limited/Corbis; **43,** David Young-Wolff/PhotoEdit; **44,** George Disario/Corbis; **48,** Tony Freeman/PhotoEdit; **52,** Richard Smith/Masterfile; **57,** Saxpix.com/AGE Fotostock; **61,** Richard Haynes; **65,** Richard Haynes; **69,** Tony Freeman/PhotoEdit; **71,** Design Pics Inc./Alamy

Data Sources

The water hyacinth data on page 2 is from "Killer Weed Strikes Lake Victoria" in The Christian Science Monitor, January 12, 1998, Volume 90, Number 32. Copyright © 1998 The Christian Science Monitor. All Rights Reserved.

Note: Every effort has been made to locate the copyright owner of the material reprinted in this book. Omissions brought to our attention will be corrected in subsequent editions.

Notes

Name _____ Date _____ Class _____

Centimeter Grid Paper

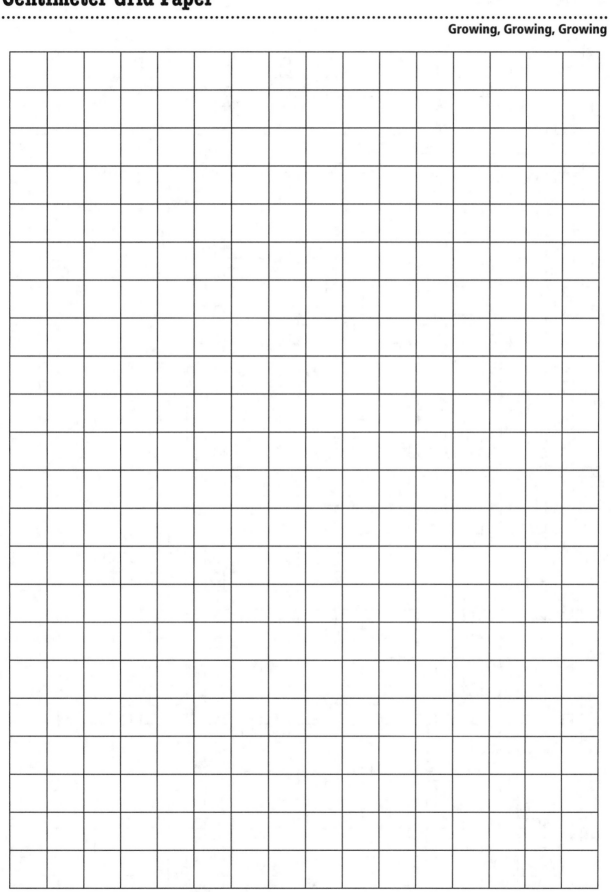

Quarter-Centimeter Grid Paper

Growing, Growing, Growing

Quarter-Inch Grid Paper

··

Growing, Growing, Growing

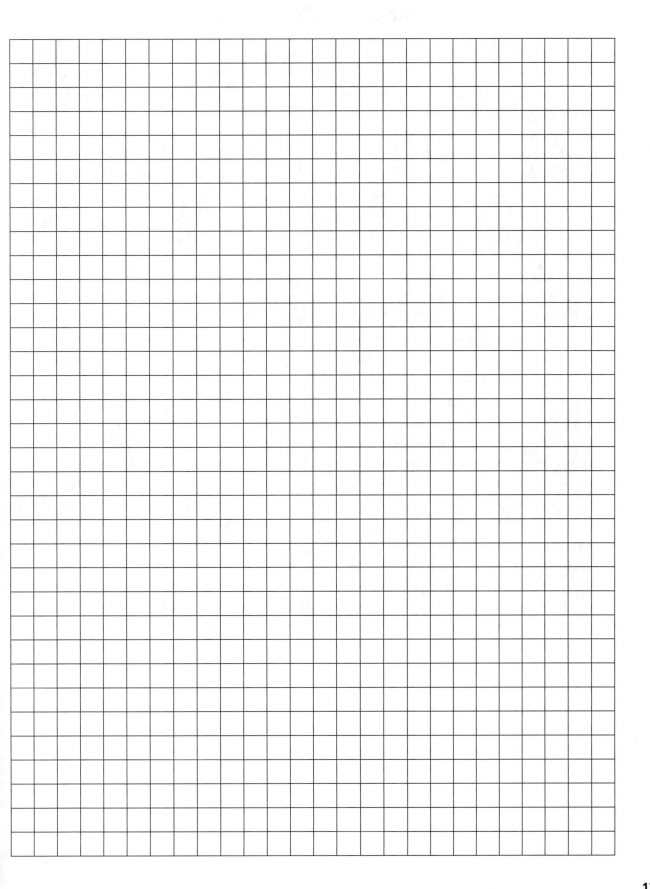

Labsheet 1.2

Montarek Chessboard

Labsheet 5.1

x	1^x	2^x	3^x	4^x	5^x	6^x	7^x	8^x	9^x	10^x
1	1	2								
2	1	4								
3	1	8								
4	1	16								
5	1	32								
6	1	64								
7	1	128								
8	1	256								
Ones Digits of the Powers	1	2, 4,								

PACING: _____

Mathematical Goals

_____

_____

_____

_____

Launch

| Materials |

_____

_____

_____

_____

_____

_____

_____

Explore

| Materials |

_____

_____

_____

_____

_____

_____

_____

Summarize

| Materials |

_____

_____

_____

_____

_____

_____

_____

Glossary

B

base The number that is raised to a power in an exponential expression. In the expression 3^5, read "3 to the fifth power"; 5 is the exponent and 3 is the base.

C

compound growth Another term for exponential growth, usually used when talking about the monetary value of an investment. The change in the balance of a savings account shows compound growth because the bank pays interest not only on the original investment, but on the interest earned.

D

decay factor The constant factor that each value in an exponential decay pattern is multiplied by to get the next value. The decay factor is the base in an exponential decay equation. For example, in the equation $A = 64(0.5)^n$, where A is the area of a ballot and n is the number of cuts, the decay factor is 0.5. It indicates that the area of a ballot after any number of cuts is 0.5 times the area after the previous number of cuts. In a table of (x, y) values for an exponential decay relationship (with x-values increasing by 1), the decay factor is the ratio of any y-value to the previous y-value.

decay rate The percent decrease in an exponential decay pattern. A discount, expressed as a percent, is a decay rate. In general, for an exponential pattern with decay factor b, the decay rate is $1 - b$.

E

exponent A number that indicates how many times another number (the base) is to be used as a factor. Exponents are written as raised numbers to the right of the base. In the expression 3^5, read "3 to the fifth power"; 5 is the exponent and 3 is the base, so 3^5 means $3 \cdot 3 \cdot 3 \cdot 3 \cdot 3$. In the formula for the area of a square, $A = s^2$, the 2 is an exponent. This formula can also be written as $A = s \cdot s$.

exponential decay A pattern of decrease in which each value is found by multiplying the previous value by a constant factor greater than 0 and less than 1. For example, the pattern $27, 9, 3, 1, \frac{1}{3}, \frac{1}{9}, \ldots$ shows exponential decay in which each value is $\frac{1}{3}$ times the previous value.

exponential form A quantity expressed as a number raised to a power. In exponential form, 32 can be written as 2^5.

exponential growth A pattern of increase in which each value is found by multiplying the previous value by a constant factor greater than 1. For example, the doubling pattern $1, 2, 4, 8, 16, 32, \ldots$ shows exponential growth in which each value is 2 times the previous value.

exponential relationship A relationship that shows exponential growth or decay.

G

growth factor The constant factor that each value in an exponential growth pattern is multiplied by to get the next value. The growth factor is the base in an exponential growth equation. For example, in the equation $A = 25(3)^d$, where A is the area of a patch of mold and d is the number of days, the growth factor is 3. It indicates that the area of the mold for any day is 3 times the area for the previous day. In a table of (x, y) values for an exponential growth relationship (with x-values increasing by 1), the growth factor is the ratio of any y-value to the previous y-value.

growth rate The percent increase in an exponential growth pattern. For example, in Problem 3.1, the number of rabbits increased from 100 to 180 from year 0 to year 1, an 80% increase. From year 1 to year 2, the number of rabbits increased from 180 to 324, an 80% increase. The growth rate for this rabbit population is 80%. Interest, expressed as a percent, is a growth rate. For an exponential growth pattern with a growth factor of b, the growth rate is $b - 1$.

S

scientific notation A short way to write very large or very small numbers. A number is in scientific notation if it is of the form $a \times 10^n$, where n is an integer and $1 \leq a < 10$.

standard form The most common way we express quantities. For example, 27 is the standard form of 3^3.

Acknowledgments

Team Credits

The people who made up the **Connected Mathematics 2** team—representing editorial, editorial services, design services, and production services—are listed below. Bold type denotes core team members.

Leora Adler, Judith Buice, Kerry Cashman, Patrick Culleton, Sheila DeFazio, Richard Heater, **Barbara Hollingdale, Jayne Holman,** Karen Holtzman, **Etta Jacobs,** Christine Lee, Carolyn Lock, Catherine Maglio, **Dotti Marshall,** Rich McMahon, Eve Melnechuk, Kristin Mingrone, Terri Mitchell, **Marsha Novak,** Irene Rubin, Donna Russo, Robin Samper, Siri Schwartzman, **Nancy Smith,** Emily Soltanoff, **Mark Tricca,** Paula Vergith, Roberta Warshaw, Helen Young

Additional Credits

Diana Bonfilio, Mairead Reddin, Michael Torocsik, nSight, Inc.

Technical Illustration

Schawk, Inc.

Cover Design

tom white.images